The Power of Example

Journal of the Royal Anthropological Institute Special Issue Series

The Journal of the Royal Anthropological Institute is the principal journal of the oldest anthropological organization in the world. It has attracted and inspired some of the world's greatest thinkers. International in scope, it presents accessible papers aimed at a broad anthropological readership. We are delighted to announce that from 2014 the annual special issues will also be available from the Wiley Blackwell books catalogue.

Previous special issues of the JRAI:

THE POWER OF EXAMPLE

ANTHROPOLOGICAL EXPLORATIONS IN PERSUASION, EVOCATION, AND IMITATION

EDITED BY ANDREAS BANDAK and LARS HØJER

This edition first published 2015
© 2015 Royal Anthropological Institute

Registered Office
John Wiley & Sons Ltd, The Atrium, Southern Gate, Chichester, West Sussex, PO19 8SQ, UK

Editorial Offices
350 Main Street, Malden, MA 02148-5020, USA
9600 Garsington Road, Oxford, OX4 2DQ, UK
The Atrium, Southern Gate, Chichester, West Sussex, PO19 8SQ, UK

For details of our global editorial offices, for customer services, and for information about how to apply for permission to reuse the copyright material in this book, please see our website at www.wiley.com/wiley-blackwell.

The right of Andreas Bandak and Lars Højer to be identified as the authors of the editorial material in this work has been asserted in accordance with the UK Copyright, Designs and Patents Act 1988.

Library of Congress Cataloging-in-Publication Data

The power of example : anthropological explorations in persuasion, evocation, and imitation / edited by Andreas Bandak and Lars Højer.
      pages cm. – (Journal of the Royal Anthropological Institute special issue series)
   Includes bibliographical references and index.
   ISBN 978-1-119-11832-9 (alk. paper)
   1. Anthropology–Philosophy. 2. Anthropology–Methodology. 3. Example. 4. Values. I. Bandak,
   Andreas.
   GN33.P68 2015
   301.01–dc23
                                    2015011674

A catalogue record for this book is available from the British Library.

Journal of the Royal Anthropological Institute.
Incorporating MAN
Print ISSN 1359-0987
All articles published within this special issue are included within the ISI Journal Citation Reports® Social Science Citation Index. Please cite the articles as volume 21(Supp) of the Journal of the Royal Anthropological Institute.

Cover image: From a photograph of Abuna Elias Zahlawi giving a sermon at the Shrine of Our Lady of Soufanieh, November 2009, taken by the editor, Andreas Bandak.

Cover design by Ben Higgins

Set in 10 on 12pt Minion by Aptara Inc.

Printed in Singapore by C.O.S. Printers Pte Ltd

1 2015

Contents

Notes on contributors

Andreas Bandak is an assistant professor at the Centre for Comparative Cultural Studies, Department of Cross-Cultural and Regional Studies, University of Copenhagen. His research focuses on the Christian minorities in Syria, where he has done extensive fieldwork primarily in and around Damascus, and more currently on the role of displacement with Syrians migrating to Lebanon. His thematic interests include Eastern Christianity, exemplarity, sainthood, authoritarianism, and belonging. *Department of Cross-Cultural and Regional Studies, University of Copenhagen, Karen Blixens Vej 4, bygning 10, 2300 Copenhagen S, Denmark. bandak@hum.ku.dk*

Lotte Buch Segal is an assistant professor in the Department of Anthropology, University of Copenhagen. She has published on the themes of intimacy, violence, security, and affect and how these are configured in the Israeli-Palestinian conflict. She is currently writing up her monograph on absence, grief, and mourning in the West Bank (to be published by the University of Pennsylvania Press). *Department of Anthropology, University of Copenhagen, Øster Farimagsgade 5, DK-1353 Copenhagen K, Denmark. Lotte.Buch.Segal@anthro.ku.dk*

Simon Coleman is Chancellor Jackman Professor at the University of Toronto. He is a former Editor of the *Journal of the Royal Anthropological Institute*, and currently co-edits *Religion and Society: Advances in Research*, as well as the book series 'Ashgate Studies in Pilgrimage'. A recent publication is 'Pilgrimage as trope for an anthropology of Christianity', *Current Anthropology*, available at *http://www.jstor.org/stable/10.1086/677766. Department for the Study of Religion, Jackman Humanities Building, University of Toronto, 170 St George Street, Toronto, ON M5R 2M8, Canada. simon.coleman@utoronto.ca*

Alice Forbess works on Orthodox monastic life, charisma, and politics in Romania, Serbia, Kosovo, and Montenegro. Her interests include the overlap of religious and political charisma, asceticism and transgression, the anthropology of institutional life, elites, expertise, and innovation. Following her Ph.D. (London School of Economics and Political Science, 2005), she completed a comparative project based in ex-Yugoslavia and funded by a British Academy Postdoctoral Fellowship. Currently she is a researcher at the LSE, working on a project which examines institutional change and innovation in legal services in the United Kingdom. *Department of Anthropology, London School of Economics and Political Science, Houghton Street, London WC2A 2AE, UK. A.I.Forbess@lse.ac.uk*

Lars Højer is an associate professor at the Centre for Comparative Cultural Studies, Department of Cross-Cultural and Regional Studies, University of Copenhagen. His previous anthropological research has focused on social, economic, religious and political aspects of transition processes in urban and rural postsocialist Mongolia, and he has also worked on minority issues related to the Uyghurs in western China. Currently, he is directing 'Escalations: A Comparative Ethnographic Study of Accelerating Change', a three-year project (2014-17) funded by the Danish Council for Independent Research in the Humanities. *Department of Cross-Cultural and Regional Studies, University of Copenhagen, Karen Blixens Vej 4, bygning 10, 2300 Copenhagen S, Denmark. lhoejer@hum.ku.dk*

Stine Krøijer is an assistant professor at the Department of Anthropology, University of Copenhagen. She is the author of *Figurations of the future: forms and temporalities of left radical politics in Northern Europe* (Berghahn, 2015) and is currently working on a new project titled 'the political life of trees' concerning the forms of politics emerging from human interaction with trees. *Department of Anthropology, Øster Farimagsgade 5, DK-1353 Copenhagen K, Denmark. Stine.kroijer@anthro.ku.dk*

Johan Lindquist is an associate professor of Social Anthropology at Stockholm University in Sweden. He is a member of the editorial committee of *Public Culture*, the co-editor of *Figures of Southeast Asian modernity* (University of Hawai'i Press, 2013), the author of *The anxieties of mobility: development and migration in the Indonesian borderlands* (University of Hawai'i Press, 2009), and the director of the documentary film *B.A.T.A.M.* (Documentary Educational Resources, 2005). *Department of Social Anthropology, Stockholm University, Universitetsvägen 10 B, SE-106 91 Stockholm, Sweden. johan.lindquist@socant.su.se*

Amira Mittermaier is an associate professor in the Department for the Study of Religion and the Department of Near and Middle Eastern Civilizations at the University of Toronto. Bringing together textual analysis and ethnographic fieldwork, her research focuses on Muslim everyday life in Egypt. Her award-winning book *Dreams that matter: Egyptian landscapes of the imagination* (University of California Press, 2011) explores Muslim practices of dream interpretation, as they are inflected by Islamic reformism, Western psychology, and mass mediation. Mittermaier's current book project examines Muslim modes of almsgiving and food distribution in Cairo since the 2011 uprising. *Department for the Study of Religion, Jackman Humanities Building, University of Toronto, 170 St George Street, Toronto, ON M5R 2M8, Canada. amira.mittermaier@utoronto.ca*

Joel Robbins is Sigrid Rausing Professor of Social Anthropology at the University of Cambridge. His work has focused on the anthropological study of Christianity, values, morality, and cultural change. He is the author of the book *Becoming sinners: Christianity and moral torment in a Papua New Guinea society* (University of California Press, 2004) and recently co-edited with Naomi Haynes a special open-access issue of *Current Anthropology* entitled 'The anthropology of Christianity: unity, diversity, new directions' (**55: S10**, 2014). *Department of Social Anthropology, University of Cambridge, Free School Lane, Cambridge CB2 3RF, UK. jr626@cam.ac.uk*

Christian Suhr is a filmmaker and assistant professor at the Department of Culture and Society, Aarhus University. He is author of the forthcoming ethnographic monograph *Descending with angels* about Islamic exorcism and Danish psychiatry based on eighteen months' doctoral fieldwork with Muslim patients, exorcists, and psychiatrists in the city of Aarhus, Denmark. He is editor of the book *Transcultural montage* (with Rane Willerslev; Berghahn, 2013) and director of the award-winning films *Unity through culture* (with Ton Otto; RAI, 2011) and *Ngat is dead* (with Ton Otto; RAI, 2009), as well as *Want a camel, yes?* (Persona Film, 2005). *Eye & Mind Laboratory, Department of Culture and Society, Aarhus University, Moesgaard, 8270 Hoejbjerg, Denmark. suhr@cas.au.dk*

Antonia Walford completed her postgraduate education at the Museu Nacional, Universidade Federal do Rio de Janeiro, where she received a grant from CNPq (Brazilian National Council of Technological and Scientific Development); and at the IT University of Copenhagen, where her doctoral thesis investigated the social, political, and ontological properties and effects of the scientific data economy in the Brazilian Amazon. She was a Research Associate at the ESRC Centre for Research on Socio-Cultural Change (CRESC), Open University, until September 2014. *walford.antonia@gmail.com*

Introduction: the power of example

Lars Højer & Andreas Bandak *University of Copenhagen*

It is the contention of this introduction that examples are important prisms through which both reality and anthropological analysis are thought and, equally importantly, reconfigured. The aim of the introduction is to redress the theoretical disregard for exemplification by exploring the persuasive and evocative power – positive and negative – of 'examples' in social and academic life while also proposing exemplification as a distinct anthropological way of theorizing. Such theorizing points to a 'lateral' rethinking of the relation between the particular and the general. Our central argument is that examples highlight the precarious tension between the example as 'example' and the example as 'exemplar'. All contributions to this special issue, in one way or another, explore this tension between the unruliness of examples and the stability-enhancing power of exemplarity. The introduction further proposes that the example serves to confuse ontological divides, such as the one between theory and ethnography, and also draws attention to the fact that theory is as much suggestive as descriptive.

A favourite example of contemporary Slovenian philosopher Slavoj Žižek is the different structure of French, English, and German toilets. Žižek observes that, in French toilets, the drain or 'hole' is located at the back of the bowl, the idea being, as Žižek eloquently puts it, that excrement should drop down and disappear as fast as possible. In English toilets, on the other hand, 'excrement floats in water' and in German ones, the most obscene according to Žižek, 'the hole' is at the front and excrement falls down onto a small 'plateau'. This, says Žižek, is in line with an old German tradition of inspecting your stools every morning, looking for symptoms of illness.[1]

While the utilitarian card is usually played to account for this difference – 'our way of doing things is simply the most practical' – Žižek immediately turns to the history of European thought for an explanation. The French tradition is strongly political, leftist even, and has a predilection for revolutions; the English is dominated by the economy and moderate liberalism; while the German is politically conservative and characterized by poetry, thinking, and contemplation. And suddenly it all makes sense. The French approach is radical politics: as with a guillotine, 'it' falls down and disappears. The Anglo-Saxons are more pragmatic: 'Let it float there and we will solve the problem'. And, last but not least, the Germans: poetry and contemplation!

The (more serious) point that Žižek is trying to make is that ideology is concrete, everyday, and to be found where you would least expect it: you go to the toilet and you are literally sitting on ideology. Žižek, in other words, exemplifies difference and the concreteness of ideology by making a funny and evocative homology between toilets, nations, and approaches to life, and an association of ideology with basic human needs. Ideology is basic and basics are ideological.

For the purpose of this introduction, however, Žižek exemplifies the *use* of exemplification and takes us to the heart of this special issue because: what can examples do? Are they, in their capacity to spread (now even in this introduction), good memory devices? Who will ever be able to go to a German toilet again without recalling the contemplative tradition of German philosophy? And are good memory devices ones that simply draw on innate cognitive dispositions (cf. Sperber 1985), refer to easy-to-remember human basics such as excrement, sex, violence, emotion, and death, or ones that beautifully simplify matters: that is, cut things down in size and complexity? Or do examples only work because they are transmitted by charismatic personalities, who may only be charismatic because they are recognizable as part of a traditionally esteemed series of, for example, 'mad genius' philosophers? Or are examples, by contrast, vehicles for the reconfiguration of thought and action, as in 'we'd never thought of it like that'? Thinking of the Žižek example, most of us have probably not, and it does undoubtedly make new analogies. Yet it also only works and convinces because it speaks to familiar national traditions and recognizable 'basic needs': that is, it works by way of repetition. Are examples, then, also 'persuasive fictions' (Strathern 1987) that we should be wary of? Žižek's account may be compelling, but it may also be more seductive than convincing.[2] And would he have come to the same conclusion if he had been talking about cars?

These are only some of the many possible questions that can be raised in relation to exemplification and the power of example. Indeed, what has struck us when working on this topic, apart from its ability to animate academics from all walks of life (anthropologists, archaeologists, philosophers, etc.), is that although 'the example' is fundamental to anthropological practice and immediately raises an almost infinite number of key disciplinary questions, it has almost never been the subject of genuine anthropological theorizing (for previous anthropological takes on exemplarity, however, see Humphrey 1997; Needham 1985). This is even more surprising in a discipline whose craft may be said to rest on the formative role of examples and exemplification. Think of Balinese cockfights, Kula exchanges, or the death of Captain Cook! Such examples have formed, motivated, and conjured up larger ensembles of anthropological ideas and discussions. They have, in Thomas Kuhn's sense, come to stand as paradigms or paradigmatic cases constitutive of anthropological knowledge as such. In a postscript to the second edition of *The structure of scientific revolutions* (1970), Kuhn even substituted the term 'exemplars' for 'paradigms'. He explains:

> Because the term [paradigm] has assumed a life of its own . . . I shall here substitute 'exemplars'. By it I mean, initially, the concrete problem-solutions that students encounter from the start of their scientific education, whether in laboratories, on examinations, or at the ends of chapters in science texts . . . All physicists, for example, begin by learning the same exemplars: problems such as the inclined plane, the conical pendulum, and Keplerian orbits; instruments such as the vernier, the calorimeter, and the Wheatstone bridge (1970: 187).

In this sense, a particular series is learned and rehearsed and gives the learner a certain confidence in how to both handle and conceive of scientific problems. In so doing,

Journal of the Royal Anthropological Institute (N.S.), 1-17
© Royal Anthropological Institute 2015

the series of exemplars, more than merely constituting a series, produces a particular way of looking at the world: it produces orientation. In this sense, exemplary examples and paradigmatic cases also direct scientific communities.[3] Yet it is equally clear that examples are an inherent part of the realities we study: 'the network' is not just an analytical tool for sociologists but has also become an exemplary organizational form (Riles 2000); the notion of precedence works by evoking authoritative examples in legal systems (Crapanzano 2000); and Fatima and Hussein are exemplary of and for practices of Shiite Muslims in Lebanon (Deeb 2009). It is through the example that both reality and analysis are thought and, equally importantly, reconfigured. The aim of this special issue, then, is to redress the theoretical disregard for exemplification by exploring the persuasive and evocative power – positive and negative – of 'examples' in social (and academic) life while also proposing exemplification as a distinct anthropological way of theorizing.

Examples and anthropology

As we have already seen, the potential strength of theorizing 'the example' is not only that it opens new avenues for anthropological analysis but also that, while doing so, it simultaneously draws on, and indeed goes straight to the heart of, age-old key discussions within anthropology and beyond. Indeed, it may be argued that Western philosophy and educational thinking were born of the grappling with exemplars and their legitimate role (Arendt 1977 [1968]; Warnick 2008: 2). In his majestic *Iliad* and *Odyssey*, Homer presented a great variety of exemplars that were used for reflection in ancient Greece and even today continue to be a source of learning in Western educational systems and literature. Socrates was an exemplar used by Plato to craft a particular philosophical system, and, in Roman thought and writing, exemplars persisted as integral to the assessment of both moral values and political action. Likewise, writers such as Plutarch, Silius, and Livy later crafted their work around exemplars that embodied Roman virtues and – at times – vices (cf. Lianeri 2011; Tipping 2010). Later still, the role of saints in much of Western Christianity took over the role of exemplars used to instil emulation of and/or ways of pleading with the divine through intermediaries (Brown 1983). While Caroline Humphrey's distinction between Mongolian and European moralities and uses of exemplars (1997) may thus be too stark, as this difference does not hinge on a lack of exemplars in Western traditions, she does seem justified in pointing to the fundamentally contested role of examples in a Western tradition. Consider, for example, the dialogue between Socrates and Meno, where Socrates in his famous maieutic style pushes Meno to define a matter, here virtue.[4] At first, Meno seems untroubled by the question and gives several examples of virtue: the virtue of a man is being able to manage the affairs of his city, the virtue of a woman to manage her house, and so on. Socrates, however, is not satisfied and exclaims:

> But come, it's your turn to pay your promised debt and say what virtue as a whole is. And 'stop making one into many', as the joke goes when somebody breaks something. Leave virtue whole and healthy and say what it is. Examples you have got from me . . . [A]s long as what virtue is as a whole is still under investigation, don't suppose that you will clarify virtue for anyone by answering in terms of its parts, or in any other terms which contain a similar obscurity (Plato 1984: 158, 162).

Socrates does not want examples or simply 'parts' and denies the role of concrete cases in his quest for pure universal forms. He looks for the definition of a 'whole': that is, a single pure standard placed above all others which can accommodate all concrete, and hence impure, cases of 'virtue'.

While it is well known that Socrates derided the role of concrete cases in his quest for pure universal forms, the debunking of cases and examples is also a familiar feature of (scientific) thought throughout history. In the age of the Enlightenment, for example, the role of exemplars was contested vigorously. The contention was that, in an era where change and upheavals were imminent, past exemplars were of no use as models for the future (Burke 2011; Harvey 2002; O'Gorman 2011). More recently, Paul de Man articulated a different, yet equally radical, critique of the logic of the example for never arriving at generality and certainty: 'Can any example ever truly fit a general proposition? Is not its particularity, to which it owes the illusion of its intelligibility, necessarily a betrayal of the general truth it is supposed to support and convey?' (1984: 276). While everything is to be expected from the general model or the pure *exemplar*, the example, on the contrary, is here reduced to 'mere *example*'. Examples are the symmetrical opposite of the general truths chased by science and can, as such, never be taken seriously in their own right. They are only real-world distortions of the real (or, rather, ideal) thing itself. In a similar vein, one may claim that while it has always been crucial to argue through examples in the anthropological tradition (Nuer segmentary lineages, Maori *hau*, etc.), such examples were at the same time discredited in twentieth-century modernist anthropology, where illustrations were rendered 'superfluous'[5] and treated simply as 'exemplars or reflections of meanings which are produced elsewhere' (Strathern 1990: 38). On the one hand, this 'elsewhere' may refer to a different layer of informants' reality (i.e. the socio-cultural system behind their actions), and, on the other, it may refer to deeper theoretical realities (sociality, culture, evolution, structure, relations of production, practice, etc.) subscribed to by theorists and claimed to be the genuine instigators of people's actions. Anthropologists made sense of 'individual incidents by putting them into their social or cultural context' (Strathern 1990: 37), and informants' actions were then seen as illustrations of a more fundamental social structure, cultural (con)text, or socio-economic reality. This particular general reality (Nuer social structure, for example), in turn, was a reflection of even more general realities (African political systems or human sociality). A movement from the particular to the general was established, and the particular was implicitly reduced to mere instantiations, or somewhat impure examples, of something more important and true. The latter was the genuine goal of scientific practice, anthropology included.

This hierarchy between the general and the particular, however, also tended to imply that some examples were promoted to the in-between position of being theoretical exemplars, simply because they were better and more pure and condensed expressions of genuine social and cultural forms. For Morgan, each evolutionary stage was 'best exemplified' by tribes and nations which had not been 'adulterated by external influence' but had worked out 'the problem of progress by original mental effort' (1985 [1878]: 16), and in the Marxist tradition, the capitalist mode of production, as exemplified by certain 'Western' regimes, or the pure Mbuti 'mode of production of the hunting band' (Meillassoux 1973) could be seen as less tainted by the confusing complexity of other, more mixed 'social formations'. In being theoretical exemplars, they were hyper-descriptive in that they described the world in more real terms than the world could do itself, and certainly did this job better than other examples would. Theoretical exemplars, then, were more accurate expressions of elementary forms (e.g. Durkheim

1995 [1912]; Lévi-Strauss 1969 [1949]), and they were – and are – found in most theoretical traditions.

It could rightfully be claimed, of course, that this is a highly simplified presentation of twentieth-century anthropology and that anthropology, more than any discipline, has been characterized by a specifying and idiographic tendency, especially in the German-American interpretative tradition of cultural anthropology, in which cultural difference (i.e. *particular* cultural examples) took centre stage. Yet the quest to understand particularities as particularities, in the Boasian tradition, implied similarly contextualizing and generalizing measures. Cultural difference was strongly tied to cultural holism, and understandings of person, time, and conduct in Bali, for example, were 'hooked together by a definable [Balinese] logic' (Geertz 1993*b* [1973]: 404). The modernist degradation of particular instances in favour of general scientific theory was replaced by the subjugation of Balinese examples – conceptions of 'persons' and 'time', for example (themselves already generalized from different Balinese naming systems and calendars) – to 'Balinese theory' (Geertz 1993*b* [1973]: 381). Again, particulars only made sense in relation to pre-specified generalities. While there was clearly an anti-modernist tendency in comparing one particular with another, the idea of the particular whole itself – culture – was elevated to the status of general theory.

Notwithstanding this, notable attempts have been made to think differently of examples and exemplification in anthropology and beyond. Max Weber's notion of ideal types entailed social scientists, on the basis of particular cultural and historical realities, constructing coherent utopian expositions of such realities against which reality could be 'measured' (Weber 2012 [1904]: 127). In other words, ideal types were generalized – and hence also different – from specific historical realities. They were constructions, caricatured exemplars made from specific realities, or 'accentuations' that our 'imagination, oriented and schooled towards the contact with reality, judges to be adequate' (Weber 2012 [1904]: 125, 127), and, in that sense, they were also a means for investigating, elucidating, and exposing the realities they were drawn from by clarifying their 'distinctive character' (Weber 2012 [1904]: 125). While subscribing neither to the logical coherence demanded of Weberian ideal types, nor to the rigid distinction between ideal types and real types, Weber does draw attention to the importance of constructed exemplars in scaling reality, and he highlights the important and never-ending circular movement between the particular and the general – their simultaneous interdependence and independence – in analytical practice. Much like the good ethnographic example or exemplar, an ideal type reveals new connections and manages to reconfigure things through a revelatory and clarifying analytical practice.

The extended case method of the Manchester School of Social Anthropology (Burawoy 1998; Evens & Handelman 2006; Gluckman 2006 [1959]; Mitchell 1983) is another exception to the modernist attempts to reduce the example to a servant of theory. Instead of using examples as an 'apt illustration of general ethnographic and analytical statements', the idea of the extended case method or situational analysis 'was to arrive at the general through the dynamic particularity of the case' (Evens & Handelman 2006: 1). The particular case was different from the apt illustration because it contained within itself 'more' than the illustration did. This 'more', it was assumed, was the practices, processes, conflicts, and ephemeral circumstances of real-life situations (Evens & Handelman 2006). The case was endorsed at the expense of the formal theories of a mainly structural-functional bent but, at the same time, the distinction between real life and formal theories (and their apt illustrations) was kept, and real life itself was promoted to theory (the theoretical axioms being process, practice, contingency, and conflict). The hierarchy between the general and the particular may have been inverted, but the verticality was kept and the particular was made the new general.

A contention of this introduction is that the example does not invert the vertical analytical movement but rather points to a 'lateral' rethinking of the relation between the particular and the general, ethnographic material and theoretical reflection. Thinking of postcolonial critique (e.g. Said 1978), the influence of post-structuralism (e.g. Bourdieu 1977; Foucault 1984) and nomadic philosophy (Deleuze & Guattari 2004), and the crisis of representation in anthropology in the 1980s (Clifford & Marcus 1986), as well as subsequent developments within anthropology, it can be said that a critique of the vertical modernist approach to exemplarity is slightly outdated. While this may be true, there are several reasons why the example may still take us in new directions. First, the idea of examples as exemplification of more general propositions is not so easily dismissed. In questioning the contextualizing practices of Western thought, Marilyn Strathern – even if only mobilizing Melanesia to make productive analogies (Holbraad & Pedersen 2009: 385) – can only resort to such contextualizing practices herself when giving multiple examples of how Melanesians in general may be inclined to 'understand encounters in terms of their effects' (Strathern 1990: 37). Examples, then – as 'mere examples', apt illustrations, or theoretical exemplars – still pertain strongly to our analytical and descriptive practices, and most anthropologists, now and again, find it necessary to qualify a general theoretical point with an example. Most of us can be 'blamed' for this, but Katherine Verdery – for example(!)[6] – while speaking of property rights and new associations in the aftermath of socialism in rural Romania, writes that, 'having joined the association, one entered a realm of intricately overlapping rights, obligations and claims. Let us take as an example a widow who is too old to manage the work on her newly acquired three hectares' (1999: 60). Verdery makes her general point about 'overlapping rights, obligations and claims' by means of other – and supposedly more accessible – material and, to the reader, it appears that an example is simply picked from among the almost infinite number of examples that the author has to hand. In this instance, the example (presumably one example among many identical ones) is the logical counterpart to the notion of the rule (the one rule creating the many examples), heavily criticized in recent decades (see, e.g., Bourdieu 1977) but nevertheless implicitly present in many of our descriptive practices.[7] Secondly, and following on from this, our aim is neither to disparage the use of examples, nor to dissolve theory in favour of a multiplicity of self-contained instances and perspectives, but to propose exemplarity in itself as a good and powerful prism for thinking anthropologically, simply because the example excels in exploring the tension between, and the instability of, the specific and the general, the concrete and the abstract, motion and structure, ethnography and theory, and it does so by never fully becoming one or the other.

In exploring this particular power of the example, we take our cue from Alexander Gelley (1995), who traces two markedly different approaches to examples and exemplarity already apparent in classical Greek thought (see also Flyvbjerg 2001). According to Gelley, the Platonic and Socratic idea of the *paradeigma* (Lat. *exemplar*) as a model, archetype, or exemplar was challenged by the Aristotelian view of *paradeigma* as an instance from which inductive conclusions could be derived:

> Whereas the Platonic model displays a vertical directionality, from a primary exemplar down to multiple instantiations, for Aristotle example involves something like a lateral movement: 'neither from part to whole nor from whole to part but from part to part, like to like, when two things fall under the same genus but one is better known than the other' (1995: 1).

Aristotle, then, would not go from part to whole, or whole to part, but rather place part and part side by side. Contrary to de Man, Socrates, and modernist anthropology, which saw particularity as a betrayal of general truth that diverts us away from the firm ground of ultimate certainty, the Aristotelian line of thought – in our rendering of it – proposes that the logic of the example, rather than putting things to rest in generalities, entails the setting in motion of particular trains of imagination, or series of particulars, that are always simply in the process of exploring and proposing generality.

In line with this Aristotelian understanding of *paradeigma* as a lateral movement that denies the distinction between the horizontal and the vertical by (only) suggesting generality, we propose that exemplarity should be taken seriously in its own right. This entails that the act of exemplification is not reduced to an unwanted distortion of pure concepts or genuine theory, although neither is it a return to the concrete or empirical reality as implicitly proposed by, for example, the Manchester School. Exemplification, rather, circumvents the distinction between the horizontal and the vertical by claiming that effective examples (i.e. exemplars) are ones that manage to theorize or assemble what lies beyond them by elucidating connections, evoking trains of thought, and persuading audiences. Such paradigmatic examples or exemplars are – paradoxical as this may sound – cases that manage to theorize the world around them, or, to cite Agamben on paradigms, they entail 'a movement that goes from singularity to singularity and, without ever leaving singularity, transforms every singular case into an *exemplar* of a general rule that can never be stated a priori' (2009: 22, emphasis in original; see also Turner 1975). From our own tradition, we only need to think of the Maori and Maussian concept of *hau*, the spirit of the gift, or the Foucauldian panopticon,[8] which are both exemplars of our kind of examples, at once part of *and* paradigmatic of more than Maori worlds and European prisons. In exhibiting its own singularity, an exemplar or paradigm 'makes intelligible a new ensemble, whose homogeneity it itself constitutes' (Agamben 2009: 18). It is a part taken from a whole and then asserted as a particular class, type, or instance, which renders a changed whole, and it thus has the capacity to constitute itself as a paradigm ('what stands beside'), that is, to become an example for other examples. As such, the exemplar never arrives at universality but points to a series of (new) resemblances by way of analogy. Gelley makes a similar point when he writes that the example/exemplar 'is oriented to the recovery of a lost whole or the discovery of a new one', and adds that the function of the exemplar is to 'induce an imitative reproduction' in audiences and thereby to 'propagate itself' (1995: 3). The example as exemplar, then, has the potential to conjure up (momentary) wholes and extend itself in series of concrete examples, and, in so doing, it reconfigures and moulds the world in its own image.

It is precisely this lateral movement of serial analogies (and digressions) that circumvents a number of problematic distinctions, because effective examples or exemplars – and this holds for both 'theory' and 'reality' – are neither simply singular cases, nor theories that transcend the world once and for all. They are only ever exemplary in their successful claims for relative generality, and they always face the danger of becoming too little – that is, being reduced to 'mere examples' (or simply bad examples that are unable to draw in other material) – or of becoming too much

– that is, 'excessive exemplars' that allow for the digestion of all other material and, in effect, turn vacuous (cf. Geertz 1993*a* [1973]: 3-4). The latter, it could be claimed, was the destiny of the Foucauldian take on the panopticon and power, and Melanesian dividualism – and, with it, the Maussian concept of *hau* – may sometimes face the same danger of being stretched too much (see, e.g., Mosko 2010; Robbins 2010). The good example/exemplar is always less than everything and more than itself and, rather than doing away with general propositions, examples and exemplars point to a constant movement – in both anthropological theory and the ethnographic worlds we attend to – between the general and the specific by suggesting, proposing, and revealing new generalized 'wholes', standing for a broader class of phenomena, while at the same time always being in danger of being shallow 'exemplars for everything' or reduced to 'mere examples', standing for nothing other than themselves.

Thus, apart from exploring 'the example' and 'the exemplar', as well as the tension between them, through a number of individual ethnographic contributions that each raise important questions in their own right, we, the editors of this special issue, suggest that thinking through examples may provide us with a number of analytical advantages. First, the example is a concrete abstraction, carved from and constituting a larger whole and, as such, proposes an attention to unruly details. Secondly, it points to analysis as being suggestive as much as descriptive. And, thirdly, the analogical logic of examples juxtaposes theory and ethnography in radical ways. We will address each of these points in turn.

The example: between stability and unruliness

The original meaning of example, deriving from the Latin *eximere*, was that of a cut, an incision, or a singling out (Arendt 1982: 77; Gelley 1995: 2; Lyons 1989: 9). This feature of alluding to singulars is closely related to a focus on detail, as the example is – etymologically speaking – synonymous with the term *detail*, which is also 'removed' and 'cut out' (Lyons 1989: 9). Attending to examples, then, is also to attend to details and, following Brian Massumi, to give in to both their dangers and possibilities:

> The success of the example hinges on the details. Every little one matters. At each new detail, the example runs the risk of falling apart, of its unity of self-relation becoming a jumble. Every detail is essential to the case. This means that the detail is like another example embedded in it. A microexample. An incipient example. ... Every example harbors terrible powers of deviation and digression (2002: 18).

While the example as exemplar may create stability by alluding to a larger whole that people (are made to) subscribe to, it may thus also contain within it a potential instability, a possibility for becoming something else, either by 'falling apart' in other details/examples or by being made to stand for other wholes. In focusing on the concrete by way of the example, we propose to focus on, and become intimate with, details that both set ethnographic worlds in motion and serve to stabilize them.

On the one hand, then, the exemplar can foster emulation, imitation, and stability, either by presenting positive ideals or by making a negative exemplar of something. This logic can be found in the penitentiary aspects of court rulings throughout history. Take the opening of Foucault's *Discipline and punish* (1977), where a vivid and rather horrifying account is given of what kind of exemplar could be made of Damiens the regicide in Paris, 1757. Damiens was to have his flesh torn from his body and limbs with red-hot pincers, and to be burned with sulphur, molten lead, boiling oil, burning resin, and wax. He was to be made an exemplar of unacceptable behaviour and of the sovereign king's exemplary power. On the other hand, however, making examples of something – by using torture to instigate fear, awe, and deterrence, for instance – has often been an inherently dangerous endeavour that does not pre-empt future effects. In a more recent context, this can be seen in the escalations in violence witnessed in Syria in 2011. The regime, wishing to remain in power, opted for the harshest measures to keep the populace at bay: first, by tearing out the nails of youngsters who – following the example of young Tunisians and Egyptians – had been spraying anti-regime graffiti over the walls of the town of Dera, and, later, at the beginning of Ramadan and ever since, by making an example of particular cities such as Hama and Deir al-Zour. The sheer use of force and violence, however, did not work as expected. Whereas the intent was to make an example of the perpetrators, of those causing civil unrest, the violence turned against the regime and made the regime itself an example of illegitimate rule and force. The effect of deterrence and fear in making examples of entire cities conjured a very different whole in the eyes of a local and global public, namely a cruel regime that would stop at nothing to achieve its goals. The making of examples, then, is not an easy task and always harbours dangers (and possibilities). It is and always will be – in the words of Gelley (1995: 14) – marked by the scandalous, if scandalous is taken to mean that the example is always insufficient yet nevertheless forces people to take a stance.

All contributions to this special issue, in one way or another, explore this precarious tension between the 'unruliness of examples' (Gelley 1995; cf. Humphrey 1997) and the disciplinary and stability-enhancing power of exemplarity. In his contribution on the Urapmin of Papua New Guinea, Joel Robbins focuses mainly on the latter by relating exemplary representations to ritual. Taking his starting-point as the claim that cultures are organized by values that are frequently in conflict in everyday life, he sees the presentation of exemplary examples in ritual as perfected representations that model, and are aimed at modelling, the realization of single cultural values. This role of the exemplary in ritual is contrasted with the role of 'failed exemplars' and examples in everyday social processes. Lotte Buch Segal's paper on the Palestinian wives of detainees held in Israeli prisons similarly looks at exemplarity – this time exemplary Palestinian motherhood – but pays particular attention to the burden of living up to ideals. The wives of detainees wrestle with the tension between who they are expected to be and who they actually are (and might be). Their return to the ordinary after the detention of their husbands, Buch Segal shows, can only ever be a descent into the *allegedly* normal. The seeming stability of national exemplarity casts shadows and 'comes at the cost of stifling personal affects that disturb the exemplary register of womanhood among Palestinians' (pp. 43–4).

Moving from Palestinians in the Occupied Territories to Christians in Damascus, Andreas Bandak analyses the singular example's relation to a series of examples of sainthood. Considering a sermon at the shrine of Our Lady of Soufanieh, he explores how the sermon takes part in and models a series of divinely inspired figures that affect the listeners and challenge them to be moved by, and be moved towards, divinely inspired change. This series is relatively open and asks for responsiveness on the part of listeners, so rather than creating clear-cut stability and repetition, the series of examples/exemplars produces a 'drift' or direction in the lives of followers. In Antonia Walford's contribution, this idea of drift becomes a problem of 'drifting away'. She explores the not-quite replication of standard measures through calibration within metrological science in Brazil. While the major concern of her informants is to produce stability (i.e. good exemplars of an international absolute standard measure), there is always an uncertainty between a unit (metre, watt, etc.) and its materialization, and being a good example can always only be an approximation. Materializations have, in Walford's words, 'a habit over time of drifting away from that which they are meant to be representing' (p. 70), and metrological exemplification, while trying to create exact copies, can only make good examples that are always exceptions. Employing Annelise Riles's expression, she suggests that stability and exception are therefore the same form seen twice.

Stine Krøijer, in her contribution, considers the example as a theory of change among left-wing radicals in Europe. While she looks at how protest actions can become exemplars for other protest actions, her major concern is the example as a possible figuration of the future. Rather than revolutionizing capitalism from without, as it were, practices such as dumpster-diving, she argues, may be seen as revolutionizing the existing from within by giving form to what is not yet. By collapsing goal and means, dumpster-diving *is* another future – or another possibility of the present, one could say – while it also directs others towards this (present) future by making an example to be imitated.

In the contributions by Christian Suhr and Alice Forbess, the unruly tends to outdo stability. Suhr's contribution exposes a curious resemblance between moving images, spirit possession, and the response to visual media among young neo-orthodox Muslims in Denmark. In all these cases, the failed example is an amplifier of invisibility that points towards the unknown, and, seen in these terms, the failed example may indeed be considered exemplary because it truthfully depicts that which cannot be depicted. As a matter of fact, unruliness may, according to Suhr, be a defining feature of all perception. That bad examples may be the best examples is a point also made by Forbess in her contribution on Orthodox Christianity in Montenegro. Despite his 'unholy' appearance – or, rather, because of it – Abbot Serafim, who is the main case in Forbess's contribution, 'renders obvious God's impenetrability and omnipotence' (p. 120) through his transgressive and unedifying behaviour. According to Forbess, paradoxical and subversive examples such as Serafim do not elucidate worlds as much as they trigger a perpetual and open-ended contemplation on the ever-elusive nature of God in an Orthodox context where mystical knowledge is privileged. She thus demonstrates how 'the exemplary can do different kinds of conceptual work in different ethical systems' (p. 116).

In Amira Mittermaier's contribution on a Sufi spiritual leader in Cairo, the example as representing an already constituted and stable whole is contrasted with the evocative dream visions of her informants. Vision stories, she writes, are not meant to be representative in a conventional modernist scientific sense but serve to invite and move listeners by gesturing towards the invisible. Rather than stabilizing meaning, the exemplar points to a realm only accessible to the imagination and as such serves to evoke the creative powers of the listener. As in Forbess's case, the introduction of 'ordinary reflection' in favour of exceptionality seems to push God further away. Much in line with this, Simon Coleman's contribution on the Anglican shrine at Walsingham uses exemplification to explore the interplay between model and instance by paying particular attention to ways in which always inchoate examples provoke rather than fix thinking. However, he also points to different ways of exemplifying – that is, different modes of making connections and constructing wholes – by drawing on two different periods in Walsingham's history. While the concern of Father Hope Patten in the

1920s and 1930s was to recover a lost whole through historical fragments, the concern of Patten's contemporary successor seems less with a specific past than with 'meta-exemplifying' the past as past and constructing an 'exegetical and historical blankness' (p. 157), which seems highly conducive to Walsingham's popularity in the present.

Johan Lindquist's contribution on the broker as an exemplary analytical figure for analysing transnational migration does not directly address the tension between the stable and the unruly but he does nevertheless use a stable analytical figure, the broker, to juxtapose dissimilar categories such as labour recruiters and NGO activists. As such, the unruly resides less in the inchoateness of the example as such – as was the case with many of the previous contributors – than in its ability to compare the previously incomparable and problematize ethical distinctions between 'bad' labour recruiters and 'good' NGO activists. The analytical exemplar, the broker, creates unruliness in the ethnographic material it subsumes. This obviously raises questions about the kind of analysis suggested by our rendering of the example and about how one may indeed conceive of ethnographic material and documentation.

The example proposes as much as it describes

A concern for evidence was the theme of another special issue of *JRAI* (Engelke 2008). Here, Matthew Engelke rightly argues that even though protocols of evidence were not given explicit and sustained anthropological attention in the past, the history of anthropological thought may nevertheless be seen 'as a series of debates over questions of evidence' (2008: S2). We have argued that the same thing applies to exemplification: 'the example' is an intriguing key to theoretical discussions and could easily serve as a prism for reading the history of anthropological theory. And, like evidence, the example is curiously absent from explicit attention in anthropological theory. Indeed, Aristotle pointed to the intimate relation between evidence and exemplification when he dealt with examples alongside enthymeme and maxim as forms of 'proof common to all' in the seminal *The art of rhetoric* (2004: 76-8/1356b-8a; 189/1393a). Examples, he pointed out, could either be taken from the fabric of real life or be invented. If taken from the fabric of real life and events, the example rested on the specific act of narration, of placing it in an argument, whereas the invented example presented a possible figuration of facts. The example in this sense was used to particular effect and to prove a point in speech. While different academic notions of the example were manifest for Aristotle, most anthropologists would not subscribe to the fictional examples often used in philosophy, such as Jean-Paul Sartre's use of 'Pierre and Paul' and their rendez-vous at random cafés (2003 [1943]), but would prefer the not-entirely fictional ethnographic example. Yet while evidence and exemplification may thus provoke a number of similar perspectives and debates, such as questions of how to establish validity, the notion of the example tends to suggest a significantly different take on analysis as such.

One key difference is that, while evidence concerns what *counts* as evidence in different disciplinary protocols (Engelke 2008), exemplification raises questions as to how analysis manages to *draw things into view*. With exemplification, the question of veracity and validity – that is, of finding proof ('What is this phenomenon proof of?') – turns into a question of how to produce imagination and potentiality ('What can this example evoke?'). The move from evidence to exemplification is thus a move from the passive provision of evidence from an already established viewpoint in a disciplinary tradition ('We know what we are looking for but can we find it?') to the active making of convincing connections *from within* the example ('Can we find other things by (imaginatively) using what we have found?'). Clearly, evidence is framed by particular protocols and exists in relation to questions (Engelke 2008: S5), and discussions of the concept of evidence are, hence, concerned with 'the historicity and disciplinary specificity of evidentiary protocols' (Engelke 2008: S1), although it tends to be evidence for what is already framed in a disciplinary horizon or for answers to questions that have already been posed (by the academy[9]) prior to the actual evidence-seeking activity; evidence is evidence for something else. Questions of evidence may thus, in the words of Engelke, be a matter of 'pattern recognition' between anthropologists and 'the social life they observe' (Engelke 2008: S9) or between different cultures: that is, between what appear to be initially separate domains. In line with this, the problem becomes a matter of translatability between different cultures and between unrepeatable field experiences and repeatable patterns (Engelke 2008: S12). Rather than immediately raising such problems regarding 'recognition' and translatability, we suggest that examples, instead of connecting what was already divided prior to the example (theory and reality, culture and culture), create their own divisions and connections. The notion of exemplification, then, points to pattern 'extension', the analytical strength of a particular example being how much it is able to proliferate, connect, and absorb. In line with this view, evidence 'makes evident' or 'recognizes' (in something outside itself) and can be gathered (the many become one), whereas exemplification multiplies, makes connections, and evokes (the one becomes many); it is a lateral self-scaling device (cf. Holbraad & Pedersen 2009: 380) that creates its own evidence, so to speak, and is explicitly imaginative and inventive (cf. Deleuze & Guattari 1994). However, while it does not concern reliability and 'getting it right' (Engelke 2008: S11-12, S16) as much as captivating and 'mind-blowing' accounts, an example also has to be convincing to be effective. Žižek, at the beginning of this introduction, may have been mind-blowing and interesting – even funny – but perhaps not very convincing.

This entails, on the one hand, that the example is more concerned with 'conviction' and 'effect' than with 'accuracy' and 'proof'. To return, once more, to Foucault and his genealogy of modern forms of disciplining. While it can surely be debated for its historical accuracy, the accomplishments of the panopticon model are harder to question. In this sense, Foucault ended up exemplifying not just a particular historical epoch but also a particular conception of a modern surveillance society that people have subscribed to. That even 'wrong' examples can be effective is a point also raised by Steven Woolgar and Geoff Cooper (1999), who discuss the property of what they term 'iconic exemplars' in the production of knowledge in scholarly communities. As ardent promoters of Science and Technology Studies, Woolgar and Cooper had long used the iconic example of Langdon Winner's famous analysis of Moses Bridge on Long Island to exemplify how technology holds political qualities. The bridge, according to Winner's analysis, was designed to exclude poor and black people from the public areas held dear to the richer sectors of the population because buses – mainly used by the poorer sectors – were too high to navigate the bridge's overpasses. But the example – as Woolgar and Cooper learn – is wrong! Buses do, in fact, cross under Moses Bridge. This has been known for many years, moreover, and yet Moses Bridge continues to be used as an iconic examplar of the political dimensions of design. And further, according to Woolgar and Cooper, a successful refutation is never possible as the story still proves a certain valid point. As they say: 'Such stories do not become exemplary simply as a result of their referential adequacy, or indeed of any inherent property. Their status is the upshot of their usage rather than the result of their internal qualities' (1999: 438). What such iconic exemplars accomplish is that they make academic readers use examples for a wide range of other examples. They do so because they are extendable and their referential adequacy irrelevant. Returning once again to Žižek: his example may not have been convincing in terms of its adequacy, but it may have been convincing – that is, capable of spreading and having effects – simply by being funny and memorable.

On the other hand, this also implies that while evidence is inherently backward-looking, by being concerned with how to prove what has already happened (e.g. evidence for murder), exemplification points to the fact that reality can be made to be something else. It is not just evidence for what *has* happened but attests to a potentially different kind of past, present, and future.[10] Examples may, indeed, be evidence for what is not yet existing (cf. Holbraad & Pedersen 2009: 384; Strathern 1999: 163), such as when Needham carves out a history of ideas devoid of history by juxtaposing a number of apparently dissimilar exemplars and thereby 'furnish[ing] a new and distinct validation of the efficacy of comparative analysis' (Needham 1985: xii). In this view, analysis – and stating examples – is also seen as suggestive: that is, as proposing worlds as much as describing them. To return once again to Agamben, '[I]n the paradigm it is a matter not of corroborating a certain sensible likeness but of producing it by means of an operation. For this reason, the paradigm is never already given, but is generated and produced ... by "placing alongside", "conjoining together", and above all by "showing" and "exposing"'. Exemplification is an analytical act that sets a new standard from which other examples emerge, and examples, from this view, *are* analysis, at once concrete and abstract, because they advance theory and, as such, encourage a particular ethnographic description. Drawing on Kuhn, we can conclude with Agamben that 'a paradigm is simply an example, a single case that, by its repeatability, acquires the capacity to model tacitly the behaviour and research practices of scientists ... the universal logic of law is replaced by the specific and singular logic of the example' (2009: 11-12).[11]

The example confuses ontological divides

We have already seen how a primary division seems to be built into the notion of evidence from the outset: evidence for what? Evidence is evidence for something else (Engelke 2008: S5, S7), such as data as evidence for a theory, a particular instance settling a wider claim, or the small as evidence for the large. When speaking of evidence in relation to scale, then, there is a tendency to stay within a terminology of 'small places, large issues' (Eriksen 2001). Engelke points to the fact that anthropologists use vignettes or anecdotes about a Tuesday morning in a market outside Timbuktu to explain the workings of globalization, that ethnographies express a *particularity* which is supposed to take *everything* into account, and that parts are used as evidence for whole representations or 'something greater' (Engelke 2008: S12-15). The example, in our understanding, tries to circumvent this occupation with – and use of language of – (spatial) 'size' (cf. Højer 2013*a*; Holbraad & Pedersen 2009; Wastell 2001). Examples may scale things and grow, as it were, but examples do not scale a world that is already small or large, part or whole, from the outset. In line with this, it may be tempting to paraphrase 'Thinking through things' (Henare, Holbraad & Wastell 2007)[12] and speak of 'thinking through examples'. Yet, while we – and many others over recent decades – share that book's ambition of overcoming oppositions between, say, representation and world, meaning and things, we believe that the notion of example, at once always already abstract and concrete, theoretical and indigenous, may do a better job than 'things', which – in that particular book – tend to be 'informants' accounts' (2007: 1), informants' 'own terms' (2007: 1), 'things' 'encountered in the field as they present themselves' (2007: 2), 'the material itself' (2007: 4), and 'things encountered in fieldwork' which should dictate their own analysis (2007: 4). According to the authors, anthropological analysis 'has to do with how *we* must think in order to conceive a world the way they do' (2007: 15, emphasis in original). It is assumed that 'they' have different 'things/concepts' than we do: '[O]ur own concepts are inadequate, and therefore need to be transformed by appeal to those of our informants' (2007: 16). The existence of a non-ambivalent and coherent 'them' and 'their things' is never questioned, and invention, it seems, always only takes place in an imagined outside. The authors thus tend to make 'their things' too definite (Højer 2013b) and to reconstitute the very divide (anthropologist versus informant, us versus them, representation versus thing) that is thought to have been overcome. The 'things' are always 'ruly' and 'theirs', whereas the example, in our argument, is always unruly and never anyone's in particular and, as such, juxtaposes analysis and 'ethnographic worlds' and enables them to move in and out of each other (see also Bandak & Kuzmanovic 2015). An effective example is in-between and has the capacity to make new connections (and divides) and conjure up particular worlds-in-the-making, and this holds as much for anthropological communities as it does for child-raisers, politicians, and priests. If ethnographic worlds, then, do not part company with the anthropological world in terms of evidential structure but rather in terms of what is brought about with the examples given, the example offers the possibility of seeing a significant correlation between the anthropological world of scholars and the ethnographic worlds explored. Just as it could be claimed that theories are only examples – Balinese cockfights as webs of significance, Maori *hau* as social life, or the panopticon as power – exemplification can also be said to be theory in the realities we study. In both cases, examples model behaviour, discourse, and thought by crafting particular series of analogies; they are not 'things' but assemblages (cf. DeLanda 2006; Deleuze & Guattari 2004; Ong & Collier 2005) that carve out trajectories. We could then follow Johnson and Needham by claiming that an exemplar is 'a pattern; an example to be imitated' (Johnson cited in Needham 1985: 1), if we specify that good examples – examples that manage to assemble things beyond themselves – are also the best theory we can hope for.

NOTES

We are indebted to Matthew Engelke, Sharon Macdonald, and two anonymous reviewers for their help and comments. We would also like to thank Mikkel Bille, Thomas Brudholm, Esther Fihl, Birgitte Scheppelern Johansen, Daniella Kuzmanovic, Benedikte Møller Kristensen, and all contributors to this special issue for their comments and suggestions. We express our gratitude to Alternative Spaces, a collaborative research project funded by the Danish Council for Strategic Research, and Copenhagen University's Asian Dynamics Initiative for funding this project.

[1] This example is given in a number of lectures broadcast on YouTube. See, for example: *http://www.youtube.com/watch?v=FJ73hLQ64Ng* (accessed 6 January 2015).

[2] Actually, one could argue that the funny and somewhat far-fetched nature of Žižek's example serves to draw attention to itself as over-simplified, thereby undermining its own seductive capability or – at least – drawing attention to itself as *just* a revelatory metaphor. And perhaps this very example, for Žižek, is not picked at random but is rather itself an expression, an example even, of a particular predilection of his also found in his musings on the anal object (cf. Žižek 2001).

[3] See Geertz (1988: 17-20) for a comparable discussion of authors as founders of discursivity.

[4] Flyvbjerg's chapter on 'the power of example' (2001: 66-87) drew our attention to this dialogue.

[5] This was not just the case in anthropology. According to Gallagher and Greenblatt (2000), for instance, a similar denigration of examples can be found in the discipline of history, where anecdotes have been considered 'no-account items' and, accordingly, have come to be associated with counterhistory.

[6] This example is simply chosen because we stumbled upon it by chance and not because Verdery is an exemplary case. As a matter of fact, this introduction may be much more exemplary with regard to using examples as illustrations of more general points.

[7] All this obviously does not apply only to anthropology. Take the study of commodity chains, for example, where some exemplars, such as 'tropical commodity chains' (e.g. coffee and cocoa) connecting South and North, may be said to hold a 'comparative advantage' over other commodity chains, because they better highlight global inequality (Bair 2008: 16). While they may, according to the theories proposing them (and in true modernist fashion), highlight the way things really are, they may equally well be seen as 'persuasive fictions' that *make* things the way they really are.

[8] Agamben writes of Foucault's panopticon model that 'it is a singular object that, standing equally for all others of the same class, defines the intelligibility of the group of which it is a part and which, at the same time, it constitutes' (2009: 17).

[9] And the academy is the main concern of Engelke's introduction.

[10] In his book on the force of example, Alessandro Ferrara (2008) speaks of the world of things and what exists – what is – and the world of ideas and normativity – what ought to be – and defines the example as the force of what is as it should be. While we agree that the example can open up new ways of going beyond the given limitations and hence holds the potential of 'expanding the reach of our normative understandings' (Ferrara 2008: 3), our take is not only concerned with a normative exemplarity pointing to new possible futures, but is also concerned with exemplification as the force of what can be made to be (of past, present, and future).

[11] In a similar vein, Lévi-Strauss – in Bruun Jensen's words – 'enjoins us to study singular cases – golden events – that somehow can count as general demonstrations' (Bruun Jensen 2011: 5; see Lévi-Strauss 1963: 288-9).

[12] A title which has itself come to serve as an example for other titles – people are now 'thinking through' a great number of things.

REFERENCES

AGAMBEN, G. 2009. What is a paradigm? In *The signature of all things: on method*, 9-32. New York: Zone.
ARENDT, H. 1977 [1968]. The concept of history: ancient and modern. In *Between past and future: eight exercises in political thought*, 41-90. New York: Penguin.
——— 1982. *Lectures on Kant's political philosophy*. Chicago: University Press.
ARISTOTLE 2004. *The art of rhetoric*. London: Penguin.
BAIR, J. 2008. Global commodity chains: genealogy and review. In *Frontiers of commodity chain research* (ed.) J. Bair, 1-34. Stanford: University Press.
BANDAK, A. & D. KUZMANOVIC 2015. Introduction: analytical displacement and the project of the humanities. In *Qualitative analysis in the making* (eds) D. Kuzmanovic & A. Bandak, 1-22. New York: Routledge.
BOURDIEU, P. 1977. *Outline of a theory of practice* (trans. R. Nice). Cambridge: University Press.
BROWN, P. 1983. The saint as exemplar in late antiquity. *Representations* **1**, 1-25.
BRUUN JENSEN, C. 2011. Comparative relativism: symposium on an impossibility. *Common Knowledge* **17**, 1-12.
BURAWOY, M. 1998. The extended case study method. *Sociological Theory* **16**, 4-33.
BURKE, P. 2011. Exemplarity and anti-exemplarity in early modern Europe. In *The Western time of ancient history: historiographical encounters with Greek and Roman pasts* (ed.) A. Lianeri, 48-59. Cambridge: University Press.
CLIFFORD, J. & G.E. MARCUS (eds) 1986. *Writing culture*. Berkeley: University of California Press.
CRAPANZANO, V. 2000. Precedent. In *Serving the word: literalism in America from the pulpit to the bench*, 304-23. New York: The New Press.
DE MAN, P. 1984. *The rhetoric of Romanticism*. New York: Columbia University Press.
DEEB, L. 2009. Emulating and/or embodying the ideal. *American Ethnologist* **36**, 242-57.
DELANDA, M. 2006. *A new philosophy of society: assemblage theory and social complexity*. New York: Continuum.
DELEUZE, G. & F. GUATTARI 1994. *What is Philosophy?* (trans. H. Tomlinson & G. Burchell). New York: Columbia University Press.
——— & ——— 2004. *A thousand plateaus* (trans. B. Massumi). New York: Continuum.
DURKHEIM, É. 1995 [1912]. *The elementary forms of religious life* (trans. K.E. Fields). New York: Free Press.

ENGELKE, M. 2008. The objects of evidence. *Journal of the Royal Anthropological Institute* (N.S.) Special Issue: The objects of evidence: anthropological approaches to the production of knowledge (ed.) M. Engelke, S1-21.

ERIKSEN, T.H. 2001. *Small places, large issues: an introduction to social and cultural anthropology.* London: Pluto.

EVENS, T.M.S. & D. HANDELMAN 2006. Introduction: the ethnographic praxis of the theory of practice. In *The Manchester School: practice and ethnographic praxis in anthropology* (eds) T.M.S. Evens & D. Handelman, 1-11. New York: Berghahn.

FERRARA, A. 2008. *The force of the example: explorations in the paradigm of judgement.* New York: Colombia University Press.

FLYVBJERG, B. 2001. *Making social science matter: why social inquiry fails and how it can succeed again.* Cambridge: University Press.

FOUCAULT, M. 1977. *Discipline and punish: the birth of the prison* (trans. A. Sheridan). London: Penguin.

——— 1984. Nietzsche, genealogy, history. In *The Foucault reader* (ed.) P. Rabinow, 76-100. London: Penguin.

GALLAGHER, C. & S. GREENBLATT 2000. Counterhistory and the anecdote. In *Practicing new historicism* (eds) C. Gallagher & S. Greenblatt, 49-74. Chicago: University Press.

GEERTZ, C. 1988. *Works and lives: the anthropologist as author.* Stanford: University Press.

——— 1993*a* [1973]. Thick description: toward an interpretation of culture. In *The interpretation of cultures,* 3-30. London: Fontana.

——— 1993*b* [1973]. Person, time, and conduct in Bali. In *The interpretation of cultures,* 360-411. London: Fontana.

GELLEY, A. 1995. Introduction. In *Unruly examples: on the rhetoric of exemplarity* (ed.) A. Gelley, 1-24. Stanford: University Press.

GLUCKMAN, M. 2006 [1959]. Ethnographic data in British social anthropology. In *The Manchester School: practice and ethnographic praxis in anthropology* (eds) T.M.S. Evens & D. Handelman, 13-42. New York: Berghahn.

HARVEY, I. 2002. *Labyrinths of exemplarity: at the limits of deconstruction.* Albany: State University of New York Press.

HENARE, A., M. HOLBRAAD & S. WASTELL 2007. Introduction: thinking through things. In *Thinking through things: theorising artefacts ethnographically* (eds) A. Henare, M. Holbraad & S. Wastell, 1-31. London: Routledge.

HØJER, L. 2013*a*. Escalations: spying and totalitarianism in Western China and beyond. In *Alternative spaces* (eds) J. Dahl & E. Fihl, 219-37. New York: Palgrave.

——— 2013*b*. Hvilke ting? Hvilke relationer? Hvilke verdener? [Which things? Which relations? Which worlds?]. *Tidsskriftet Antropologi* **67**, 47-9.

HOLBRAAD, M. & M.A. PEDERSEN 2009. Planet M: the intense abstraction of Marilyn Strathern. *Anthropological Theory* **9**, 371-94.

HUMPHREY, C. 1997. Exemplars and rules: aspects of the discourse of moralities in Mongolia. In *The ethnography of moralities* (ed.) S. Howell, 25-47. London: Routledge.

KUHN, T. 1970. *The structure of scientific revolution.* Chicago: University Press.

LÉVI-STRAUSS, C. 1963. Social structure. In *Structural anthropology,* vol. 1 (trans. C. Jacobsen & B.G. Schoepf), 277-323. London: Penguin.

——— 1969 [1949]. *The elementary structures of kinship* (trans. J.H. Bell, J.R. von Sturmer & R. Needham). Boston: Beacon.

LIANERI, A. 2011. *The Western time of ancient history: historiographical encounters with Greek and Roman pasts.* Cambridge: University Press.

LYONS, J. 1989. *Exemplum: the rhetoric of example in early modern France and Italy.* Princeton: University Press.

MASSUMI, B. 2002. *Parables for the virtual.* Durham, N.C.: Duke University Press.

MEILLASSOUX, C. 1973. On the mode of production of the hunting band. In *French perspectives in African studies* (ed.) P. Alexandre, 187-203. London: Oxford University Press.

MITCHELL, C. 1983. Case and situation analysis. *Sociological Review* **31**, 187-211.

MORGAN, L.H. 1985 [1878]. *Ancient society.* Tucson: University of Arizona Press.

MOSKO, M. 2010. Partible penitents: dividual personhood and Christian practice in Melanesia and the West. *Journal of the Royal Anthropological Institute* (N.S.) **16**, 215-40.

NEEDHAM, R. 1985. *Exemplars.* Berkeley: University of California Press.

O'GORMAN, E. 2011. Repetition and exemplarity in historical thought: ancient Rome and the ghosts of modernity. In *The Western time of ancient history: historiographical encounters with Greek and Roman pasts* (ed.) A. Lianeri, 264-79. Cambridge: University Press.

ONG, A. & S.J. COLLIER 2005. *Global assemblages: technology, politics, and ethics as anthropological problems.* Oxford: Blackwell.

PLATO 1984. The Meno. In *The dialogues of Plato*, vol. 1 (trans. R.E. Allen), 151-86. New Haven: Yale University Press.

RILES, A. 2000. *The network inside out.* Ann Arbor: University of Michigan Press.

ROBBINS, J. 2010. Melanesia, Christianity, and cultural change: a comment on Mosko's 'Partible penitents'. *Journal of the Royal Anthropological Institute* (N.S.) **16**, 241-3.

SAID, E.W. 1978. *Orientalism.* London: Penguin.

SARTRE, J.-P. 2003 [1943]. *Being and nothingness: an essay on phenomenological ontology* (trans. H. Barnes). London: Routledge.

SPERBER, D. 1985. Anthropology and psychology: towards an epidemiology of representations. *Man* (N.S.) **20**, 73-89.

STRATHERN, M. 1987. Out of context: the persuasive fictions of anthropology [and comments and reply]. *Current Anthropology* **28**, 251-81.

——— 1990. Artefacts of history: event and the interpretation of images. In *Culture and history in the Pacific* (ed.) J. Siikala, 25-44. Helsinki: The Finnish Anthropological Society.

——— 1999. *Property, substance and effect: anthropological essays on persons and things.* London: The Athlone Press.

TIPPING, B. 2010. *Exemplary epic: Silius Italicus' Punica.* Oxford: University Press.

TURNER, V. 1975. Social dramas and ritual metaphors. In *Dramas, fields and metaphors: symbolic action in human society*, 23-59. Ithaca, N.Y.: Cornell University Press.

VERDERY, K. 1999. Fuzzy property: rights, power, and identity in Transylvania's decollectivization. In *Uncertain transition: ethnographies of change in the postsocialist world* (eds) M. Burawoy & K. Verdery, 53-81. Oxford: Rowman & Littlefield.

WARNICK, B. 2008. *Imitation and education: a philosophical inquiry into learning by example.* Albany: State University of New York Press.

WASTELL, S. 2001. Presuming scale, making diversity. On the mischiefs of measurement and the global: local metonym in theories of law and culture. *Critique of Anthropology* **21**, 185-210.

WEBER, M. 2012 [1904]. The 'objectivity' of knowledge in social science and social policy. In *Max Weber: complete methodological writings* (eds) H.H. Bruun & S. Whimster, 100-38. London: Routledge.

WOOLGAR, S. & G. COOPER 1999. Do artefacts have ambivalence? Moses' Bridges, Winner's bridges and other urban legends in S&TS. *Social Studies of Science* **29**, 433-49.

ŽIŽEK, S. 2001. *On belief.* New York: Routledge.

Introduction : le pouvoir de l'exemple

Résumé

L'introduction part de l'idée que les exemples sont des prismes importants pour penser aussi bien la réalité que l'analyse anthropologique et, ce qui est tout aussi important, pour les reconfigurer. Son objectif est de remédier au manque d'intérêt théorique pour l'exemple, en explorant le pouvoir persuasif et évocateur (aussi bien positif que négatif) des « exemples » dans la vie sociale et universitaire. L'introduction propose également de considérer l'administration d'exemples comme une méthode particulière à l'anthropologie d'élaboration de la théorie. Ce type d'élaboration théorique pointe vers un réexamen « latéral » de la relation entre le particulier et le général. L'argument central est que les exemples mettent en lumière la tension précaire entre l'exemple en tant qu'« exemple » et l'exemple en tant qu'« exemplaire ». Toutes les contributions à ce numéro spécial explorent, d'une manière ou d'une autre, cette tension entre la turbulence des exemples et le pouvoir stabilisateur de l'exemplarité. L'introduction avance en outre que l'exemple peut servir à brouiller les frontières ontologiques telles que celles qui existent entre théorie et ethnographie, et attire l'attention sur le fait que la théorie suggère autant qu'elle décrit.

1

Ritual, value, and example: on the perfection of cultural representations

JOEL ROBBINS *University of Cambridge*

For modes of thinking influenced by the fact/value distinction, values are often defined as in some sense unreal. Against this view, I argue that values exist in the form of socially concrete, enacted examples. In making this argument, I define examples as representations that model the realization of single values in full form – forms that are not common in daily life because most actions are driven by a mix of diverse value considerations. I further suggest that rituals are a key social form in which exemplary representations of values are made socially available. I illustrate this argument by analysing two important rituals among the Urapmin of Papua New Guinea, and by exploring several innovative Urapmin rituals that have failed to become established because, I suggest, they do not provide examples of fully realized values.

As the editors note in their introduction, anthropology has always been a field that leans heavily on examples and the exemplary in its analytic work. This is true in at least two senses. Think first of cultural forms such as the *kula*, which become singular examples from which widely applicable theories are crafted – in this case theories about exchange and reciprocity. And then think of those exemplary cultural forms such as the Iatmul Naven rite or the Balinese cockfight which become analytic keys for the broader discussion of the cultures in which they are practised. As sociocultural anthropology is often allergic to explaining its data in terms of universal laws, it is not surprising that the example should do so much work in this field – for it is precisely the possibility to work up from, or perhaps (to refer again to the editors' introduction) sideways from, the particular, rather than down from the law or principle, that reasoning by example affords to thought. Given this, I think it is reasonable to hope that anthropologists will never give up their interest in the example.

But even if reasoning by example is a condition of doing anthropology, one can argue that the field needs the example now more than ever. To explain why this is so, I want to make a move that is at the centre of my argument in the rest of this paper. This move involves defining the example in terms of value – defining the example, that is to say, as a cultural form that realizes a specific value to the fullest extent possible. It also involves the claim that the discovery of the existence of examples in social life (and not just in our analytic practice) is the answer to a pressing theoretical question about values. Most scholars do not define the example in terms of value, and once I make this move, my argument becomes admittedly idiosyncratic. But I want to suggest that if we do define the example in this way, it becomes clear why anthropology is at the moment particularly in need of its services.

So let me start with values. As it happens, the use of the term 'value' with which we are familiar is not ancient. It first takes off in the middle of the nineteenth century, when philosophers borrow it from political economists (Frondizi 1963; Joas 2000; Schnädelbach 1984: 161). From that point on, discussions about the nature of value play a key role in German philosophy in particular, and in the emerging social sciences as well, until the 1920s, after which, with a few exceptions, they largely fade from the scene outside of their original home in economics. For our purposes, it is important to note that value became a preoccupation in the late nineteenth century just as the scientific-materialist worldview finally entrenched itself as the dominant modern understanding of the nature of existence. In that worldview, all that exists is matter, and matter is in itself devoid of meaning or purpose. What exists is not good or bad, beautiful or ugly, true or false (a classic triumvirate of value dimensions) – it simply is. In this worldview, as is well known, there is no intellectually legitimate way to move from is to ought, or, as we now more often put it, from fact to value. This way of construing matters left philosophers with a key question – what is the mode of existence of values? If the good, or the beautiful, or the true by definition cannot exist, since what exists is matter and matter is meaningless or without value in itself, then what is their mode of being in the world? It is this question that gets the philosophy of value off the ground.

As social scientists, we are most familiar with this set of problems from Weber, who was steeped in some of the German debates about the nature of value to which I just referred. He bequeathed to the social sciences the enormously influential view, one that comes out of this philosophical problematic (and ultimately out of Protestantism, but that is another story – see Albrow 1990, Scheler 1973: 67), that the world (including human existence) considered in material terms is a chaotic flux which only acquires meaningful shape when human beings impose their values upon it (for a classic statement of this position, on which Weber drew, see Rickert 1986). In this view, values exist in human thought and are expressed in human action, and such action in turn orders the world in ways humans can comprehend. The claim that values are ideas that motivate action is thus one answer to the question of the mode of being of values. But as an answer to the question of how values exist that aims to explain why human beings do not live in a chaotic, meaningless world, it leaves one problem unresolved. This is the problem of why it is that each human being does not impose his/her own unique set of values on the world, leading social life to take the form of a cacophony of opposed projects each based on wholly singular meaningful structurings of the chaos of material existence. This would only lead to another kind of unformed meaninglessness – a human war of all against all. The anthropological notion of culture is a solution to this second problem of how values as ideas that motivate action can create an orderly world, for it suggests that values are shared between members of a society. People who share values will, on this model, all impose order on the chaos of existence in similar ways, thus allowing them to live relatively orderly lives together.

Various versions of this cultural solution to the problem of how values exist in the world and order it in meaningful ways served anthropology well for much of the twentieth century. But in the last twenty-five years or so they have in many quarters been abandoned. For a large number of contemporary anthropologists, the proximate cause of this abandonment has been the postmodern turn (a term that already sounds nostalgic, but which is precisely the right one to use in the context of this historical argument). It was this turn that made notions of shared culture seem too deterministic, too disrespectful of the reality of chaos and complexity and of the true individuality of persons – each of whom many anthropologists now believe does have his or her own individual perspective on the world. In a longer view, one that is just now coming into focus, it may well prove to be the case that the abandonment of notions of shared culture was in fact the result of another strong turn of the screw of the scientific worldview with its denial of the meaningfulness of what exists, a turn to which the postmodern critique of meaning and structure unwittingly lent a hand and which is evidenced, for example, in the contemporary ascendancy of scientizing models across the social sciences and humanities. But regardless of the reasons for our current situation, it is certainly true that these days many anthropologists are not inclined to see the idea of shared culture as a good answer to the question of how values exist in the world, and are more interested in documenting the world's chaotic aspects than those we might take to be ordered by values. What I want to propose here is that if we accept that this is in fact the dominant state of play in contemporary anthropology, then we need the example now more than ever because it can give us a way of thinking about the existence of values and the emergence of order in social life that does not rely on the kinds of strong models of shared culture that are so much out of favour at the moment.

On examples, values, and social action

As I noted at the outset, my argument for the contemporary importance of the example for anthropological theory depends on a definition of the example in terms of values. To develop this definition, let me start with the important work of the Italian philosopher Alessandro Ferrara (2008). In a book whose title – *The force of the example* – is quite close to that of this collection, Ferrara argues that we easily recognize two kinds of forces in the world. There is the force of what exists, or what he calls the force of things (2008: 1). And there is also, at least for human beings, the force of 'what ought to be the case – the force of ideas' (2008: 2, emphasis removed). These two forces, Ferrara recognizes, align with the modern dichotomy between fact and value, or the real and the ideal (2008: ix). But as we have seen, this leaves us with the problem of the nature of the existence of value – for if the ideal or values are defined precisely by not existing as material things, then where do they exist? And if they exist only in individuals' minds, why is the world not a chaotic mess of persons each pursuing wholly unrelated projects? Though Ferrara's questions are close to these, he does not pose them in quite this way. But he none the less does offer us some help with our own problems when he proposes that the two sides of the dichotomy between what is and what should be need to be supplemented by a middle term – 'the force of what is as it should be or the force of the example' (2008: 2–3, emphasis removed). '[T]he force of the example', he goes on to assert, 'is the force of what exerts appeal on us … by virtue of the singular and exceptional congruence that what is exemplary realizes and exhibits between the order of its own reality and the order of the normativity to which it responds' (2008: 3). To put this in the terms I will use from now on, an example is a realization of a value in the world, and it solicits our attention for precisely this reason.

When I claim that an example is the realization of a value in the world, I mean this in a somewhat special sense. In some respects, all human action realizes, or at least aims to realize, something the actor defines as valuable in the context in which he or she undertakes it. This is a very common view of human motivation that I do not intend to counter here. But given this view, is it also right to say that every action, as the realization of a value in the world, is an example? If this is true, then I cannot be saying anything very useful about examples.

As a response to this problem, I want to sketch much too briefly an account of how values operate in action that suggests that most actions, even if motivated by values, do not fully realize any one of them and thus do not stand as examples. Let me start by simply asserting, rather than taking time to argue, that in any social milieu there are numerous values in play. Some of these work together such that realizing one value helps you towards realizing another one you count as even higher, and so on in chains of what Nancy Munn (1986) refers to as 'value transformation'. So on Gawa Island, Papua New Guinea, for example, if you are a man, you plant taro and yam gardens to give over to the husband's family of one of your female relatives so that this family can eventually give you a *kula* valuable and a canoe that you can further exchange along *kula* paths in order to increase your range of spatio-temporal control and thus bolster your fame (Munn 1986: 123–9). At each step you are acting in terms of a value, though the ultimate purpose of the whole chain is only given by the final transformation, which realizes its overall value of increasing your fame. Much of the time, you are realizing only lower-level values, such as behaving appropriately to your affines through your female relatives, in actions that will have been of limited import if the chain is never completed. Other values do not link up in chains, but rather conflict, such that realizing one precludes realizing the other. A gift given to one's affines to gain access to valuables, for example, is not a gift given to one's clan-mates to secure support in disputes. When faced with an exclusive choice between values of this kind, people often hedge, realizing both values partially but neither one of them fully. In this way, values are often, perhaps usually, compromised in action. Most actions either do not realize a value that is in itself of great importance, but only one that is a link in a chain orientated towards realizing another value, or they are driven by a mix of partial value considerations. This is why not every action is an example, even if all actions are motivated by values.[1]

Against the background of this argument that most actions do not realize people's most important values, or realize them only in limited ways, I want to suggest that some actions stand out for accomplishing the opposite. There are some actions or products of action that realize important values in their fullest forms. It is these actions and their products that become examples and that have, as Ferrara puts it, a 'force' that solicits a special kind of attention or demand for participation from people. One social form that very routinely produces such actions, I want to suggest, is ritual.[2] Rituals often are, that is to say, actions that fully realize a specific value or values and therefore stand out in social life as exemplary and command people's attention on that basis.

That rituals at least sometimes enact an idealized picture of the world, one that is more fully realized in one or other respect than is usually the case, is not a new insight. It is also frequently linked to the claim that ritual enactments of such idealized images are meant in one way or another to inform life outside of ritual. Jonathan Z. Smith, for example, some time ago defined ritual as 'a means of performing the way things ought to be in conscious tension to the way things are in such a way that this ritualized perfection is recollected in the ordinary, uncontrolled course of things' (1982: 63). Bruce Kapferer, more recently, has argued for a view of ritual as constituting a space of virtuality which 'allows people to break free from the constraints or determinations of everyday life'

(2006: 673), not in order to leave everyday life and its concerns behind, but to slow 'down its flux and speed' (2006: 676) so they can examine and perhaps transform its elements. In keeping with Kapferer's and Smith's analyses, I want to argue that some rituals accomplish this process of slowing down the production and perfecting the shape of representations in relation to values. They allow people, that is, to suspend the complex relation between values and action that holds in daily life, where one is mostly making only small progress in the middle stretches of attempts to realize more or less lengthy chains of value transformation, or is acting in ways that realize a number of values at once but only in compromised forms, and instead to experience what it is like to realize one or more values fully. These values are realized in a space that has been in some respects simplified and slowed down, but their ritual accomplishment none the less remains in play in the rushed flux of everyday life; indeed, it remains in play in the form of people's possession of examples that will henceforth solicit some of their energy towards further realization of the value(s) involved.

On this analysis, the point of a ritual is not to compel people to realize fully the value it represents throughout the course of their daily life outside of ritual. This, we know, is impossible, since everyday life is marked by the need to juggle a number of values simultaneously, make choices between them, and work towards the realization of lower-level values as a means to the potential eventual realization of higher ones. That rituals do not demand continual realization of the values they represent is why they should be described as producing examples of fully realized values, rather than rules one must apply outside of ritual in order to realize such values regularly. Rituals show people the values that exist in their community by providing realized representations of them, but they do not expect people to live lives singularly devoted to reproducing these values in such pure form. In this way, ritual action, rather than (or perhaps alongside of) cultural imposition (if you believe in such a thing), helps develop people's understandings of what their community's values consist in, and it solicits people's interest in these values. It accomplishes this by means of the provision of examples.

In order to illustrate the analytic potential of this model of ritual as a means of providing fully realized representations of values, I turn in the next section to some examples taken from my fieldwork among the Urapmin of Papua New Guinea.

Ritual and value among the Urapmin

The Urapmin are a group of roughly 400 people living in the West Sepik province of Papua New Guinea. The Urapmin were never directly missionized by Westerners, though they became familiar with many of the tenets of Christianity by sending a number of young people to study with Baptist missionaries who came to work with their neighbours in the 1960s. Then, in the late 1970s, a Protestant revival movement spread throughout Papua New Guinea. When it reached Urapmin territory in 1977, the entire adult population converted to charismatic Christianity. By 1978, Urapmin was in its own self-understanding a completely Christian community. Since that time, working towards Christian salvation has been the dominant theme of Urapmin public life, and of most people's private lives as well. I have described the conversion of the Urapmin in great detail elsewhere and, more crucially for my discussion here, I have argued that Urapmin Christianity defines salvation as ultimately an individual matter – something each person has to work out for him/herself (Robbins 2004). In Urapmin, Christianity thus promotes a particular brand of individualism as the most important value one can dedicate oneself to realizing.

Journal of the Royal Anthropological Institute (N.S.), 18-29
© Royal Anthropological Institute 2015

At the same time as the Urapmin have come to take a version of Christian individualism as their most important religious value, much of their social life continues to be shaped by the value that was traditionally paramount in the community. This is the value of what I have called 'relationalism' – a value that defines the creation and maintenance of relationships as the most important goal one can work towards achieving (Robbins 2004). In contemporary Urapmin life, people often find themselves caught between realizing the value of individualism, which in their understanding requires something of a withdrawal from social life in order to avoid sin, and that of relationalism, which requires sustained social engagement directed towards bringing others into relationship and keeping them involved in such relationships once one has connected with them. People's failure to realize either value fully most of the time leaves them in a state of moral frustration, a frustration they describe in Christian terms as a strongly felt sense of their own sinfulness. This feeling of moral frustration well illustrates my point that in daily life people generally find their actions to fall short of fully realizing the values they hold to be most important.

Yet even as most Urapmin find it difficult to realize any of their values very fully in daily life, there are ritual settings in which they are able to do so. To make this point, I want to consider two of the rituals Urapmin find most dramatic and important: a Christian ritual called a 'Spirit disco' (Spirit disko)[3] and a traditional one referred to as a 'pig sacrifice' (*kang anfukeleng*). These rituals make a nice pair in terms of the argument of this paper, for the Spirit disco is an unusually full realization of the value of individualism, while the pig sacrifice fully realizes the value of relationalism. In addition to discussing these two rituals, in the next section I will consider one attempt to produce an innovative Christian rite and a similarly novel attempt to transform a traditional death rite in order to demonstrate that rituals that fail to function as examples by fully realizing any specific value in a complete way tend to fade from social life because they do not solicit people's attention and commitment in the way exemplary rituals do.

I will begin with the Spirit disco. Urapmin prepare themselves for salvation by participating in a wide range of rituals, from attending church services, to studying the Bible, to praying regularly throughout the day. The goals of all Christian ritual activities are to strengthen a person's heart (*aget* – the seat of all thought and feeling) so it will not be tempted to answer the call of sin and to cleanse the heart of the sins it has committed. Understood as parts of a chain of value transformations leading to the creation of a self that is prepared for Jesus' return, many Christian rituals can be seen to point to the performance of the Spirit disco, a ritual the Urapmin undertake infrequently relative to most other Christian rites. The Spirit disco stands at the apex of Urapmin ritual life because it fully accomplishes a goal other Christian rituals contribute towards realizing but do not themselves wholly bring about: it renders its participants as individuals free of sin and ready to be taken by Jesus to heaven should the Second Coming transpire near to the time of its conclusion. The Spirit disco does this by removing the residues of committed sins from the hearts of those who take part in it.

Spirit discos are circular dances performed at night inside the church. Most members of the church attend when one is held. During the dance, some of the dancers become possessed by the Holy Spirit. Once this happens, they begin to flail wildly and will be 'controlled' by other dancers who hold them and do their best to prevent them from hurting themselves or others. During a successful dance, several people will become possessed in this way for up to an hour. At the height of the rite, the scene inside the church can be chaotic, with all of the possessed people careening unpredictably around the room as others struggle to keep up the circular pattern of the dance. Eventually, the Spirit will leave the possessed dancers one by one. When the Spirit leaves a dancer, he/she collapses on the floor, completely limp, unconscious, and, as the Urapmin see it, at peace. After possession, people will lie on the church floor in this state for some time as the dancers slow down and eventually stop. Participants remain with those who were once possessed until they regain normal consciousness. Then everyone will pray together and the ritual ends.

In Urapmin understanding, the violence of possession during the Spirit disco is due to a battle within the possessed person's heart between the Holy Spirit and his/her sins. The conclusion of possession happens when the Spirit finally succeeds in 'throwing' the person's sins out of his/her body. Before commencing the Spirit disco, all participants must confess their sins to a pastor or deacon who prays over them and tells God that the sins have been given to Him. But it is only during the Spirit disco and the possession that is central to it that the sins are finally removed from the body. This leaves the person ready for salvation. As the Urapmin see it, the previously possessed person lying still and alone on the church floor represents the full realization of the saved individual. Since, as someone once crystallized the general Urapmin understanding for me, 'once people leave the church building they will start sinning again' – they will, to put it otherwise, be caught again in the sinful snares of trying to realize a range of different values at once – it is only at this moment at the end of the rite that one can be sure of one's own or someone else's salvation. It is thus the only time in Urapmin social life that the value of becoming an individual worthy of salvation is fully realized. The Spirit disco is, then, an example of the value of Urapmin Christian individualism in its fullest form.[4]

If the Spirit disco stands as the capstone of a wide range of Christian rituals, pig sacrifice in Urapmin is a more singular institution, less linked to other rites the Urapmin practise as parts of institutionalized chains of value transformation. In fact, pig sacrifice is the only 'traditional' ritual the Urapmin still enact. As I have discussed elsewhere (Robbins 2007), many Urapmin are for this reason ambivalent about performing it and question whether they are led to do so by the promptings of evil spirits (sinik mafak). But it is also true that they have been unable to give it up. My argument here is that this is so because it is, in the terms of this paper, a key example of the full realization of the value of relationalism, a value which, despite the Christian promotion of individualism, still remains important in their lives.

Pig sacrifices are offered to nature spirits (motobil) whom the Urapmin formerly believed owned every significant part of their natural environment: land, major trees, rivers, large rocks, and the game animals people hunt. In the past, the nature spirits allowed Urapmin people to use these resources provided they observed various taboos put in place by the spirits who owned them. Among other things, these taboos forbade the Urapmin from talking loudly or laughing while they hunted and gardened, lest they offended the spirits. If the Urapmin did offend the spirits by violating these taboos, the spirits would 'hold' (kutalfugumin) them and make them sick. As Christians, Urapmin now say that God created and owns everything and that He wants people to use the resources He provides. There are no more taboos. Instead, they say, now is 'free time' (fri taim), and people should in principle be able to use the earth's bounty without fear of the nature spirits' retribution.

Yet even as the spirits have lost their position as the original owners of all of the resources of the Urapmin landscape, the Urapmin continue to recognize their existence.

As in the past, whenever people become sick, it is assumed that they have disturbed the spirits in some way. Generally, friends and family respond to sickness by praying to God to remove the offending spirit from the sick person, and sometimes they engage Christian ritual specialists to help them in this endeavour (see below). Yet when illnesses linger, especially in children (who, unlike adults, can die from illness caused by nature spirits), people will sacrifice a pig to them, asking them to take the 'smell' (*tang*) of the pig and let go of their human victim. This gift of a pig to a spirit is a very full expression of Urapmin relationalism – which is elaborated through exchange in many different ritual contexts – because it realizes this value in the face of the nature spirits' general failure to do their part in the making and maintaining of relations. Unlike people, spirits do not give generously. They hedge their gifts with taboos, and their generosity is unreliable. Mostly they would prefer to be left alone. It is by virtue of realizing the value of relationalism in connection with the spirits, and this in the face of the spirits' lack of interest in this value, that pig sacrifice stands as a key example of relationalism in Urapmin culture. By continuing to perform this ritual, despite their fears that it is sinful in Christian terms, the Urapmin present themselves with a thoroughly realized version of the relationalism that continues to figure in so many areas of their lives.

To this point, my discussion of Urapmin ritual life has been orientated towards showing how some of their most important rites realize in particularly clear form the key Urapmin values of individualism and relationalism. As members of a society that has recently undergone rapid and extensive cultural change, Urapmin also present us with a number of examples of ritual innovations that have failed to catch on. In the next section, I examine two such failed ritual innovations with the aim of showing how their inability to realize any single value fully can help account for their failure to become enduring features of Urapmin social life.

Failed ritual and the absence of the example

Turning now to two rituals that do not produce exemplary expressions of value and hence have not established themselves in Urapmin practice, let me start with one man's attempt to redesign traditional death rites. Traditional death rites in Urapmin have a number of parts, which include gifts of food from those who lived with the deceased to his or her other relatives, who in good relationalist fashion take the food they have been given home to share with those among whom they live. The rites also involve the exchange of exactly equivalent goods between those who lived with the deceased and his or her other relatives (see Robbins 1999 for a fuller discussion of these exchanges). Exchange rituals of various kinds that, like this one, revolve around the exchange of exactly equivalent goods are relatively frequent exemplary performances of Urapmin relationalism. The whole complex of rites around death is thus taken up with realizing relationalism in one of its fullest forms – an appropriate response to the way death by its nature threatens to destroy the kinds of relational networks the Urapmin so highly value by removing one of their nodes.

The innovative death rite I want to discuss dispenses with the traditional rituals' emphasis on the value of relationalism. The development of the new rite needs to be understood in relation to the fact that the Urapmin territory is quite remote. The community has no electricity, road, or airstrip, and there is very little local involvement with the cash economy. But Urapmin is located five days' walk away from Ok Tedi, a very large gold and copper mine that is situated in the town of Tabubil. Since the mine opened in the 1980s, many Urapmin men have worked there for short stints as labourers. And one Urapmin man whom I will call Docsi is unique for having lived in Tabubil for over fifteen years. Although he has remained a low-paid labourer who lives in a squatter settlement (rather than in the more prestigious company housing), he is the Urapmin person with the single greatest experience of the market economy and the more modern or 'white' world of Tabubil. For this and other reasons, he is widely respected in Urapmin. When his elderly parents died within days of each other, he came home to Urapmin and announced that he was going to perform a new kind of death ritual for them. The ritual he had in mind was patterned after how food is served and eaten in the Ok Tedi mess hall in Tabubil. He had the younger men of his village build a serving counter along which people would walk and receive individual-sized portions of food at different stops – a serving of cooked taro at one stop, of pig meat at another, and of greens further down the line. Then, once people had filled their plates, they would all sit around Docsi's parents' village and eat, just as everyone eats together in the Ok Tedi mess hall. As far as I ever learned, this would be the entirety of the ritual – there would be no accompanying exchange of exactly equivalent goods.

Docsi's authority was such that people were initially excited about the proposed new-style rite. On the day of the ritual itself, the younger men of Docsi's parents' village manned the serving line and people walked along it with their individual plates and collected their food. Then they sat down. But the scene was very quiet, and it appeared no one was comfortable eating together publicly, as if in a cafeteria. In traditional feasts, one always takes the food away, redistributes most of it, and then eats the rest in the privacy of one's own house. The idea of eating individual portions in public was too shameful (*fitom*) for people. One senior man eventually stood up and walked off with his plate in the direction of home. Others quickly followed suit, and soon the village was empty. The innovative death ritual had been an utter failure.

In analysing the failure of the new rite, it is important to realize that it had every chance to succeed. Urapmin generally find anything new and connected with what they call the 'white' world to have some appeal, and everyone in the community respected Docsi as an important local representative of that world. The rite failed not because it was new, but rather because it did not realize to any extent the value of relationalism of which traditional death rites provide such powerful examples – gifts were one way, given piecemeal by young people of little standing, and neither redistribution nor reciprocation was part of the ritual plan. Nor was the ritual a robust representation of the newer value of Christian individualism, for it made no contribution towards the Christian salvation of those who participated as individual consumers of Docsi's one-way gift of food. Lacking in the crisp, full realization of a single value that defines successful rituals, it solicited in practice little positive attention from the Urapmin, and no commitment at all. Quickly forgotten, it never came to serve as an example of any particular end one might pursue.

The second ritual I want to discuss has to this point failed in a different sense than Docsi's new death ritual. Though people sometimes talk about this rite and how they would go about performing it, they have never brought themselves to the point of actually carrying it out. Docsi's rite did generate enough interest to warrant a performance, though one suspects this had as much to do with Docsi's high standing in the community as with people's excitement about the potential of the rite itself. The ritual I turn to now exists only as an occasional topic of conversation, never as a project into which people pour any sustained energy.

Journal of the Royal Anthropological Institute (N.S.), 18-29
© Royal Anthropological Institute 2015

The ritual in question is a Christian one that would rid key parts of the Urapmin landscape of all nature spirits, allowing the Urapmin to use the resources to which the spirits attached themselves with no fear of spiritual reprisal for taboo violation. This rite of spiritual removal, for which the Urapmin have not settled on a name, is in some respects similar to rites they do regularly perform.[5] When people first become ill, ritual specialists known as 'Spirit women' (Spirit meri) are called in. These Spirit women become possessed by the Holy Spirit, who shows them which nature spirit is causing the illness. They then pray with God's power to command the nature spirit to let go of its victim and they ask God to bind the spirit far from Urapmin territory, so it cannot afflict the patient or other people in the future. It is only in those rare cases where repeated attempts at such spiritual healing over time have failed to bring about an improvement in the patient's condition that Urapmin resort to the pig sacrifice rituals discussed in the previous section. Treatment by Spirit women is far more common, and it is the routine way of handling illness in Urapmin.

Like the treatments performed by Spirit women, the ritual of spiritual removal the Urapmin sometimes discuss but never undertake would involve seeking God's help to remove nature spirits from Urapmin territory. But it would do so on a much grander scale than the treatment of afflicted individuals. As the Urapmin imagine this rite, it would unfold as a number of Spirit women worked together to clear all of the nature spirits out of broad areas of the Urapmin territory they densely inhabit. This would include formerly sacred (taboo – awem) spaces and other spaces the Urapmin hope might be used in the future for intense resource extraction such as gold mining (there has been some prospecting by mining companies on their land, as there has been on the land of many of the groups in their region).

Even as the basic pattern of these imagined rituals has much in common with that of the regularly practised healing rites of the Spirit women, however, it is important to note that the rituals have markedly different ends. Healing treatments aim to redress the illnesses of single individuals that they have contracted by disregarding the relational demands of the nature spirits. In successful cases, the patient is returned to living a normal Urapmin life, one in which he/she will have to balance the realization of both relational and individualist values. The nameless rite, by contrast, aims not to redress past conflicts between people and nature spirits, but rather to allow all Urapmin completely to disregard the relational claims nature spirits currently make (even if illegitimately, from a Christian point of view). As was the case with Docsi's new funeral rite, if successful, this rite also makes no contribution to people's efforts to realize their Christian individualist projects of freeing themselves from sin. Instead, it simply liberates them to exploit the world around them as fully as they might like in a frenzy of uncontrolled desire and consumption, an outcome that is for the Urapmin a potent image of an undesirable, even sinful, kind of individualism. In this respect, this rite does not fail because it only partially realizes any one value, but rather because it realizes in full terms something that is disvalued. It is what we might call a negative example, and as such it bears discussion among the Urapmin for the fantasies of unfettered consumption it brings to the surface, but it does not solicit performative engagement.

Conclusion

By way of a brief conclusion, let me start by noting that I have in this paper urged us to consider the possibility of defining the example in terms of value. Lying behind this is a conception of social action as motivated by values, but only in complex ways that leave a lot of room for contradiction and compromise in their realization. It is the cross-cutting play of values in people's lives that gives social experience its fluid, occasionally unpredictable, and perhaps sometimes even chaotic character. At the same time, however, people in all societies also find themselves drawn to certain kinds of repeated actions that serve to give their social worlds at least minimally orderly shape. We tend to call 'rituals' the most elaborate and well-ordered versions of such repeated actions. As rituals, I have suggested, they solicit interest and participation for the way in which they allow people to slow life down so that they can at least sometimes work on realizing one or a few values very fully, or on setting out in clear terms to themselves and others what it would mean to do so.

Urapmin encounter the values that give shape to life in their community in their Spirit discos, where Christian individualism becomes liveable in the figure of the dancer spread out in perfect repose on the church floor, and in their pig sacrifices, where they demonstrate their commitment to the value of relationalism by repairing relationships with the very worst social partners they know. These ritual accomplishments of value stand as examples not so much by providing models of or for how to live outside of ritual, but rather by offering concrete images of fuller realizations of particular values than are usually possible in everyday life. Realized in ritual, a form of 'actual' as opposed to merely 'imaginary' social life, these values gain 'real' as opposed to simply 'ideal' force in moving people into the future.

It is this point about the example as a mode of real existence of values that has been at the heart of this paper. As representations that actually *are* as they should be, in Ferrara's terms, examples help us escape the difficulties that come with assigning values an only ideal existence. These difficulties, at least for social thought, manifest themselves as problems one encounters in explaining the orderly qualities of social life if one assumes that neither values nor the cultures once thought to house them have a real existence. In finding an ontological home for values in actually existing examples that people encounter in the course of their social lives, rather than in a model of culture as seamlessly organized and exhaustively imposed on the members of any given society, I hope to have offered a path out of these difficulties that does not run afoul of the core intuitions of contemporary anthropology.

NOTES

[1] I would also note in passing that the fact that there are always numerous values in play, combined with the fact that most actions do not fully realize the values people find most important, is what gives social life the kind of complexity that leads so many anthropologists to abandon notions of order and culture. But this complexity is not proof of the absence of values, but rather follows from the existence of more than one value in any given community (see below).

[2] I should stress at this point in my argument that I do not think rituals are the only places one finds values represented in relatively fully realized form in social life. Some myths and other narrative forms surely work out similar representations. And in another, as yet unpublished paper that is in some respects a sibling of this one, I draw on the work of Humphrey (1997) and Scheler (1987) to argue at length that certain kinds of people also stand as socially existing exemplars of values they realize far more fully than most of the people among whom they live (Robbins n.d.).

[3] In this paper, terms given in Tok Pisin, the most common lingua franca of Papua New Guinea, are underlined, while those in the Urap language are given in italics.

[4] As I have shown elsewhere, the Spirit disco also contains relationalist elements, seen most clearly in the way all participants are understood to be saved when the ritual is a success (Robbins 2004). However, they are all saved as individuals, and the image of the previously possessed person lying in calm repose on the church floor is one Urapmin understand as the most moving example of the saved individual they encounter

in the course of their lives on earth (*towal diim*). It is for these reasons that it makes sense to analyse the Spirit disco as offering a fully realized image of the value of individualism, even as it partially addresses the value of relationalism as well.

⁵ Both the rites the Urapmin do perform and the ones they talk about but as yet do not undertake are very similar to globally widely diffused kinds of charismatic-Pentecostal rituals associated with what is known as 'spiritual warfare'. The Urapmin, however, do not refer to them using these terms. (I discuss the history of the globally diffused form and the Urapmin engagement with it in detail in Robbins 2012.)

REFERENCES

ALBROW, M. 1990. *Max Weber's construction of social theory*. New York: St Martin's Press.

FERRARA, A. 2008. *The force of the example: explorations in the paradigm of judgment*. New York: Columbia University Press.

FRONDIZI, R. 1963. *What is value? Introduction to axiology* (trans. S. Lipp). Lasalle, Ill.: Open Court.

HUMPHREY, C. 1997. Exemplars and rules: aspects of the discourse of moralities in Mongolia. In *The ethnography of moralities* (ed.) S. Howell, 25-47. London: Routledge.

JOAS, H. 2000. *The genesis of values* (trans. G. Moore). Chicago: University Press.

KAPFERER, B. 2006. Virtuality. In *Theorizing rituals: classical topics, theoretical approaches, analytical concepts* (eds) J. Kreinath, J. Snoek & M. Stausberg, 671-83. Leiden: Brill.

MUNN, N.M. 1986. *The fame of Gawa: a symbolic study of value transformation in a Massim (Papua New Guinea) society*. New York: Cambridge University Press.

RICKERT, H. 1986. *The limits of concept formation in natural science: a logical introduction to the historical sciences* (trans. G. Oakes) (Abridged edition). Cambridge: University Press.

ROBBINS, J. 1999. 'This is our money': modernism, regionalism, and dual currencies in Urapmin. In *Money and modernity: state and local currencies in contemporary Melanesia* (eds) J. Robbins & D. Akin, 82-102. Pittsburgh: University Press.

——— 2004. *Becoming sinners: Christianity and moral torment in a Papua New Guinea society*. Berkeley: University of California Press.

——— 2007. You can't talk behind the Holy Spirit's back: Christianity and changing language ideologies in a Papua New Guinea society. In *Consequences of contact: language ideologies and sociocultural transformations in Pacific societies* (eds) M. Makihara & B.B. Schieffelin, 125-39. New York: Oxford University Press.

——— 2012. On enchanting science and disenchanting nature: spiritual warfare in North America and Papua New Guinea. In *Nature, science, and religion: intersections shaping society and the environment* (ed.) C.M. Tucker, 45-64. Santa Fe, N.M.: School for Advance Research Press.

——— n.d. Where in the world are values? Exemplarity, morality, and social process. Unpublished manuscript.

SCHELER, M. 1973. *Formalism in ethics and a non-formal ethics of values: a new attempt toward the foundation of an ethical personalism*. Evanston, Ill.: Northwestern University Press.

——— 1987. *Person and self-value: three essays* (trans. M.S. Frings). Dordrecht: Martinus Nijhoff.

SCHNÄDELBACH, H. 1984. *Philosophy in Germany 1831-1933*. Cambridge: University Press.

SMITH, J.Z. 1982. *Imagining religion: from Babylon to Jonestown*. Chicago: University Press.

Rituel, valeur et exemple : de la perfection des représentations culturelles

Résumé

Dans les modes de pensée influencés par la distinction entre fait et valeur, les valeurs sont souvent définies comme ayant un certain caractère irréel. Prenant le contrepied de cette définition, l'auteur avance qu'elles existent sous la forme d'exemples socialement concrets et mis en actes. Dans cette optique, il définit les exemples comme des représentations qui modèlent la réalisation de telle ou telle valeur sous sa forme pleine et entière, une forme qui n'est pas courante dans la vie quotidienne parce que la plupart des actions sont motivées par un mélange de diverses considérations de valeur. L'auteur suggère en outre que les rituels sont une forme sociale cruciale dans laquelle sont mises à la disposition de la société des représentations exemplaires des valeurs. Il illustre cet argument en analysant deux rituels importants des Urapmin de Papouasie-Nouvelle-Guinée et en explorant plusieurs rituels innovants qui n'ont pas réussi à prendre souche parce que, suggère-t-il, ils ne donnent pas des exemples de valeurs pleinement réalisées.

2

The burden of being exemplary: national sentiments, awkward witnessing, and womanhood in occupied Palestine

LOTTE BUCH SEGAL *University of Copenhagen*

This paper offers an analysis of how Palestinian wives of detainees are made into examples, both by themselves and by the people they are intimate with, whilst considering also the context of these women's awkward place in Palestinian narratives of national becoming. The main objective is to examine the burden of being an example, and what that implies for those who aspire to or are subtly coerced into inhabiting the position of an 'exemplary' woman in Palestine. Particular modalities of being an example are expected from Palestinian wives of detainees in order to sustain a shared version of the ordinary under military occupation. Not surprisingly, the emotional labour it takes to appear exemplary is necessarily eliminated from public as well as intimate registers of speech in order to keep up the collective aspiration to maintain a so-called 'ordinary life' during ongoing conflict.

> You know there is a film about me on YouTube? Two students from Birzeit University asked me if they could make a film about me because Ahmad[1] is in prison. And so they visited me and my family and slept in the village for twenty-four hours and came with me to work. It was when I was still working in the Palestinian Authority. They joined me at work, where we had a public ceremony, and came back home with me, cooking and eating with us, just like you. They wanted to know how I cope, even without him.

Aisha told me this one afternoon in her new American kitchen as we were preparing lunch. The meal was late that day because of the stream of visitors who had come to express their concern for and solidarity with one of the most respected prisoners' wives in the Occupied Palestinian Territories (OPT). Aisha's husband is serving a life sentence in a high-security prison in Israel for participating in armed resistance during the second Intifāda, also known as the al-Aqsa Intifāda. This makes him one of the 5,527 Palestinians who are currently detained in Israel for armed attacks against the Israeli state (B'Tselem 2014).

According to the Office for the Co-ordination of Humanitarian Affairs, around 800,000 Palestinians have been detained in Israeli prisons for varying lengths of time since 1967.[2] These Palestinians have been the focus of a considerable amount of local and international political agitation and, to a lesser extent, academic scrutiny.[3] Esmail Nashif

(2008), for example, has published a study of community-building among Palestinians in Israeli prisons between 1967 and 1993, and Abeer Baker and Anat Matar's recent (2011) anthology discusses the people considered a threat to the security of the Israeli state. Less attention has been paid, in lay as well as in academic writing, to the wives, mothers, and children of these men. This paper offers a rare glimpse of the emotional labour that is implicit in being an exemplary relative of Palestinian prisoners in Israel, with particular emphasis on the wives of these men. The argument is based on ethnographic fieldwork carried out during alternating periods between 2007 and 2011 among the families of high-security, long-term Palestinian detainees like Aisha's husband.

My focus here is on the tensions between what everyday life can be like during the absence of a detained husband and what is expected socially of the abandoned wives. Husbands' absences can span from three months of administrative detention to a life sentence, and may demand a great deal of labour – emotional, financial, and social – on the part of those left behind. I will explore how Palestinian wives of detainees are made into an example, by themselves, by their intimate relations, and by the national narratives of Palestinian becoming that pervade social life in the OPT. The main argument entertained here is that particular modalities of being an example are expected of the Palestinian wives of detainees in order for the collective of Palestinians to keep up what we may think of as the ordinary under occupation. In addition, the burden of being exemplary must be kept hidden to sustain the aspiration of the ordinary during ongoing conflict.

Aisha's husband has been imprisoned for almost twelve years now, which is why she lives alone with her two children in a newly constructed house next to the family compound of her in-laws. Formerly she lived in a flat further away from her relatives, although neither Aisha nor her family thought that ideal, since a woman living on her own is vulnerable, both in the physical sense and in terms of the rumours that can spread around her, potentially unsettling her image as a loyal and patriotic prisoner's wife. Owing to her husband's heroism, and because Aisha herself holds an important moral position in this West Bank village, there are regular visitors at her house. They stop by to ask how her husband is doing in prison, if there is any news about the ruling of the Israeli court, or if Aisha has obtained permission to visit her husband recently. She has not. She visited him in the autumn of 2010 and still has not received further permission. It has been twelve years at the time of writing, and it is a well-known fact that Aisha and other wives of detainees belonging to this political cell should count themselves lucky if they get to visit their husbands at all during their sentences. Indeed, everyday life just goes on even without a husband. The question worth asking, though, is what this kind of life is for Aisha and what forms of labour of the self she engages in to actually be able to live it. Like the university students who chose Aisha to star in their film, I will investigate here both how Aisha experiences her husband's confinement and how she willingly created an example of how to cope with a detained husband's absence.

That Aisha offers an example of how to be a Palestinian woman in the face of hardship is stating the obvious. She is 37 years old, she has an MA in gender studies, she occupies a prestigious job in the local government, and she has raised her 16-year-old girl and 13-year-old boy on her own, albeit with the help and advice of her native and conjugal kin. Aisha is known by people across the occupied West Bank as a strong yet humble woman. She is also pious, observing Islam closely, wearing modest dress, and praying five times a day. She is cherished in her home village for her gentle nature and way of caring for others in need. Not least she is admired for helping other detainees'

families and wives, with whom she openly sympathizes even though they are from less
fortunate backgrounds than she is and have lived through their husbands' detentions
less successfully than Aisha herself, say by falling out with their in-laws or failing to
make a life for themselves. In the eyes of her neighbours, her colleagues, her family, and
in fact Palestinians more broadly, Aisha is indeed well suited to serve as an example.
First and foremost, however, what sets her apart as an example across a broad spectrum
of different religious and political groupings in Palestinian society is the way in which
she deals with her husband's life sentence.

Women and national becoming

To understand the meaning of womanhood during a husband's incarceration requires
attentiveness to how a form of life like Aisha's and the distress written into it are
expressed in or eliminated from the way in which the effects of the occupation is put
into words in contemporary Palestine. Collective language about Palestinian national
becoming, although admittedly emptied of life in the current climate, revolves around
suffering and heroism (Allen 2009; Buch Segal in press; Kublitz 2013). This language
is informed by the gendered organization of Palestinian society. At its centre are the
young men who sacrifice their lives and are therefore perceived to be the primary heroes
of the resistance against military occupation (Asad 2007; Hage 2003; Jean-Klein 2000;
Khalili 2007). They are martyrs, while the detainees have put their lives on hold, all
in the name of a Palestinian nation-state (cf. Khalili 2007; Massad 1995; Nashif 2008;
Peteet 1991).

Women, too, figure in discourses about Palestinian national becoming. In contrast
to the men, who fight, women are described as the soil in which 'manhood, respect and
dignity' grow (Massad 1995: 474). In national discourse, historically, mothers, daughters,
and sisters appear as those who are supportive in the Palestinian narrative (Massad 1995:
473). Through an analysis of the constitutional documents of the Palestine Liberation
Organization and political communiqués from the first Intifāḍa, Massad shows how
women are primarily represented as mothers destined to deliver the new warriors and
mourn their loved and lost sons. Important work in anthropology has documented how
Palestinian women have historically participated directly and indirectly in activities of
resistance in the public domain, for example Leila Khaled or other political heroines
of particularly the first Intifāḍa (Jean-Klein 2000; Peteet 1991; Sayigh 2008). Meanwhile
the general exhaustion of Palestinian society after the failed Oslo Accords and the
second Intifāḍa has meant, among other things, that the new forms of gendered, social
organization gained under the first Intifāḍa have evaporated (Johnson, Abu Nahleh
& Moors 2009). The way in which the gendered organization of resistance activities
is configured in contemporary Palestine resonates with Veena Das's reflections on the
intersection of gender and war: '[S]ex and death, reproduction and war, become part
of the same configuration of ideas and institutions through which the nation-state sets
up defences to stave off the uncertainty emanating from dangerous aliens and from
the ravages of time' (Das 2008: 285). In Palestine one defence against the uncertainty
that permeates the anticipation of the future life of the Palestinian collective has been
to crystallize womanhood into figures who adopt a role of working for the care of the
nation. One example of this is the role of the Palestinian mother in poetry of resistance:

> Oh Mother, if they forbid you to visit me, I will send my heart to you
> And I will ask my heart to gently kiss your hand and to take care of your flowers and garden
> Oh mother, do not be confused ... all Palestinian men are eagles

Please Mother, I ask you to remain as I always knew you
Free and strong, with your faith in God.[4]

Whereas the mother here may refer to a specific mother, she could, in the words of the Arabist Nathalie Khankan (2009: 122), represent the 'woman as Palestine'. In this vein, Massad argues that owing to Palestinians' failure to secure a territory, a reconfiguration of 'Palestinianness' has taken place: to be Palestinian formerly implied to be born in the territorial motherland, whereas being Palestinian now is hinged on the agnatic line, thereby making kinship, rather than territory, the stronger tie (Massad 1995: 472). We see this mothering of nation-building in song (cf. Kanaaneh & Thorsén 2013 for elaboration on this point), where women, in the sense of mothers of heroic detainees, stand out as emblematic of the contemporary Palestinian discourse of belonging, as do the mothers and widows of martyrs, who mourn while still keeping the household and the family together despite frequent destitution. How these gendered nodes in Palestinian discourse are vindicated in everyday interaction was made clear to me on several occasions during my fieldwork. Upon visiting acquaintances, who were often wives of detainees, women would subtly ask me, 'Do you want to speak with my mother-in-law too?' The question was rhetorical – it was rather a reminder to me not to upset intimate relations of hierarchy between the mother and her daughter-in-law. This tiny speech act reminds us that even though I as an anthropologist turned the spotlight on prisoners' wives, the local distribution of attention could not be circumscribed. Whereas talking to the mothers of the detainees was part of my interest already, it was also a necessary gesture on my part as the anthropologist.

Given this context, we must try to understand what the national emphasis on heroic men and on suffering, nurturing mothers means for how the detainees' wives perceive themselves as (Palestinian) women and how this intersects with others' perceptions of them. In terms of understanding the porous line between self and other, Das quotes Wittgenstein in *Life and words*: 'The ideal as we think of it, is unshakeable. You can never get outside it, you must always turn back. There is no outside; outside you cannot breathe' (Das 2007: 62).

Wittgenstein's formulation of the permeability between the inner and the outer can be seen in how the formerly described language of Palestinian national becoming is not located outside the intimate sphere of the individual detainees' wives. Rather, the heart of female subjectivity is located in how women and exemplary Palestinian womanhood are enunciated and perceived collectively. On this note I turn to an analysis of how some particular registers of Palestinian womanhood become examples for women to live by, and what is necessarily muted in order for a woman to stand out as exemplary.

Outside and inside the example

As mentioned above, Aisha receives many visitors to her new premises. But these visitors often come on errands other than paying her a visit of respect. They also come to learn how nice Aisha's new house is, to find out how she got the money to build it, and to see how many new pieces of furniture, rooms, and items of décor Aisha has bought with the money that they, erroneously, presume she must have taken from the Palestinian Authority's budget, just as – allegedly– many a former employee or politician has done. Patiently, Aisha sits down to receive the visitors' greetings and politely answer their questions by taking them around the house, showing them each piece of furniture, each picture and pedestal, saying: 'This I brought from my old house, and this is a gift from my aunt'. Though Aisha is grateful for the visitors' solidarity, her demeanour still reveals an intangible annoyance: Aisha has constantly to prove herself as a moral being in both the financial and intimate registers of her life. She allows visitors to see that she has left the arrangement of her bedroom décor the same as it was at the time of her husband's capture twelve years ago, even though she has been sleeping there on her own for almost the same length of time and has, moreover, moved house. Despite her annoyance, Aisha never refuses unexpected visitors, whether from inside or outside her close circle; she invites people to see for themselves that she cultivates the Palestinian and Arab cultural value of hospitality to perfection (Bille 2010). This figures, if subtly, in the way in which she allows her visitors a glimpse of both the public and private rooms in her house. As such, she signals a radical case of transparency that allows visitors also to conclude that, with Aisha, the outside is in fact the inside. The mutual configuration of ultimate transparency tells us how the process of becoming an example is a gesture of co-creation between a woman and her social relations.

Womanhood both becomes and fails to become exemplary across a range of social forums in which detainees' wives participate. This section examines the gulf between the idealized expectations of inhabiting social space as an example and the actual experience of this inhabitancy, including the loss of feelings of self, sensuality, and womanhood. Yasmin's husband has been sentenced to one hundred years in an Israeli prison owing to both his political affiliations and his participation in activities of resistance against Israel. During a conversation that I had with Yasmin, we spoke about her experience with a group therapeutic project with other detainees' wives. Such groups proliferate in the OPT as a popular psychosocial intervention targeted at the relatives of prisoners or martyrs by Palestinian NGOs funded by both Western and Arab donors (for elaboration of this point, see Buch Segal 2014a).

When Yasmin compared the participation in such a group with regular social forums with her female friends and relatives, I asked her to elaborate what her situation – being married to someone who would be imprisoned for a hundred years – meant for her in her ordinary social interactions. Yasmin said that it made her feel excluded. She was quiet for a while and then added, 'From my own experience'. Her words refer to the fact that she is married and therefore in theory may participate in regular conversations with other women who frequently talk and gossip about their husbands, including their faults and their whereabouts. Yasmin explained that she felt that she could not contribute anything to such interactions. If she revealed to other women how it felt to be in her situation – her physical loneliness in tandem with being the sole person responsible for their children – she was sure to be the focus of gossip among her near and distant peers for some time. This is because such feelings are at odds with the affect permeating Palestinian national sentiment, in which women such as Yasmin are viewed as the proud and honourable wives of heroic resistance fighters. Rather than only feeling a sense of pride, as is expected of her as an exemplary wife of a detainee, Yasmin sometimes felt empty and lonely. The notion of the ideal detainee's wife permeates self and social relations, but it does not cover the entire spectrum of feelings that living in an uncomfortable situation may evoke.

Paul Sant Cassia's work on the missing in Cyprus can lend some clarity to this situation. He argues that situations with unsettled affect pose a challenge to anthropological understanding, since we are disciplined to think that ritual, and I would also add local vernacular, covers and indeed offers solace for all forms of feeling

(Sant Cassia 2005: 153). Both Yasmin's and Aisha's stories, as well as subsequent cases below, testify that this is not always the case.

'In the group [with the other detainees' wives]', Yasmin said, 'I can speak about everything that didn't happen'. Yasmin here indicates how her everyday life lacks the small and not so small events that are perceived as making up a life together with a husband. Yasmin can participate in regular social forums with her in-laws, sisters, and friends by talking about her children, but she cannot share in conversations concerning husbands. She can't even complain about him, because it would compromise not only her own image but her support for the national struggle too.

Yasmin recognizes a gap between the pride that is supposed to fill the void of her absent husband and the way she actually feels. According to a therapeutic assumption about the healing potentiality of groups, Yasmin supposedly would feel better among women in situations similar to her own, where the absence that saturates their lives can help the group to bond (Bion 1996 [1961]). But from my participation in a similar therapeutic group for other detainees' wives, it seems that such intended creation of social bonds on the basis of shared experience captures only part of the affective discourses in and around therapeutic groups. In this second therapeutic group, the women did not talk about 'everything that did not happen' but about what structured and filled their lives. The content of the therapeutic sessions concerned problems bringing up the women's children, trouble with pleasing their families-in-law, and sometimes financial issues, like how to find the time for a job when one still had to care for children. The concerns were confirmed in the women's diaries,[5] the pages of which were full of worries about their children and about what other people thought of them as wives and mothers. Frustrations as to how to deal with gossip and 'intruders' who transgress personal boundaries when pretending to help were also described at length.[6]

Any mention of the women's husbands in this group were few and far between. Only in the context of an upcoming or recent visit to a husband in prison were they mentioned. In the women's diaries, these passages expressed intense emotions of frustration, joy, and anger. Once the affective reverberations of a visit had settled in the self and the collective, however, any mention of a husband quickly evaporated from the pages. It appears that only the people and activities most present in the women's everyday lives – namely children, family, and social networks – would be shared in a forum with women in similar situations, as well as in the women's writings, which were addressed to no one but themselves (for comparison, see Ross 2001).

Meanwhile, talk about detainees takes up a great deal of social conversation in everyday life outside group therapy. But what is absent from such talk, including by the family or close friends of a detainee, is the fact that, apart from being a detainee, he is also a husband. This must be seen against a backdrop of a general social ethos that marital problems and conflicts pertaining to the extended family are best kept within the couple or family in question (Muhawi & Kanaana 1989). The relationship between an imprisoned husband and his wife is therefore not an issue that is spoken about in any forum, particularly not when the man is absent owing to detention. As Tobias Kelly (2010) writes on the relation between knowledge and intimacy in the OPT, people know all too well what such an absence means for the people involved and, in this sense, conversation about marital difficulties could only leave the woman embarrassed. Whenever friends, family, or social acquaintances thus greet the wife of a detainee, the question asked is: 'Kīf al-asīr' (How is the detainee)?

This question actualizes the woman's relationship to her husband, yet it is an actualization that leaves aside the conjugal aspect of that relationship (for elaboration on this point, see Buch Segal 2013). One reason for the lack of reference to the married couple's relationship in talk about detainees and their relatives is that the Palestinian family is seen as a stronghold against Israel. And whatever is seen to threaten this stronghold, both in the concrete and in the symbolic register, is hidden away and contained within the family or within the personal relationships that are affected (Buch Segal in press).

In comparison to the collective silence about a conjugal relationship marked by detention, a mother or widow mourning a martyr who died for the Palestinian cause is not considered a threat to relational texture. As Nathalie Khankan writes in her analysis of the female voice in post-Oslo Accords Palestinian poetry, female poets – who often adopt masculine forms of writing while leaving experimentation of form to male writers – are included in the Palestinian cultural canon through writing as *ritha* (elegy) (Khankan 2009: 112). Mourning, however, is not possible for the wives of detainees, in brief because they are not considered to have (properly) lost their husbands as the widows of the martyrs have (Buch Segal in press). In reference to Freud (1957 [1917]), American philosopher Stanley Cavell describes mourning thus:

> The world must be regained every day, in repetition, regained as gone. Here is a way of seeing what it means that Freud too thinks of mourning as an essentially repetitive exercise. ... Freud regards mourning as the condition, that is to say, of allowing its independence from me, its objectivity (Cavell 1988: 172).

Of relevance here is how Freud thinks of mourning as both a repetitive, daily regaining of the world and as something that creates the possibility of separating mourning from one's self. Whereas the everyday must be created and regained every single day, for the detainees' wives it is impossible to separate themselves from the void left by their incarcerated husbands. This attribute of the conjugal relationship, I argue, is part of bearing the burden of being an example. The corollary of bearing this burden is that the words available to the detainees' wives to voice their experience are hinged on a national rhetoric of perseverance, steadfastness, and political sacrifice rather than an individual woman's feeling of hardship. As such there is a particular register of speech available for the women to speak within whether or not their experiences are felt to be contained with this register. This complex of frayed acknowledgement strikes a chord with Robert Orsi's work on the disabled members of a Catholic congregation in the United States, who are seen to body forth the suffering of the group yet without actually voicing what it feels like to be the body that lives this vexed representation (Orsi 2004). The intricacy of acknowledging without verbalization is gestured at in the following section.

Weaving pillows – stitching the inside/outside
It was Friday and the third day of *Eid al-Fitr*, and life was slowly returning to normal after the end of the holy month of *ar-Ramadan*. The three sisters, Amina, Reema, and Layla, were baking bread for the entire week in the backyard of Reema's house, one of the oldest houses in the village. Reema is the oldest of three sisters, in her early forties, married with four girls and two boys. That particular Friday, she, Amina, and their younger, unmarried sister Layla were waiting for Aisha to come by for lunch. Aisha's husband had orchestrated the political event that led to his life sentence and Amina's

husband's seventeen years in a high-security prison in Israel. Aisha's husband's sentence of life plus seventy years had been handed down by the Israeli military court a week earlier. Layla was sitting on the wall between the courtyard and the garden, peeling cucumbers for the salad with me. Amina was watching the last loaves in the wood-fired oven when Reema came out of the house, slightly annoyed because lunch had already been ready for a long time. Reema asked rhetorically, 'Where is Aisha? When is she coming? She was supposed to be here by now. Lunch is ready, it is almost three o'clock, *yalla Imm Yasser*'.[7] Amina answered her vaguely, saying, 'I called her one hour ago, she said twenty minutes; she will be here soon'.

Layla:	I called her too; she said she had to clean the bathroom because of *al-Eid* and all the visitors.
Reema:	She is always cleaning her bathroom; that was also her excuse last week. She is nervous, very nervous.
Layla:	Yeah, she has been very nervous lately, always doing something, cleaning, visiting, driving the kids around, always busy.
Amina:	Nervous? Well, what can she do, what do you want her to do, lifetime plus seventy years . . . what is she supposed to do?

Aisha had changed in the wake of her husband's sentence. Something had happened – she was more anxious, more restless, and she avoided eye contact. When I went to Aisha's house with her after the lunch with Amina, Reema, and Layla, she said to me that, after seven years of imprisonment, the fact that her husband had received his final sentence had caused feelings she had never experienced before, feelings that did not go away, no matter what she did to keep herself busy, be it cleaning or even praying. According to her self-perception as a devout Muslim, the lack of any effect on the part of her prayer unsettled her. She kept herself busy, performing her role with sincerity and persistence, giving every available hour that was not spent caring for family or studying with her two children to visiting and receiving visits from villagers wanting to ask her a favour or pay her their respects. In one of our first conversations, she stated adamantly with regard to the then undecided length of her husband's absence: 'This is not a loss. It is missing. Loss is miserable, missing is romantic'. Yet what she felt during the weeks after the final sentence was handed down to her husband was, she said, like being lost.

In her attempts to contain her feelings of being lost within the romantic connotations of longing, Aisha eclipsed the aspect of herself as a wife with an absent husband by keeping herself busy with everyday activities. To some extent, she wrote down what was detached from her subjectivity in her diaries and in the letters she composed to her husband. Through these expressive media, she partially actualized herself as a wife. Even in the letters, though, Aisha does not tell her husband about how her self unravelled when she was informed of the sentence. She writes only that Palestine will be victorious some day (for a detailed analysis of such letters, see also Buch Segal 2013; 2014*b*). Her affective expressions are thus immaculately kept within the language of national struggle in order to legitimate any kind of personal loss or suffering. Thus whatever feelings, even sorrow or mourning the loss of a particular way of being (together), that a wife of a detainee may experience, they have to be left out of her story and way of inhabiting a social world. She must stand out as an example of how she as a woman also bears the brunt of her husband's detention and the military occupation at large. This form of implicit self-censorship of particular feelings could be seen as an act of blinding that which could actually potentially threaten social life in Palestine. Or, in other words, inhabiting the position of the example stifles feelings that are not exemplary.

Another example of the entanglement between subjective feelings and the example one wishes to set can be seen in how Amina expresses herself as a wife to her husband through the photos of herself she sends or asks her children to take to her husband in prison. Usually, as a seasonal farmer and a weaver with little money, Amina dresses very simply, never displaying any sign that could be taken as vain or as wanting to attract a new man. In contrast, the photos she sends her husband show a woman with her hair done simply but elegantly by the hairdresser. In these photos, Amina is not wearing the *hijab*, since her husband is allowed to see her unveiled. And she is dressed in smart womenswear that connotes discreet sensuality. However, in the part of Amina's everyday that is not about herself as a wife in an expressive relationship with her husband – by far the majority of her time – there is no trace of this woman.

A further example of this contrast can be seen in a stanza from the poem 'My messengers to the desert' by the Palestinian poet Ghada al-Shafi'i.

> Like this
> from a day that departs in the tolling [sound] of gold
> to a day that swims in clouds
> they walk
> inheriting [their] longing
> storing it in clay jugs [made to hold drinking water].[8]

Khankan describes al-Shafi'i's poetry as pondering over the nexus of lack and want (2009: 129), for instance with regard to the national homelessness of the Palestinians (2009: 133). Longing in the poem above is contained in the everyday objects of clay jugs, perhaps suggesting that the only materialization such a longing can assume is that of ordinary objects. While the longing subject matter of the poem is not personal longing but rather the collective longing for statehood and freedom on the part of the Palestinians, two aspects of the poem are relevant for the present analysis: first, the transfiguration of longing into everyday objects; and, secondly, the image of containing longing.

Longing that is reconfigured into everyday objects is somewhat crudely illustrated by Amina's work as a weaver in a small local factory to sustain her family. In this factory, she produces pillows that bear the image of Che Guevara, the global symbol for a heroic figure who not surprisingly also symbolizes resistance to the occupation by the Palestinian people. This was made clear to me on a quiet afternoon, when I had been picking olives with Amina, her children, and two of her sisters on her family's fields near her village. When we were done, Amina's nephew Ibrahim, who came to pick us up in a run-down car, asked me, tongue in cheek, 'Do you know Che?', clearly hoping for a discussion about the legitimacy of the Palestinian freedom fighters in the light of the revolutionary icon of Che Guevera. Having participated in this genre of discussion numerous times before, I said, 'Yes', and then shrugged my shoulders when Ibrahim asked me what I thought of him. Not happy at all with my lack of spirited counter-argument, he went on to tell me why Che was a hero in occupied Palestine. Ibrahim need not have explained, since Che Guevera is in fact so iconic that his image figures on tapestries, woven pillows, as well as the letters and pieces of handicraft produced by the Palestinian prisoners in Israeli detention that one finds on display in the living rooms of their relatives across occupied Palestine.

I wish to dwell on how both the woven pillows featuring Che and the letters and photos women send to their detained husbands are no less ordinary objects than the clay jugs storing longing in al-Shafi'i's poem. For Amina and Aisha, wowen images of Che and letters sent to a prison refer to the entanglement of the ordinary and the extraordinary in their everyday lives, namely their husbands' physical disappearance from the everyday owing to confinement. The personal longing of Amina and Aisha is inseparable from the inherited, collective longing for freedom. In the quotidian lives of these women, such longing, however, gives way to acts of care for their children and relatives around them in order for there to actually be a collective for whom the heroes are fighting. The pillows showing Che Guevara are thus emblematic of the revolutionary struggle in the double sense and their production is a dual act of national solidarity and making a living. In fact I would argue that Amina's motivation for weaving such a pillow is less a desire to make a heroic contribution to the fight for national liberation than it is the task of nurturing and sustaining a home and a life for her family.

The above poem's containment of longing in clay jugs may be, in the cases of Amina, Aisha, and other women in similar situations, likened to the way in which they contain their loneliness and emptiness in objects, namely in their diaries, photos, and letters. Containment of such feelings is necessary, as has been described elsewhere, notably in Lila Abu-Lughod's sensitive work on emotions among the Awlad-Ali in Egypt and more broadly on gender in the Middle East (Abu-Lughod 1986; 2013). If the feelings were actualized in public rather than in private, they would severely compromise the example detainees' wives are supposed to set (Nashif 2008). Loneliness and emptiness are thus best kept at a distance from words because they have no home in the standing language. Containing these feelings, one may speculate, is therefore woven into Aisha's constant cleaning of the bathroom, Amina's weaving, and Yasmin's restless attempt to come up with errands she can run in her big Land Cruiser. The results of the ongoing effort to contain un-exemplary feelings may do the job on a subjective level, but, as shown in Amina, Reema, and Layla's discussion of Aisha's restless cleaning, these efforts produce other cracks in the example otherwise set by Aisha. The question is whether the obligations of the detainees' wives help to fill the abyss in their everyday lives or constantly tear open that emotional void, which the women's mundane acts of containing through cleaning, weaving, and driving around on errands attempt to mend.

Antigone and awkward witnessing

In order to cast the above ethnography in a different light, I turn to an exemplary figure of thought who has informed social analysis of women balancing the silver lining of heroism and its consequences: Antigone (Butler 2000; Das 2007; Willner 1982). In an act intended to secure the heroic burial of her brother, Antigone defies her uncle Creon and, as a consequence, is walled up in a tomb, where she commits suicide. By insisting on burying her brother, Antigone chooses kinship over the state at the cost of her own life. To Judith Butler, Antigone's choice is a conflict between the law of the state and the law of the family (2000: 6).

Antigone's choice also informs Veena Das's examination of how the violence of the partition between India and Pakistan in 1947 is folded into kin relations through women's silence about that violence in their attempts to stitch together split families (Das 2007). What makes Das's analysis of Antigone salient here is how she references Lacan critically to frame Antigone as a female witness who finds her voice in the zone between two deaths (Das 2007: 61). In Das, voice 'is a spectacular, defiant creation of the subject through the act of speech' (2007: 61). Voice, then, is other than speech in the sense that speech, as we have seen, does not always allow for subjective experience to be expressed. To Das, the voice of Antigone emerges in the moment of transgression; transgression here refers to the instant in which the crime of the law is realized by the killing of Antigone's brother, to which Antigone is a witness (2007: 61). In what sense, may we ask, is Antigone as a female witness of transgression relevant to an analysis of exemplary womanhood in Palestine? Though the link to Palestinian widows of martyrs is all too easy to make, I flag it none the less because it shows precisely the kind of exemplary witness that women who have (only) lost their men to imprisonment can never become. Like Antigone, martyrs' widows indeed live through the transgression caused by their husbands' deaths in the name of the Palestinian state-to-be. In contrast, the wives of detainees find themselves balancing on the knife edge of a transgression that has not (yet) fully occurred. That which has not happened, of course, is death. An exemplary witness is the one standing beside the death of a near one, whereas what detainees' wives witness is not death, only its possibility. This is what makes it impossible even for an apparent example like Aisha to stand out as a truly exemplary witness. All women like her can hope for is to become awkward witnesses.

I wish to point to a further resemblance between the portrayal of humans' and gods' failures in Greek tragedies and how Palestinian women are supposed to inhabit the world in the wake of detention. The premise of this argument is that my interlocutors are primarily understood by intimates, counsellors, and indeed international observers through what they are not. Thus, the difference between the Greek tragedies and the situation of my interlocutors is that the linearity of the tragedy and the way in which death offers a solution to the tension, albeit a tragic one, does not offer a framework for comprehension for Palestinian wives of detainees. Cavell, interestingly, asserts that Shakespeare's tragedies are distinctive in that they are imbued with what he terms a 'skeptical structure'. According to Cavell, the skepticism in Shakespearean tragedies refers to the withdrawal of the world as one knows it (1987: 19). Cavell analyses the tragic story of Othello and Desdemona as being about a man whose tragedy is not a lack of knowledge of the other but a lack of trust in such knowledge. How can he be sure of what he knows – how can he be sure of Desdemona's virginity upon their marriage (Cavell 1979: 490)? Of importance in Othello's attempts to prove that his doubts in his wife are grounded in her infidelity is his demand for visual proof of her intactness, a proof Desdemona fails to deliver owing to a conspiracy between Othello's aide Iago and Iago's wife Emilia (Cavell 1979: 495). The only thing that can prove Othello's doubts wrong is Desdemona's death. Othello kills her, and she is metaphorically turned into a stone, intact as only the inhuman can be (Cavell 1979: 481). By turning his wife to stone, Othello attempts to keep his knowledge of her outside the register of skepticism, thus allowing death to bring about a degree of certainty that human life is never endowed with. Othello's final act of suicide underlines the tragic juxtaposition of death and clarity.

The image of Othello desperately trying to secure his knowledge about Desdemona by metaphorically turning her to stone may further our understanding of the lack of acknowledgement of what it means emotionally to be a detainee's *wife* in Palestine, derivative honour aside. The emphasis on exemplary womanhood in Palestine could be conceptualized as a national requirement to turn certain types of emotion to stone – an allegory that was often used by my interlocutors, albeit in a different sense, namely that their strength was '*zay al-jabal*' – like the mountain. No matter what occurred, they would endure. Amalia Sa'ar (2006) argues that local expressions of women as *qawiyya* (strong) are used as a mode of praise that positions the women's strength as affirming shared values of, in the Palestinian case, national revolution. The tragic structure of such praise lies in the way that praising a woman's strength turns her into an example, whilst at the same time denying feelings like loneliness, despair, or even a wish to divorce. What is denied is precisely what can be endured because it does not count as tragic, compared to being the widow of a martyr (Khalili 2007). How some feelings are left out of the representation of womanhood that comes with being an example to others illustrates the burden that appears to lie in setting an example. Even though women are considered exemplary national heroes when they display strength through their husbands' detentions, this is an ambiguous heroism.

Antigone, while heroic in the face of her brother's burial, breaks the law of the state. For the wives of detainees, it seems to be the other way around. They reproduce the nation and live up to its requirements by displaying heroic strength while hiding their longing behind a public face of exemplary womanhood. In ethnographic terms, the cracks nevertheless figure in how even an exemplary woman such as Aisha is questioned: she is at the centre of rumours of financial fraud, she constantly feels nervous, and she regularly has to prove that she guards her husband's memory in the most intimate of domestic locations – the bedroom.

Children – underlining exemplary womanhood

One day, I went to the town hall with Amina in order to pick up her children, who where in the children's club downstairs. The children's club was run by Reema, Amina's sister. After she had taken me on a tour of the premises, Reema asked my assistant Rawan and me to sit down in front of the television and watch a video. The video showed Zeinab, Aisha's 11-year-old daughter, on stage agitatedly singing and half-shouting a song to the glory of the detainees. Around her were children who enacted being held in an Israeli prison. As the song neared its end, they broke their chains, symbolizing the freedom of Palestine. The video was recorded on the Palestinian Prisoners' Day that takes place every year on 17 April all over the OPT. In Dar Nūra, which at that time had just over one hundred of its four thousand citizens detained in Israel, the day is celebrated at the school, where the children perform songs, plays, and recitals to a crowd of their parents, detainees' families, and official representatives of the community. Reema, Amina, and Zeinab observed me intensely as I watched, eager to hear my reaction to the show. This instance made clear that, though wives of detainees are the focus of this paper, the children of detainees are no less affected by the situation. With the conjugal relationship cut, and permission rarely granted to visit detainees, the child or the children step in as a mediating relation between mother and father. Indeed, women sometimes pass on letters to their husbands through their children. It is the children who carry the photos, presents, and letters back and forth between their parents, thereby inhabiting a central position in attempting to keep together the fragmented family.

'Ādi: absence, skepticism, and the ordinary

A frequent response in everyday conversations to questions such as, 'Kīfik?', (How are you?), 'Šu akbārik?' (f) (What's your news?), and 'Kīf aḥsāsik?' (How do you feel?) was "Ādi', which literally means 'Normal' or 'Standard', but is used to signal nothing unusual or spectacular. "Ādi' was also a response to my question concerning if and how life had changed after a husband had been sent to prison. Yet, as was obvious to me from knowing the wives of long-term detainees, the way in which their lives were stitched together was of course not the same as before their husbands' detention. How could they answer "Ādi' to a life that had become uncanny at its seams (cf. Freud 2003 [1919])?

This actualization makes relevant a return to the politicized and nationalized image of the exemplary suffering and nurturing mother who sustains everyday life in the absence of a son (Jean-Klein 2000). For the wives who emphasize those aspects of womanhood that are connoted by motherhood, life remains recognizable even in the absence of a husband. A mother still has to keep the family together by making sure that everyday life is normal in its structure: getting children ready for school, cooking for them, studying with them, earning money for their livelihood, and caring for them. During the absence of a husband, these things still function routinely, hereby recalling how to Freud mourning and its termination are made possible only in the repetition of the quotidian acts that make up one's life. As such, even though a violent event has happened, the mother is what makes life safe in the midst of chaos. The symbol of 'the Palestinian mother' therefore secures Palestine as a homeland while her sons engage in resistance to the occupation. Reducing womanhood to motherhood becomes a means of sustaining the Palestinian struggle for a nation-state through nurture and support, making sure that violence does not fragment the Palestinian collective. Returning to Das, then, the sole possible way for detainees' wives to turn back, to reinhabit not only their social world but themselves too, is by allowing motherhood to stand in for other aspects of womanhood.

In a sense, the women are captured in epitomizing stability. Conceiving womanhood as motherhood during male absence owing to incarceration is a collective attempt to defeat skepticism. Here, skepticism refers to world-shattering doubt as to the worth and value of the national struggle for statehood. Skepticism in this register renders it impossible to know and to acknowledge the loss of a life as a holy sacrifice and a thirty-two-year prison sentence as a necessary price to pay. In this light, the image of the Palestinian mother achieves more than keeping Palestine intact for the collectivity of Palestinians. The descent into the ordinary through motherhood is a way of constructing a life that is still 'normal' in the absence of the husband because motherhood in fact eclipses skepticism.

If we, the detainees' wives themselves, and their near and distant relations were to focus only on the absence of a husband, then nothing would be "ādi' or normal in his absence. If womanhood were eclipsed by the aspect of subjectivity connoted by marital relations, the image of the Palestinian collective as practising patience (ṣumūd) and supporting activities of resistance would be shattered, thus allowing profound doubt as to the national project of becoming to seep into the social texture. To keep the notion of a nation-state intact, it is necessary to replace conjugal womanhood with motherhood. Whereas motherhood may be said to be part and parcel of the conjugal relationship owing to its objective of reproducing warriors (Massad 1995), the slight tilt that makes motherhood overshadow conjugal womanhood in this case is significant for understanding what is altered in the lives of women who live with an incarcerated husband. Reminiscent once more of Sant Cassia's work on public secrecy and Kelly's writing on similarity and suspicion, the intimate and collective but not publicly voiced knowledge of that alteration is what constitutes a looming threat to collective hope and faith in Palestinian national becoming.

Crafting the example and its shadows through the work of anthropology

My concern here has been with the emotional labour done by the women who stand out as examples of national, heroic womanhood in the face of their husbands' detention. Now what, may we ask, is the academic value of attending to women who, I have argued, can in fact never become truly exemplary owing to the perilous position they inhabit in the Palestinian national imaginary? The prisoners' wives about whom this paper is written compel me to scrutinize aspects of human life that challenge the systems of thought we have available to understand them, like resistance, religion, or ideology, so often flagged in analysis of Palestinians. João Biehl, facing a similar concern in his continuous return to his main protagonist Catarina, contends that 'ethnographic subjects allow us to return to the places where thought is born' (2014: 99). The figures of the prisoners' wives in Palestine are so structurally, emotionally, and relationally compelling that I do not think that anthropological knowledge about them is exhausted, despite studies on Palestine being a well-ploughed field. On part of the anthropologist, it does, however, require an impulse to look beyond the templates of understanding available already in the literature on gender and resistance in Palestine and emphasize that the premise for any analysis is an acknowledgement of the deep entrenchment of female heroism with everyday life. This analytical anchoring has brought to the fore how to these women, the descent into the ordinary is only possible by detaching from the partial aspect of gendered subjectivity involved in marriage in order to make everyday life ordinary or "*ādī*" in the face of their husbands' incarceration.

Cavell, however, reminds us that this descent is only a return to the allegedly normal:

> The return of what we accept as the world will then present itself as a return of the familiar, which is to say, exactly under the concept of what Freud names as the uncanny. That the familiar is a product of a sense of the unfamiliar and of the sense of a return means that what returns after skepticism is never just the same (1988: 166).

This paper has revealed that the ordinary, as sited in the sphere of the domestic, also becomes the uncanny for the detainees' wives.

The descent into the ordinary on the part of the women figuring here is only obtainable by detaching that part of subjectivity that made Amina and her peers therapeutic subjects and patriotic women in the first place, namely the relationship to their heroic husbands. Replacing conjugal womanhood with motherhood is a way of sustaining and nurturing not only their children, but also the Palestinian collective. Through this substitution, the importance, necessity, and legitimacy of engaging in resistance remain in focus. This is a way of knowing that allows only the Palestinian mother and the male hero to occupy the position of the example. It is this that necesssitates the described aspect-blindness of many other aspects of subjectivity such as loneliness, sensuality, and longing (Wittgenstein 2009 [1953]: PPF § 157). The shadows created in this process are required in order to sustain the idea of a nation. Yet the shadow that casts detainees' wives in the light of motherhood is as important for the women themselves in order to stay themselves, and to be able to live ordinarily in the face of an altered ordinary. In order for them to do this, they paradoxically have to embrace themselves as exemplary mothers, thereby keeping at bay personal knowledge of what the cost of incarceration in fact amounts to. My broader argument is thus based on the fact that examples and the production of examples are powerful, necessary, and evocative ways in which a collective thinks and acts within itself and towards others. Yet such examples, at least in the ethnographic context of Palestine, come at the cost of stifling personal affects that curb the register of womanhood among Palestinians. This paper's attention to some of the less spectacular figures of the Palestinian collective has given access to how exemplary being is in fact a way of breathing for wives of Palestinian detainees in Israel. The immanent tragedy of this mode of breathing is that it cannot inhale the entirety of what detention has meant for subjective feelings of womanhood, leaving the women in the role of awkward witnesses to the skepticism of the future of the Palestinian project.

NOTES

I would like to thank Aisha, Amina, and Yasmin for opening their hearts, homes, and thoughts to me in the course of my work in Palestine. The ethnographic research was generously funded by a Ph.D. scholarship from DANIDA and postdoc funding from the Carlsberg Foundation. I also wish to extend my gratitude to the editors of this special issue, Andreas Bandak and Lars Højer. First of all, thank you for including me in the initial seminar and inviting me to be part of this fine collection of contemporary anthropology. But thank you also for being at once thorough, productive, demanding, and inspiring editors. Sharon Macdonald, Veena Das, and the anonymous reviewers have at different stages of this paper helped clarify my thinking on the subject through their thoughtful and generous comments.

[1] Ahmad is a pseudonym, as are all names of people, places, and institutions in this paper.

[2] See *http://www.ochaopt.org/annual/c1/7.html* (accessed 15 January 2015).

[3] See, however, Laleh Khalili's recent book *Time in the shadows* (2012) for an analysis of the workings behind incarceration in Israel and the United States.

[4] The song was written by former detainee Ayman Ramadan in 2005.

[5] As part of my fieldwork I gave my interlocutors diaries in which I asked them to write about big and small events and emotions in their everyday lives. The intent was for me to read the diaries at different intervals, though I also made it clear that if the women felt that the diaries were too private to share or they did not write at all, they were still theirs.

[6] Regarding the women's frequent use of the notion of 'intruder', one of the reviewers made the most relevant comment whether such a remark was in fact targeted at the anthropologist. Naturally I do not know whether that was sometimes the case. Yet, based on the ways in which the women described what was intrusive about the intruders, I do not think so. To them, intruders were people who in discreet and indiscreet ways tried to make them change their behaviour or indeed tried to influence the life-choices they made, whether in terms of remarrying, dressing appropriately modestly, or running errands unaccompanied by a chaperone. For instance, one woman described how her aunt urged her to remarry whilst she was still mourning her martyred husband (see also Buch Segal in press for elaboration of this point). Intrusion was thus used in relation to people trying to change a woman's manners and expressions.

[7] Aisha also goes by the name of Imm Yasser, since she is Yasser's mother.

[8] Ghada al-Shafi'i: 'My messengers to the desert', in *Eternal guests of fire* (1999) in Khankan (2009: 135). The poem has been translated by Khankan and transcribed by Christina Copty.

> w-hākaḏā . . .
> min yaum ḏāhib fī ranīn al-ḏahab
> ila yaumin 'a'imin fī as-saḥb
> yasīrūna
> w-humm yatawāratūna al-ḥanīn
> w-yukazinūnahu fī il-jarār il-mu'adat li-ma'i iš-šurb

REFERENCES

ABU-LUGHOD, L. 1986. *Veiled sentiments: honor and poetry in a Bedouin society*. Berkeley: University of California Press.
———— 2013. *Do Muslim women need saving?* Cambridge, Mass.: Harvard University Press.
AL-SHAFI'I, G. 1999. Rusuli ild al-sahra [My messengers to the desert]. In *Duyuf al-ndr al-da'imuna: shucara min Filastin* [The eternal guests of fire: poets from Palestine] (ed.) G. Zaqtan, **99**. Ramallah: Bayt al-shi'ir.
ALLEN, L. 2009. Martyr bodies in the media: human rights, aesthetics, and the politics of immediation in the Palestinian intifada. *American Ethnologist* **36**, 161-80.
ASAD, T. 2007. *On suicide bombing*. New York: Columbia University Press.
BAKER, A. & A. MATAR 2011. *Threat: Palestinian political prisoners in Israel*. London: Pluto.

Biehl, J. 2014. Ethnography in the way of theory. In *The ground between: anthropologists engage philosophy* (eds) V. Das, M. Jackson, A. Kleinman & B. Singh, 94-118. Durham, N.C.: Duke University Press.

Bille, M. 2010. Seeking providence through things: the word of God versus black cumin. In *An anthropology of absence: materializations of transcendence and loss* (eds) M. Bille, F. Hastrup & T.F. Sørensen, 167-84. New York: Springer.

Bion, W. 1996 [1961]. *Experiences in groups and other papers*. London: Routledge.

B'Tselem 2014. Statistics on Palestinians in the custody of the Israeli security forces (available on-line: *http://www.btselem.org/English/Statistics/Detainees_and_Prisoners.asp*, accessed 7 January 2015).

Buch Segal, L. 2013. Enduring presents: living a prison sentence as a wife of a detainee in Israel. In *The times of security: ethnographies of fear, protest, and the future* (eds) M.A. Pedersen & M. Holbraad, 122-40. New York: Routledge.

——— 2014a. Why is Muna crying? Acknowledgement and criteria for evaluating suffering in the Occupied Palestinian Territories. In *Histories of victimhood* (eds) H. Rønsbo & S. Jensen, 179-97. Philadelphia: University of Pennsylvania Press.

——— 2014b. Disembodied conjugality. In *Wording the world: Veena Das and scenes of inheritance* (ed.) R. Chatterji, 55-68. New York: Fordham University Press.

——— in press. Mourning, grief, and the loss of politics in Palestine: the unvoiced effects of military occupation in the West Bank. In *An anthropology of living and dying in the contemporary world* (eds) V. Das & C. Han. Berkeley: University of California Press.

Butler, J. 2000. *Antigone's claim: kinship between life and death*. New York: Columbia University Press.

Cavell, S. 1979. *The claim of reason: Wittgenstein; skepticism; morality and tragedy*. Oxford: University Press.

——— 1987. *Disowning knowledge in six plays of Shakespeare*. Cambridge: University Press.

——— 1988. *In quest of the ordinary*. Chicago: University Press.

Das, V. 2007. *Life and words: violence and the descent into the ordinary*. Berkeley: University of California Press.

——— 2008. Violence, gender and subjectivity. *Annual Review of Anthropology* **37**, 283-99.

Freud, S. 1957 [1917]. *Mourning and melancholia* (trans. J. Strachey). London: Penguin.

——— 2003 [1919]. *The uncanny* (trans. J. Strachey). New York: Penguin.

Hage, G. 2003. 'Comes a time we are all enthusiasm': understanding Palestinian suicide bombers in times of exighophobia. *Public Culture* **15**, 65-89.

Jean-Klein, I. 2000. Mothercraft, statecraft, and subjectivity in the Palestinian intifada. *American Ethnologist* **27**, 100-127.

Johnson, P., L. Abu Nahleh & A. Moors 2009. Weddings and war: marriage arrangements and celebrations in two Palestinian Intifadas. *Journal of Middle East Women's Studies* Special Issue: War and transnational Arab families (eds) P. Johnson & S. Joseph, **5**: 3, 11-35.

Kanaaneh, M. & S.-M. Thorsén 2013. *Palestinian music and song: expression and resistance since 1900*. Bloomington: Indiana University Press.

Kelly, T. 2010. In a treacherous state: the fear of collaboration among West Bank Palestinians. In *Traitors: suspicion, intimacy and the ethics of statebuilding* (eds) T. Kelly & S. Thiranagama, 168-87. Philadelphia: University of Pennsylvania Press.

Khalili, L. 2007. *Heroes and martyrs of Palestine: the politics of national commemoration*. Cambridge: University Press.

——— 2012. *Time in the shadows: confinement in counterinsurgencies*. Stanford: University Press.

Khankan, N. 2009. *Breathing sun-drenched horizons: the possibility of poetry in post-Oslo Palestine*. Ph.D. thesis, University of California (Berkeley).

Kublitz, A. 2013. Seizing catastrophes: the temporality of Nakba among Palestinians in Denmark. In *The times of security: ethnographies of fear, protest and the future* (eds) M.A. Pedersen & M. Holbraad, 103-21. London: Routledge.

Massad, J. 1995. Conceiving the masculine: gender and Palestinian nationalism. *Middle East Journal* **49**, 467-83.

Muhawi, I. & S. Kanaana 1989. *Speak bird speak again: Palestinian Arab folktales*. Berkeley: University of California Press.

Nashif, E. 2008. *Palestinian political captives: identity and community*. Abingdon, Oxon: Routledge.

Orsi, R. 2004. 'Mildred, is it fun to be a cripple?': the culture of suffering in mid-twentieth century American Catholicism. In *Between heaven and earth: the religious worlds people make and the scholars who study them*, 19-47. Princeton: University Press.

PETEET, J.M. 1991. *Gender in crisis: women and the Palestinian resistance movement*. New York: Columbia University Press.

ROSS, F. 2001. Speech and silence: women's testimony in the first five weeks of public hearings of the South African Truth and Reconciliation Commission. In *Remaking a world: violence, social suffering, and recovery* (eds) V. Das, A. Kleinman, M. Lock, M. Ramphele & P. Reynolds, 250-80. Berkeley: University of California Press.

SA'AR, A. 2006. Feminine strength: reflections on power and gender in Israeli-Palestinian culture. *Anthropological Quarterly* **79**, 397-431.

SANT CASSIA, P. 2005. *Bodies of evidence: burial, memory and the recovery of missing persons in Cyprus*. Oxford: Berghahn.

SAYIGH, R. 2008. *The Palestinians: from peasants to revolutionaries*. London: Zed.

WILLNER, D. 1982. The Oedipus Complex, Antigone, and Electra: the woman as hero and victim. *American Anthropologist* **84**, 58-78.

WITTGENSTEIN, L. 2009 [1953]. *Philosophical investigations* (trans. G.E.M. Anscombe). Chichester: Wiley-Blackwell.

Le fardeau de l'exemplarité : sentiments nationaux, inconfort du témoignage et statut de femme dans les territoires occupés de Palestine

Résumé

Le présent article analyse la manière dont les épouses de détenus palestiniens sont transformées en exemples à la fois par elles-mêmes et par leurs proches, tout en examinant le contexte de la place inconfortable de ces femmes dans les narrations de la destinée nationale palestinienne. Son principal objectif est d'examiner le fardeau que constitue le fait d'être un exemple et ce qu'il implique pour celles qui aspirent à la position de femme « exemplaire », ou y parviennent sous de subtiles pressions, en Palestine. On attend des femmes de détenus palestiniens certaines modalités d'exemplarité afin d'entretenir une version partagée de la vie ordinaire sous occupation militaire. Il n'est dès lors pas étonnant que le travail émotionnel nécessaire pour paraître exemplaire soit forcément occulté dans les registres du discours public aussi bien qu'intime afin de conserver l'aspiration collective à garder une vie que l'on pourra qualifier de « normale » en temps de conflit.

3

Exemplary series and Christian typology: modelling on sainthood in Damascus

Andreas Bandak *University of Copenhagen*

In this paper, I explore the way in which examples are used in sermons among the pious followers of Our Lady of Soufanieh in Damascus, Syria. In the sermons, a particular logic of seriation functions to present specific models and exemplars as prisms of lives to be imitated. The framing of these lives takes place through entextualizations, whereby the life of some is made into texts that others are told to emulate. The process of making life into text and text into life is explored in the production of examples at the weekly Saturday sermons in Soufanieh. While directly related to life as lived, such sermons also stand for a broader class of life as *forma vitae*, that is, lives to be followed. I thus explore the example as exemplum, a particular moral story used for edification and didactic purposes, one which situates the listener at the centre of the story by integrating the miraculous happenings in Soufanieh with the response of the individual. The sermons thus serve to examine exemplification and the modelling of sainthood in Damascus in the years preceding the current civil war.

> How are we taught the word 'God' (its use, that is)? I cannot give an exhaustive systematic description. But I can, as it were, make contributions toward the description; I can say something about it and perhaps in time assemble a sort of collection of examples.
>
> Wittgenstein 1998 [1977]: 94

'The Gospel is always new!' Abuna Elias Zahlawi proclaims in his always eloquently delivered sermon. The 80-year-old priest looks at the congregants through his heavy glasses. 'The Gospel is always new, even if we have heard it one hundred times before!' he continues, only to make a rhetorical pause to let the effect of his words be felt. The whirring sound of the fans on the ceiling can be heard. A couple of youngsters wriggle around on their plastic chairs, which make a noise as they scratch on the tiles. The inner courtyard of the house of the Nazzour family, where the weekly service is held, is packed this Saturday. People of all ages are present: children, young men, old ladies, and even whole families are assembled in the house. The rosary has been said in front of the icon of Our Lady of Soufanieh, which is customary and has been so almost ever since the miraculous happenings began in the home more than two and a half decades ago. The miracles started in late November 1982 as Myrna Akhras prayed for

Journal of the Royal Anthropological Institute (N.S.), 47-63
© Royal Anthropological Institute 2015

her ailing sister-in-law. The sister-in-law was cured and, in the following days, Myrna both witnessed an icon in her home ooze oil and saw apparitions of the Virgin Mary. Abuna Zahlawi and several others were part of the miraculous happenings from the very start and the phenomenon was soon named Our Lady of Soufanieh after the area of Damascus in which the events took place. Subsequently, Myrna received messages from the Virgin Mary on numerous occasions and sometimes from Jesus, focusing on three words: faith (*imān*), love (*maḥabba*), and unity (*waḥda*). Later still, Myrna suffered stigmata, the wounds of Christ upon his crucifixion, on five occasions. The home concomitantly developed into a shrine and a centre for devotion and pilgrimage. During the last of the five repetitions of the rosary on this January Saturday in 2010, Abuna Zahlawi slowly descends the steps from the living room and walks past the people sitting there. He halts in front of the icon, where he silently says a prayer. People touch his white gown decorated with a cross in red satin. He takes some steps further and exchanges a few words with two of the elders before assuming his stand in front of the altar. A microphone is switched on by one of the two elders, who walks to the side of the room and adjusts the sound on the stereo. Abuna Zahlawi is silent for a moment as the congregants all await his initiative. He then leads the liturgy and thereby signals the start of the service proper. Some know the liturgy by heart, while others use books following the liturgy of the Melchite Catholic Church to aid their memory of the patterned practice. Later, during Eucharist, hymns and devotional songs in praise of the Virgin Mary, Christ, and the happenings in this very house add yet another layer of words to those already uttered. The singing of hymns and the recitation of prayers liturgy, and the Bible, as well as the sermon delivered by Abuna Zahlawi, all emphasize the role of words in the formation of the Christian character.

In this paper I shall address the formation of character as a modelling on sainthood. I explore the specific models and exemplars presented in sermons as prisms for lives to be imitated. The framing of these lives is made through entextualizations, whereby the life of some is made into texts which others are told to emulate. The process of making life into text and text into life is explored in the production of examples at the weekly Saturday sermons in Soufanieh. While directly related to life as lived, such sermons also stand for a broader class of life as *forma vitae*, that is, lives to be followed. I thus explore the example as exemplum, a particular moral story used for edification and didactic purposes, one which situates the listener at the centre of the story by integrating the miraculous happenings in Soufanieh with the response of the individual.

Exemplifying the Gospel: repentance and change

Abuna Zahlawi begins his sermon this Saturday by clearing his throat. People are all ears. He clears his throat once more and starts with the words spoken by Jesus in today's text from Matthew 4:12-17. 'If we listen to what is in the Gospel today, Jesus says: "*Repent, for the kingdom of heaven is near*"'. He pauses briefly before continuing: 'Perhaps you think that this is something Jesus said two thousand years ago. And perhaps you think that this was probably fine for those living then, but we ... What should we change? That nothing changes in our lives.' Abuna Zahlawi glances out over the people assembled. The narration goes on at a steady pace without the assistance of a manuscript. Abuna Zahlawi holds the microphone in his hands, which are joined in front of him. The hands shake slightly but no shaking is heard in the voice of the experienced priest. If people are reluctant regarding the message of Soufanieh, it is difficult not to be, if not

Journal of the Royal Anthropological Institute (N.S.), 47-63
© Royal Anthropological Institute 2015

persuaded, then at least affected by the work of words delivered by this priest. From the outset, the importance of change is underscored as the theme for today.

> When I discuss with some people, they say to me: 'Abuna, what do you want from me?' I say how long is it since you confessed? 'Uff, pihhh … I haven't confessed for a very long time!' And the person is old. Very well, so there is nothing problematic in your life? 'No, not really!'

By giving this brief description of a person who does not confess, it is possible for Abuna Zahlawi to address a more general problem: 'Man's problem is that he wants to see his situation as from afar … If one stands in front of a mirror, even if he is a pretty person, the closer he gets his reaction is: "Uff, is it me?!"' Steadily and engagingly, Abuna Zahlawi builds up his sermon and frames the importance of the Gospel for today. The first move is to situate the problem of mankind as such. From here the relevance of the Gospel for today can be assessed. The priests's line is very clear as he takes his listeners on a tour of the scriptural context, and from this context to examples in Damascus, and finally ends in this house with the grace of God bestowed upon it and perforce on the listeners: God wants change! He has done it in history, and history has been made on the very soil where people are now present.

'I don't know if your situation is like this', Abuna Zahlawi continues. 'The problem in us is that our life feels distanced'. He continues this line of thought and relocates the problem in relation to Jesus a little later: 'Jesus is in our hearts, but very often, we don't let this reality enter our families or our behaviour. We pray. We go to church … We go to the Eucharist far away from other people, and everybody goes to Eucharist without confession'. The problem now is addressed in moral terms, that a life devoid of attentive listening and ensuing action is dangerous and that the very moment of the sermon is precious for each person present.

> Believe me, we need time to see the daily importance of this sentence from the Gospel, because there is very much in our lives that needs to be brought into being (*takwīn*). Jesus' words – '*Repent, for the kingdom of heaven is near*' – are not just for those living two thousand years ago. They matter here, too!

Apart from stating that the basic problem is still the same, Abuna Zahlawi now couples Jesus' first recorded public message with the first message the Virgin is reported to have imparted to Myrna: '*Repent and believe and remember me in your joy*'.'In the first message! Who of you know the messages? … I want you all to know the messages. Let us pause and examine some of the words the Virgin and Jesus said. *Repent*. From what should we *repent*?' The priest repeats the sentence: 'From what should we *repent*? … I and you. There are things in our lives that he wants us to repent from'. The doubling and crafting of the relationship between Jesus' first message and the Virgin's first message here in Damascus adds weight to the proximity of God in this location, and to the focus on personal change as tied to repentance.

'*Repent, for the kingdom of heaven is near!*' Abuna Zahlawi recursively repeats the first public words of Jesus, before centring on the role of Soufanieh and Damascus yet again.

> We may think that God is far away, even if we know that he is close. Sometimes we can feel as if he is far away … God is closer than we imagine! And Jesus is closer than we imagine! And the demonstration (*al-burhān*), the happenings of this house twenty-seven years ago. Who of you would have expected that? Not me.

Abuna Zahlawi explains this as he includes this very locality and the characters in the very house where the sermon is delivered in the divine plan of redemption. The listeners include people who have been part of the extended family of Soufanieh from the outset, and they all have vivid memories of the first time the extraordinary events happened. Abuna Zahlawi places himself firmly in the chain of events. He explains how he was told of the first apparition. 'I rejected it', the experienced priest explains. He underscores his personal scepticism when the rumours of the first apparition spread and how he rejected their veracity not just once but three times.[1]

Exemplifications: crafting the series

'I don't know each of you. God alone knows what is in your hearts!' Abuna Zahlawi says as he glances over the congregants. He takes his time while he attentively looks at specific people and not just the crowd. At once mildly and fervently, he turns his near-bald head from the left side of the courtyard to the right. 'However, I am convinced that most people live as if God were far away from them'. The focus on the distance between personal experience and God's reality is addressed in the part of the sermon that follows, where Abuna Zahlawi first emphasizes God's love for the individual person. He ties this to the message of the Virgin at this very locality: 'The Virgin says: *Remember God, because God is with us!* This means he loves all of us. There are no exceptions. The words of Jesus in the Gospel for today are: "*Repent, for the kingdom of heaven is near*". We need to attend to this'. To make this simpler, Abuna Zahlawi underscores how God sees the individual: 'He is with me, but am I with Him? And if I died, in which condition (*wadʿa*) would I arrive? How would he see me? In his eyes, how would I fare? This could happen to us at any moment, whether we are big or small, no one knows'. The implication of these words is that the focus on God's vision is tied both to the comforting voice of the Virgin here in Soufanieh and also to an afterlife with or without God. However, the sermon does not dwell on these aspects of the afterlife, but rather the choice and situation of the moment are underlined: 'We in particular know that the Lord is with us! You are children of Soufanieh. Here in Soufanieh we are closer than so many other people that don't know Soufanieh'. Abuna Zahlawi continues his exhortation: 'This is the secret of Soufanieh, the love of Soufanieh, the existence of Soufanieh in our lives'.

Abuna Zahlawi starts to focus on another part of the passage read from the Gospel: 'The second word from the Gospel for today says this: *The people living in darkness have seen a great light; on those living in the land of the shadow of death a light has dawned*'. The priest now fashions another important series resting on locality.

> In the Gospel for today, Jesus approaches Capernaum from Nazareth, where they tried to kill him. They tried to kill him! Because of this Jesus once said:[2] 'No prophet is respected in his own country.' Do you know this saying? 'No prophet is respected in his own country'.

Abuna Zahlawi repeats this quote. The words here are important, as one of the features that is difficult to grapple with is the miracle of Our Lady of Soufanieh and the many locals who do not care (see also Bandak 2013). In the sermon, this is mirrored in the situation in Nazareth and Capernaum. The reluctance is a sign of weak minds not wanting to change. Abuna Zahlawi continues: 'In Damascus, to this day there are people talking badly about Soufanieh. They talk about those who believe in Soufanieh. But people are travelling from the ends of the world to pray here'. The global relevance is hence inscribed to counter the local lukewarm attitudes. It is a matter of seeing things from God's perspective: 'We hope that the Lord will open their eyes', says Abuna Zahlawi. To make this even more pertinent to his listeners, he uses a recent incident to highlight the importance of Our Lady of Soufanieh and, by extension, Myrna. He recounts a trip just undertaken to Amman, the capital of Jordan, where a large number of people wanted to see Myrna, and where, more significantly, many of them had travelled from Nazareth to do so: 'Recently Myrna was in Amman. A hundred and four people came from Nazareth. From Nazareth, from the town of Jesus!' He explains the details of the meeting and continues:

> They wanted to listen, they wanted to understand. From the first to the last moment we were with them. And here this is not necessarily the case. *In the shadow* means hidden from the world. God will open our hearts. Each one of us wants from Jesus the change to become messengers. Ask Jesus to change you. And try from your home. Then you will become his apostle. And today he needs messengers.

What Abuna Zahlawi accomplishes is to craft a series whereby the villagers from Nazareth who rejected Christ now accept Myrna, whom many in Damascus still do not endorse.

Change and saintly models: seriation performed
Damascus is mirrored in Nazareth, in the lack of receptivity in Nazareth in the past but not today, and this allows Abuna Zahlawi to create one last series that attests to the possibility of change. He uses particular lives to frame this.

> We know Saint Augustine. He died in the year 430 AD. His father was an officer and lived in Tunis, in North Africa. His mother believed very strongly. His father was very rich. He was very handsome and very clever. His mother was crying. His mother was crying: "What are you doing with your life?" And it so happened that his uncle became a Christian and tried to form his faith. And it happened in the area where he lived that he heard that in Milan there was a bishop who was a wonderful speaker. So he said I want to go to his school. He was just a youngster. He went to Milan and asked where this man was. The name of the bishop was Ambrose. He was close to the emperor and had taught him everything. And therefore he had been given the seat as bishop of Milan. At that time it was the capital of the Roman Empire. Ambrose felt that something was going to change. They had a conversation and the conversation changed Augustine's mind. He wanted to live the life God wants. Now he wanted to live it. Here began a complete transformation. He went back to the home of his uncle. He read the Bible for a year. And, after this year, people wanted to see him; they knew him as he had been famous before. After a year, the local bishop died. At that time it was the people who decided who was to become bishop. The greatest priest among the priests would ask who they wanted to be the next bishop. They would say we want this one or that one. Thus was the opinion of the people. But there was a child who said: we want Augustine. Augustine, however, doubted that this would be the right choice. Me? Never, me I'm the last human to do so! But, in time he became a priest, he became a bishop, and so the Lord can change people. But patience, patience. If you feel your situation is weak. If you are tempted by sins . . .

Abuna Zahlawi now forcefully adds a number of new people to the series by focusing on the possibility of change for God: 'As he changed the disciples, as he changed Mary Magdalene, as he changed Thomas, as he changed Augustine, as he changed John of Damascus'. Having presented this series, he explains:

> John of Damascus was head of the ministers among the Umayyads. The ruler of the Umayyads was in his hands, he was responsible for everything. He left and went to Bethlehem. And there he used his time in prayer and writing. The church today still uses his hymns and his poetry and theology. How long has he been dead and he is still influential? God's change really transforms a person. And

in Soufanieh we know how he changes people. Each of you knows what he has changed in you. In truth, he wants you to change more ...

He pauses and later elaborates: 'We ask Jesus for healing and the Virgin changes us'.

The logic of seriation

Abuna Zahlawi is frequently on national television, and even received a prize from the Syrian First Lady in the summer of 2009 for his work for the country. The priest elaborates on his theme, that he himself would be able to discern only some of the faces of those present, but that God, being all-knowing, would know not only all the faces but all the hearts as well. Abuna Zahlawi goes on to talk about the many Christians in Syria who are not confessing and the problems that evolve in abstaining from this sacrament. He continues with the topic of change. He recounts the life and change of Augustine and continues with John of Damascus. Change in every single person is thus underscored as urgent and necessary. He brings in Soufanieh and the first message as well as other features of particular importance to his exposition. By drawing these themes together, people are placed in a particular time-space whereby personal change is tied to God's planning and human response. Not all are well trained in reading practices, but all have the faculty for listening, and listening is here emphasized as a profound way to relate to God. The different lives presented in the sermon all embody the qualities of a changed and charged life and, in this sense, each is exemplary of a certain type of sanctified life. As these figures were moulded by God, every single listener is challenged to let his or her life be changed, just like Saint Augustine, Saint John of Damascus, Saint Francis of Assisi, or local types in contemporary Damascus, Myrna being the foremost example. These examples are used by the priest to flesh out the Christian character to be strived for. Not – as he emphasizes – because each person necessarily so wants it, but because God wants it. Personal change in this sense rests on dual ground: the divinely ordained and inspired life and the human response. Life in this sense can become charged and sanctified and used as an example to follow for others. The examples given in this sense do not rest on human perfection but Godly election and sanctification. The saintly exemplars, modelled by the words of the skilled priest, are placed in a series of divinely inspired figures, all of whom were changed, and this perforce allows the listeners to see themselves reflected and challenged to become part of the same series. Even the story of Myrna features the classic motif of her wanting to flee upon the first apparition, which fits, or is fitted, into the biblical standard. The Bible contains a host of such examples whereby the chosen prophet either reluctantly follows the Lord or, stricken with panic, is seized by Him (e.g. 1 Samuel 3; Isaiah 6; Jeremiah 1). This model renders credible the source, in that it is presented not as something that could have been made up by the human imagination, but as a task enforced upon the individual against his or her previous knowledge or anticipation. In this regard, only the manner in which this election is received can be lauded, as with the Virgin Mary, who in peace and quiet received the words from the Archangel on the annunciation of her becoming the mother of Christ (cf. Luke 1:26 ff.; more generally, see Christian 1981: 200).

Example and exemplar: ex-sample and ex-sampling

To understand the working of the example in the sermon, it is instructive to note that, in Arabic, there exists an intricate relation between representation, example, ideal, model, parable, and resemblance, all of which derive from the three root letters *m-th-l* (*mathala*). In general, the root designates what stands for something else. According to Abraham Mitrie Rihbani, *mithāl* is sociable and carries the meaning and weight of storytelling (2003 [1922]: 90; see also Mittermaier, this volume). Persons, stories, proverbs, and sayings can stand for and sum up human conditions. It is this quality of standing for something else that has been examined by Nelson Goodman (1981). Goodman lists several forms of reference, one of them being exemplification, which he terms an overlooked but extremely important form of non-denotational reference (1981: 124). Exemplification is not a simple denotation but rather 'reference by sample to a feature of it' (1981: 124-5). A part of a whole is taken to stand for it, to express it. Exemplification is in this sense to use a part, which is made to stand for the whole. Extending this in a series of examples, each of the parts may not be understood as identical but they are subsumed in a category which they are made to represent and, in this process, they are juxtaposed. Saint Augustine is not identical to Saint John of Damascus but they are both used by Abuna Zahlawi to point to a particular reality. Exemplification in this sense emphasizes the capacity of particulars to relate to universalities, albeit in very different manners. However, the quality that the example represents has, from the inception of Greek thought, resulted in two markedly different approaches to the category and status of examples and exemplarity. As argued by Alexander Gelley, Plato, on the one hand, thought of *paradeigma* as a model or exemplar, whereas Aristotle, on the other, considered it as an instance from which inductive conclusions can be derived (Gelley 1995: 1). The relationship between the example as an instance or instantiation and the exemplar as the ideal form highlights a certain tension in the way particularity and universality relate. As a mere example, nothing much is to be expected and a reduction to the particular case seems possible. As an exemplar and model, conversely, everything is to be expected. In *Writing and difference* (2001 [1967]), Jacques Derrida writes of the two different senses of the example, namely as a sample and as a model. And to Derrida it is fundamental to consider what we mean when using examples, as he writes: 'To pose the problem of its exemplarity: are we concerned with an example among others or the "good example", an example that is revelatory by privilege?' (2001 [1967]: 51). To Derrida and to the classical tradition, what we are presented with appears a choice. Either we go with the 'mere' example or we go with the exemplar. What if there is no choice to be taken, however, but rather lines of force to be followed? In the sermon, Abuna Zahlawi crafts a crucial series of examples. He is, in other words, *ex-sampling*, taking something out of the sample – that is, drawing from the stock of divinely ordained figures to paint with words particular characters to emulate. The series does not, however, indicate that the sample is merely a collection of singularities as they add up to a larger field in which each instantiation is worthy of attention in its own right but also, and further yet, adds to the divine glory in and through human response. Here the sample is also the model. Seriality is modelling. Abuna Zahlawi accordingly is not merely adding more examples of the same but is modelling a series, which opens up and extends so that the listener can become a part of it.

Examples and words: fleshing out examples

In the exposition of the sermon above, central features of genre and authority conjure up a specific configuration of practices. As pointed out by Eric Hoenes del Piñal (2009: 88), the Catholic sermon may very well function as disciplining within the universal church, following the same calendar and biblical readings, but the exhortation may depart a good deal from the reading, allowing different interpretative modulations.

In the sermon by Abuna Zahlawi, a particular interpretative modulation consists of linking models past and present to personal change in imitation of these models. By drawing upon both highly acclaimed persons already authorized as saints, such as Saint Augustine, Saint John of Damascus, Saint Francis of Assisi, Myrna, and ordinary people from Damascus, the sermon aims to mould the character of the listener. Presented with these examples, each individual can test his or her own life. Examples and models are used as evidence for sanctity both on a mundane and on an extraordinary basis, but also as instigators of life change. The basic insecurity, that only God knows the heart, can be used to let Him mould one's character not only in the joint prayers and confession of faith but also in the labour of living oneself as an example, and – as Abuna Zahlawi implies in the sermon – confessing one's sins in not being able to live up to the model. The use of words, in this sense, relates to a particular understanding of Christ as the Word incarnated. In this vein, the Christian tenet from the opening of the Gospel according to John is significant. In the very opening of this Gospel, John says: 'In the beginning was the Word, and the Word was with God, and the Word was God' (1:1), and later: 'The Word became flesh and made his dwelling among us' (1:14). Words are, in this sense, conceived not just as surface or letters devoid of spirit, but as holding the capacity to change hearts. More generally, words are always ideologically framed in various Christian traditions (see also Robbins 2001; Tomlinson 2014), not only in sermons but also in the example of lives made text and text made life. This is where stories of Christ, Mary, and the saints merge with mundane persons, and flesh and blood participates in divine labour. Words are a distinct way of human action in the world, one that Hannah Arendt (1998 [1958]), who was also deeply inspired by Augustine (Arendt 1996 [1929]; see also Bandak 2012), claimed holds the potential for opening the space for natality, a space where something new can be initiated. To Augustine – one of the figures used as exemplifying God's change in Abuna Zahlawi's sermon – memory and grace go together. And memory for Augustine was critical in that it opened up the scrutiny of the self, albeit not in the modern sense as a life regarded as unique and individual but rather as *exemplary* life (cf. Arendt 1994 [1930]). Augustine crafts an exemplary line to be followed: as my life testifies, it is possible for everybody to change, as I have been changed so you can be changed. Memory and grace are hence intertwined as life can be separated into a clear before and after.

Example, exemplar, exemplum: webs of exempla

Following recent studies of reading (J. Boyarin 1993) and the social life of scriptures (Bielo 2009; see also Engelke 2009), I will argue that the Bible, more than being mere letters read and used in social contexts, is a web of exempla, of figures to imitate and reflect upon. And that this web is extended in the sermons delivered by Abuna Zahlawi. The specific examples given, however, are not just positive. The scriptural edifice or repository abounds with examples not to be imitated. One of the most severe examples is given by another priest, Abuna Elias Saloun, in one of the weekly Tuesday evening novenas, in Myrna's home. Abuna Saloun here refers to Ananias and Saphirah, who, according to the Acts of the Apostles, were both struck dead when they lied in front of the disciples (Acts 5:1–11). This rather dark tale is used as an admonition to the followers of Our Lady of Soufanieh neither to lie to themselves nor to lie to God. The examples in this sense do not just comfort and soothe but critically challenge the lives of the listeners. Normally, though, the examples given would be of emphatic virtue, as in the lives of Saint Augustine, Saint Thérèse of Lisieux, Saint Bernadette Soubirous, Saint

Francis of Assisi, and Saint John of Damascus. Precisely because the transmission of the words to individuals is not simply direct but fraught with danger, we often hear criticisms of those who hear without hearing in the biblical record (e.g. Matt. 13:13). Rather than just one series, two series are crafted in the sermons: one extending the logic of the bad listener, the other the logic of the good listener.

A critical aspect of the work of words found in Soufanieh is to present examples that people can see through and hence mould their own character after. It is precisely due to this tradition that Caroline Humphrey, in her work on exemplars, appears not to take her conclusion far enough. In asserting that general moral rules and not exemplars govern Western and Christian practice, Humphrey (1997) places greater focus on rules than has typically been the case. Moral rules may appear to govern in fast formulations of ethics but, in practice, Western traditions abound with exemplary figures giving content and form to these rules (Warnick 2008). From antiquity onwards, human learning has been focused on exemplars. The Christian innovation was to place a centre in the series. As the eminent historian Peter Brown writes of Christianity, its novelty was the proposed central figure: 'The Exemplar of all exemplars, a being, Christ, in Whom human and divine had come to be joined' (1983: 6). The saints were conceived as exemplars, not necessarily perfect ones, but mediators and intercessors between God and men (Forbess 2010: 142–3; Gudeman 1976: 712; Kleinberg 1992: 134). The importance of the series in a Christian sense was the extendability from past to future and the double constitution of exemplar in relation to Exemplar. The exemplar rendered the Exemplar credible, and vice versa. This was, in a particular way, captured by John of Damascus – whom Abuna Zahlawi draws upon in the sermon. John of Damascus, in a formative way, formulated the relation between archetype and copy in his defence of holy images and icons: 'An image is a likeness depicting an archetype, but having some difference from it; the image is not like the archetype in every way' (2003 [726–30]: 25). The image bestows glory upon the archetype by way of transfer, which in a Christian tradition means prayer. Later, Hans-Georg Gadamer, in *Truth and method* (2004 [1960]: 130–8) argued that the copy never merely reproduces the original but rather adds to it, given that the former is seen through the latter, and vice versa. In hagiographical writing and sermons – as Derek Krueger (2004) has emphasized – the importance of the double constitution was profound. Krueger's point is that not only is the sanctity of the saintly prospect invigorated by the text, but also the author assumes a particular relation to his subject by the very act of writing. By writing the life of the saint, sanctity is bestowed upon the author (Krueger 2004: 9). Writing and holiness therefore mutually follow and accomplish each other. Accordingly, a whole *typology* exists in biblical and saintly tradition whereby biblical and saintly figures, as in a series, bestow credence upon each other. This is a classical pattern, which precedes the Arab conquests in the first half of the seventh century and which, in early Eastern Christianity, has been reflected in the discussions of the importance of the Christian as made in God's image. Here, the Greek term originally used was *graphein*, which carries the meaning of both writing and painting. This dual meaning, in a striking way, attests to what the relation between word and image in a Christian tradition crafts as exemplary: the word paints an image, a story, a narrative, as the divine ordeal is fleshed out in types across time and space – something which, in Catholic and Orthodox traditions, is very tangible in the form of statues and icons which materialize and make tangible the words of the sermon in physical form (Morgan 1998; Orsi 2005). But the opposite also holds: images and icons render the word of God accessible as a scripted story that one can become a part of.

Journal of the Royal Anthropological Institute (N.S.), 47-63
© Royal Anthropological Institute 2015

More than example and exemplar, we here encounter the exemplum, the moral tale used for edification, and it is to the exemplum that we shall now turn.

Filling in the gaps: exemplification and interpretation

John Lyons has, with great erudition, traced the genealogy of the example in rhetoric. In his elaborate tracing of the various roles allotted to the example throughout a primarily European tradition, Lyons points to the word 'exemplum' and how it came to be associated with the Greek *eikon*, meaning image or likeness, just as much as *paradeigma*, meaning pattern or sample (1989: 10). This is a significant point as it attests to a broader movement between words and images, such as the one just noted above. Lyons asserts:

> This movement, which is entirely consonant with the rhetorical function of example in Aristotle, permits the spread of example from linguistic to non-linguistic forms. At the same time the visual form of the example leads to the ontological consequence that examples have the quality of seeming rather than of being, they are associated with *species* and *imago*, and are therefore within the realm of all that is specious and imaginary (1989: 10).

The example as exemplum had its origins in Greek and Roman tradition but found a particular Christian form as a moral tale to instruct the masses (see also Demoen 1997: 126). In Christian tradition and, in particular, in the medieval usage of the exemplum, it was a tool for didacticism. As argued by Jacques Le Goff (1988: 78–80, 181), the exemplum was a specific genre that was developed in medieval Europe. The exemplum was now rendered as a narrative that crafted a particular form of persuasiveness alongside biblical exhortation. Wholesale collections of exempla were circulated for use in sermons (Gelley 1995: 4; Kemmler 1984: 12; Kleinberg 1992, 2008). The lives of the saints used as exempla played a crucial role in the sermon, where they could be appropriated as a particular, condensed genre, as short moral stories used for instruction and edification. In Joseph Mosher's words: 'The exemplum may be briefly and conveniently described as a short narrative used to illustrate or confirm a general statement' (1911: 1). More recently, however, this view has been challenged, in that, more than merely a genre, the exemplum has been described as a device (Kaufmann 1996; Lyons 1989: 9). As a device, the exemplum is more powerful than the designation 'genre' allows for. It is used to effect something in the listener, to illustrate, persuade, and convince. And, as such a device, the exemplum is a powerful tool which asserts authority in and through a narrative modelling (Scanlon 1994).

The exemplum is a device used to train certain sensibilities, but also, and more importantly, it is a device which endows the listener with a responsibility of judgement. Abuna Zahlawi deliberately places the listener at the centre as he or she is presented with various examples of change. The listener is to pass judgement and, by this judgement, he or she will be placed in the series of the good or the bad listener. In his exploration of rabbinic readings of the Bible and the use of examples to corroborate understanding, Daniel Boyarin has made a strong case for a dual working of exemplification. Boyarin asserts that word-pictures denote something that again exemplifies a label, which, in turn, denotes and exemplifies something else: 'The process of interpretation by exemplification is thus a picking out of the feature to which the exemplification will refer' (1995: 35). This is what I have designated as a series and what, in various ways, can be seen to be put in action Abuna Zahlawi's sermon. He uses the different persons in distillated versions where each feeds back into the series. The action rests on concretion, not abstraction, as the part relates to other parts. Or, perhaps better, it works by making Christian abstraction concrete. The exemplification, then, works not only by being set in motion in and of itself, but by making other wholes feasible as both model and part. Exemplifications can, in this sense, be highly productive for other exemplifications. This is so because the example is not finished, but rather the reading by example produces and procures knowledge and asks the listener to fill in the gaps (D. Boyarin 1995: 35). It is precisely this process of filling in the gaps in narratives that Susan Harding (2000) has argued characterizes the art of language of the fundamentalist Christians surrounding Jerry Falwell's Baptist community. Harding addresses the use of biblical figures in witnessing and preaching among fundamentalist Christian Baptists in the United States. Actually, what Harding shows is what I have designated the logic of seriation. In an interview with Reverend Campbell, one of her interlocutors, he places Harding in a mirrored relationship with biblical figures such as Moses, Nicodemus, Isaac, Adam, Eve, Jesus, John the Baptist, and himself as preacher. Harding writes:

> Narratively, that is, looking at the form his argument took on the surface of his whole juxtaposition of stories, Campbell emphasized the importance of spoken language, of dialogue, in making the passage from one world to the next. He repeatedly relied on dialogue – between Jesus and Nicodemus, himself and me, Isaac and Abraham, John the Baptist and the disciples – to set up the dilemma of human choice (2000: 50).

Biblical figures are placed in a sequence and Reverend Campbell attempts to insert the listener, Harding, in the series – that is, to move her from being a listener to being a speaker. The example in this case points not only to precedents but also to a structure of fulfilment (Harvey 2002: 93) which rests upon a particular dialogue in which the listener, and more broadly the audience, is made to participate. The links made are, in this sense, 'typological' or 'figural', as Harding later writes (2000: 55, 85). The series breaks off with the invitation and demands the filling in of the gaps of the stories by the listener adding to the series. In other words, the stories, figures, and examples presented by Abuna Zahlawi fulfil each other but only in soliciting interpretative action on the part of the listener.

The responsive listener: neither hot nor cold

As Abuna Zahlawi approaches the end of his sermon, he carves out the gravity of the listener's response. Having established the need for change through different figures, by biblical precedent and authority he uses the words of Jesus to enforce a choice on the individual listener: 'Jesus says in Revelations:[3] "*You are neither hot nor cold, but lukewarm* ...*"*. Abuna Zahlawi stops and looks out over the faces, inviting a response: 'Who knows the continuation?' He pauses again and sees the finger of a young boy go up. 'Hana!' Abuna Zahlawi invites him to answer. Hana answers with the clear and high-pitched voice of a child: '*So I am about to spit you out of my mouth!*' Abuna Zahlawi repeats the sentence. '*I am about to spit you out of my mouth!*' Abuna Zahlawi pauses a moment and then repeats the words again: '*You are neither hot nor cold, but lukewarm, therefore I am about to spit you out of my mouth!*' The gravity is felt even if he is not adding to it in terms of gestures, and neither is he taking any kind of joy in the dire consequences. The words are allowed to effectuate their own weight before he elaborates: 'Who of you want to be lukewarm, who of you wants to be cold? *Inshallah* no one. *Inshallah* every one of us wants to be hot. But in the power of the Lord and by your spirit'. The weight of the address is felt as every listener is now placed in the centre. What will the response be? The series is to be extended. Abuna Zahlawi glances yet again over the assembled people of all ages, and then adds his: 'Amen!'

Forma vitae

Pivotal work has been done by Giorgio Agamben in elaborating on and formulating a theory of the example. Agamben's first formulation of a theory of the example is found in his book *The coming community*. Here, he very aptly locates the example between the particular phenomenon and the universal class

> One concept that escapes the antinomy of the universal and the particular has long been familiar to us: the example. In any context where it exerts its force, the example is characterized by the fact that it holds for all cases of the same type, and, at the same time, it is included among these. It is one singularity among others, which, however, stands for each of them and serves for all. On the one hand, every example is treated in effect as a real particular case but, on the other, it remains understood that it cannot serve in its particularity. Neither particular nor universal, the example is a singular object that presents itself as such, that *shows* its singularity. Hence the pregnancy of the Greek term, for example: *para-deigma*, that which is shown alongside (like the German *Bei-spiel*, that which plays alongside). Hence the proper place of the example is always beside itself, in the empty space in which its undefinable and unforgettable life unfolds. This life is purely linguistic life. Only life in the word is undefinable and unforgettable. Exemplary being is purely linguistic being. Exemplary is what is not defined by any property, except being-called (1993: 9–10).

Where Agamben rightly asserts the radical singularity, he does not focus on the formative role of the sample. Exemplary being may be linguistic but, in a Christian sense, such being transcends the letter and fleshes out God's image refracted in personal life. The example holds the potential to flesh out, illustrate, and persuade. Accordingly, in the working of the sermon by Abuna Zahlawi, the example is tied to both identities and properties, here as Christians and followers of Our Lady of Soufanieh, as both are modelled in a particular and not a general series. The modelling of life by words and words by life are two series of effects that bridge the world of the listener and God's reality and let it become inhabitable. The examples given by Abuna Zahlawi are, in this sense, all part of the same sequence, but they do not point only in one direction. The virtue of particular examples is, of course, to be emulated, but some aspects, more than imitation, demand awe and wonder (Kieckhefer 1988; Macklin 2005; Woodward 1990). Myrna's piety may well be imitated, whereas her stigmata, conversely, are believed vicariously to stand for the community in a sacrificial economy. Likewise, saints such as John of Damascus, Augustine, Padre Pio, and Francis of Assisi are all part of a series which, at the same time, is extendable. The relationship with the saint is specifically crucial, therefore, as friend, benefactor, intermediary, and intercessor.

Agamben recently returned to the example to give it a much more exquisite rethinking in his book *The signature of all things: on method* (2009). Here, Agamben devotes the first essay, entitled 'What is a paradigm?', to questions on the working of the example. Of particular interest is his outlining of monastic orders and their foundations in a Catholic tradition. Agamben asserts how monastic orders, through the ages, have been formed around the life of the founder. In this regard, the life of the founder was moulded as a *forma vitae*, an example to follow, where '[t]he founder's life is in turn a sequel to the life of Jesus as narrated in the gospels'(Agamben 2009: 21). A formalization of the life of the founder would, however, often find its penultimate form in the meaning of a written text. Life is, in other words, turned to text. The life of the individual monk or novice is moulded upon the example set by the founder: 'At least until Saint Benedict, the rule does not indicate a general norm, but the living community (*koinos, bios,* cenobio) that results from an example and in which the life of each monk tends at the limit to become paradigmatic – that is, to constitute itself as *forma vitae*' (Agamben 2009: 22). The paradigmatic relation does not merely occur between sensible objects or between these objects and a general rule; it occurs instead between a singularity (which thus becomes a paradigm) and its exposition (its intelligibility). In a very significant move, Agamben contrasts the working of the example with that of the exception. Where the exception works by exclusion and thereby is included, the example works by exhibiting its inclusion, which makes up for its exclusion. The working of the example, the ex-sampling, renders intelligible a series of phenomena that would otherwise have been unaccounted for. In this sense, what Agamben has made is a paradigmatic ontology.

Extensions of the series: to catch the drift

The extendability of Christian exemplary series therefore goes beyond the work of words undertaken by Abuna Zahlawi. The exemplary series works as a paradigmatic ontology, or, perhaps better, a paradigmatic typology, its logic resting on the very seriation whereby each instantiation, as well as the series as a whole, embodies the Christian logic. And, furthermore, the logic of the series works by having an adversary series of anti-exemplarity, figures such as Ananias and Saphira as used as admonition by Abuna Saloun, in apposite form attesting to the importance of the singular listener's response. The priest Abuna Zahlawi himself is rendered a part of the series, and this particularly so as he is often used in media on Christian topics. The priest himself is known as a confessor of Myrna and a prime intellectual, but also as exemplary in his piety. The role of the priest is therefore evaluated by the listeners, and the priest is moulded by the sermons he delivers. Where recent work on the role of charismatic preachers has underscored the transgressive nature of their social persona as constitutive of their reputation (e.g. Coleman 2009; Harding 2000), exemplary piety is shown by the humility of Abuna Zahlawi in his sermon. By effacing himself as nothing but a witness, he assumes the saintly character of the confessor. Moreover, when actually adding his own corresponding deeds and actions to his words, Abuna Zahlawi is admired as a priest to be listened to. This is contrary to many priests and even bishops, who are criticized for not following their own words, thereby making them devoid of exemplary force. The series, however, extends to individuals, to rosaries, prayer cards, and to the whole family of Soufanieh, which are believed to have an exemplary role in the Middle East and the world as such. The series opens up as it refers to other examples: Myrna as another Mary or visionary such as Bernadette, as another stigmatic such as Francis of Assisi or Padre Pio, and Soufanieh as another Lourdes or Fatima, famous locations for Marian apparitions, and hence accordingly the listener as another Myrna, another Mary, another Christ-carrying exemplar. The challenge to the listener, then, is to catch or 'guess' what Wittgenstein in his *Philosophical investigations* called the 'drift' of the series (2009 [1953]: 90). The series and the motion of the example then open up and ask for the responsiveness and judgement of the individual. As Jacques Derrida says in *Specters of Marx*:

> An example always carries beyond itself: it thereby opens up a testamentary dimension. The example is first of all for others, and beyond the self. Sometimes, perhaps always, whoever gives the example is not equal to the example he gives, even if he does everything to follow it in advance, 'to learn how to live', as we were saying, imperfect example of the example he gives – which he gives by giving then what he has not and even what he is not. For this reason, the example thus disjoined separates enough

from itself or from whoever gives it so as to be no longer or not yet an example *for itself* (1994: 34, emphasis in original).

The purpose of the sermon, then, is not to be an example of itself but rather to capture and move the listener to a change in which novelty, natality, is bestowed upon him or her as a *forma vitae* for others.

Exemplifying Soufanieh: on the social production of examples and types

A paradigmatic ontology is highly relevant to thinking through the methods by which both anthropology and Soufanieh produce examples. Persuasion rests in both fields on the creation of viable examples that move us in such a way that each instantiation reflects both its particularity and something more general, universal even, about social phenomena. In the logic of seriation, I as an anthropologist was addressed very early on by several of the ardent followers of Soufanieh and advised as to whom to talk to and whom not to talk to. I was told not to interview divorcees. I was led towards Myrna, her family, and other 'good' examples. And even I was addressed as an example to become. 'You didn't choose to come here yourself!', Salwa, one of the followers of Our Lady of Soufanieh, said one day after a service in Myrna's home. 'God chose you! He wants you to spread the message with your dissertation'. After this, Salwa went on to paraphrase some of the messages Myrna had received, emphasizing one sent by Jesus on Easter Saturday, 10 April 2004: 'This is my last commandment to you: each one of you, return back home. However, hold the East in your hearts. From here a light emerged anew. You are its radiance in a world seduced by materialism, sensuality and fame, so much as to have lost its values'. Emphasizing that a light from the East will emanate and spread to the West, followers of Our Lady of Soufanieh generally interpreted this message as referring to their own particular location as the source. To Salwa, I was the obvious answer to this prophecy and was urged to become a part of the series and extend it in even wider circles. More than extending the series, however, the anthropologist here was also functioning as an example of the importance of Our Lady of Soufanieh beyond Syria proper.

In anthropology and the social sciences more broadly, Max Weber's work on ideal types can help us situate the production of examples. Both in his methodological essays and in his analysis of the Protestant ethic and the capitalist spirit, Weber used a framing of certain characteristics to describe developments of a certain Christian character (cf. Cannell 2006). The character he crafted was that of Calvinistic Christians used to frame a broader Northern European work ethic. The ideal type Weber hereby presented was a distillation of traits into a single figure of a very general purview. But by this crafting of an ideal type, Christianity was encapsulated in a particular form which rendered other forms more opaque. Recent attempts in anthropology to analyse Christianity have shared similar tendencies in that a great number, with Joel Robbins (2007) as the prime proponent, have transposed the focus on Christianity from a basically Protestant ideal type, and Calvinistic at that, to a novel ideal type of Christianity which is basically Pentecostal. This is not a problem in itself since, numerically, Pentecostalism is the most expansive form of contemporary Christianity. The problem, though, is whether Pentecostal types of Christianity are taken to embody Christianity as such. The problems raised by Pentecostal ideal types are worthy of investing analytical labour on, but also invite further reflection on the varieties of Christian formulations of types. An examination of types in churches as well as in anthropology therefore critically needs to engage types or examples as informative but in different domains (cf. Schmitt 1996 [1923]; Weber 1992 [1904]). In this sense, which types are used in research as well as in the life of the church is as much a theoretical as it is a methodological question. And this – as argued in the introduction to this special issue – offers a way of exploring how different worlds make use of examples and exemplification, even if the goals may be a better understanding in the one domain, and the salvation of souls in the other. Roman Catholicism or the varieties of Eastern Catholicism and Orthodox Christianity as found in Damascus and Syria need to be read as culturally more nuanced in their formulation of types when opposed, both deliberately and unconsciously, to Protestant varieties. Here the promulgation, discussion, and development of types in the Catholic Church can be seen as a significant inventory of different ideals and examples as they have percolated throughout history and persist to this day. The modelling of sainthood in words and images has its exemplary force in the extendability and spread in and of a series. Here, in different ways, anthropologist, interlocutors, and Christian tradition all appear to be participating.

NOTES

I thank my co-editor Lars Højer as well as Tom Boylston, Matthew Engelke, Alice Forbess, Christian Suhr, and the two anonymous reviewers for productive readings of this paper. Funding for the research for this paper was given by the Danish Council for Independent Research in the Humanities.

[1] You could draw parallels between this and Peter's three rejections of Christ, even if this is not drawn upon overtly in the sermon.

[2] See Matt. 13:57; Mark 6:4; Luke 4:24; John 4:44.

[3] See Rev. 3:15-16, where the topic is addressed in relation to the church in Laodicea. The address here is grave and the response even more so.

REFERENCES

AGAMBEN, G. 1993. *The coming community* (trans. M. Hardt). Minneapolis: University of Minnesota Press.
———— 2009. *The signature of all things: on method* (trans. L. D'Isanto with K. Attell). New York: Zone.
ARENDT, H. 1994 [1930]. Augustine and Protestantism. In *Essays in human understanding 1930-1954*, 24-7. New York: Schocken.
———— 1996 [1929]. *Love and Saint Augustine*. Chicago: University Press.
———— 1998 [1958]. *The human condition*. Chicago: University Press.
BANDAK, A. 2012. Problems of belief: tonalities of immediacy among Christians of Damascus. *Ethnos: Journal of Anthropology* **77**, 535-55.
———— 2013. Our Lady of Soufanieh: on knowledge, ignorance and indifference among the Christians of Damascus. In *The politics of worship in the contemporary Middle East: sainthood in fragile states* (eds) A. Bandak & M. Bille, 129-53. Leiden: Brill.
BIELO, J. (ed.) 2009. *The social life of scriptures: cross-cultural perspectives on biblicism*. New Brunswick, N.J.: Rutgers University Press.
BOYARIN, D. 1995. Take the Bible for example: Midrash as literary theory. In *Unruly examples: on the rhetoric of exemplarity* (ed.) A. Gelley, 27-47. Stanford: University Press.
BOYARIN, J. (ed.) 1993. *The ethnography of reading*. Berkeley: University of California Press.
BROWN, P. 1983. The saint as exemplar in late antiquity. *Representations* **1**, 1-25.
CANNELL, F. 2006. Introduction: the anthropology of Christianity. In *The anthropology of Christianity* (ed.) F. Cannell, 1-50. Durham, N.C.: Duke University Press.
CHRISTIAN, W.A., JR 1981. *Apparitions in late medieval and Renaissance Spain*. Princeton: University Press.
COLEMAN, S. 2009. Transgressing the self: making charismatic saints. *Critical Inquiry* **35**, 417-39.
DEMOEN, K. 1997. A paradigm for the analysis of paradigms: the rhetorical exemplum in ancient and imperial Greek theory. *Rhetorica: A Journal of the History of Rhetoric* **15**, 125-58.
DERRIDA, J. 1994. *Specters of Marx: the state of debt, the work of mourning and the New International* (trans. P. Kamuf). New York: Routledge.
———— 2001 [1967]. *Writing and difference* (trans. A. Bass). New York: Routledge.

ENGELKE, M. 2009. Reading and time: two approaches to the materiality of scripture. *Ethnos: Journal of Anthropology* **74**, 151-74.

FORBESS, A. 2010. The spirit and the letter: monastic education in a Romanian Orthodox convent. In *Eastern Christians in anthropological perspective* (eds) C. Hann & H. Goltz, 131-54. Berkeley: University of California Press.

GADAMER, H.-G. 2004 [1960]. *Truth and method* (trans. J. Weinsheimer & D. Marshall). New York: Continuum.

GELLEY, A. 1995. Introduction. In *Unruly examples: on the rhetoric of exemplarity* (ed.) A. Gelley, 1-24. Stanford: University Press.

GOODMAN, N. 1981. Routes of reference. *Critical Inquiry* **8**, 121-32.

GUDEMAN, S. 1976. Saints, symbols, and ceremonies. *American Ethnologist* **3**, 709-29.

HARDING, S.F. 2000. *The Book of Jerry Falwell: fundamentalist language and politics.* Princeton: University Press.

HARVEY, I.E. 2002. *Labyrinths of exemplarity: at the limits of deconstruction.* Albany: State University of New York Press.

HOENES DEL PIÑAL, E. 2009. How Qéqchi-Maya Catholics become legitimate interpreters of the Bible: two models of religious authority in sermons. In *The social life of scriptures: cross-cultural perspectives on biblicism* (ed.) J. Bielo, 80-99. New Brunswick, N.J.: Rutgers University Press.

HUMPHREY, C. 1997. Exemplars and rules: aspects of the discourse of moralities in Mongolia. In *The ethnography of moralities* (ed.) S. Howell, 25-47. London: Routledge.

JOHN OF DAMASCUS 2003 [726-30]. *Three treatises on divine images.* Crestwood, N.Y.: St Vladimir's Seminary Press.

KAUFMANN, W.O. 1996. *The anthropology of wisdom literature.* Westport, Conn.: Bergin & Garvey.

KEMMLER, F. 1984. *'Exempla' in context: a historical and critical study of Robert Mannyng of Brunne's 'Handlyng Synne'.* Tübingen: Gunter Narr Verlag.

KIECKHEFER, R. 1988. Imitators of Christ: sainthood in the Christian tradition. In *Sainthood: its manifestations in world religions* (eds) R. Kieckhefer & G.D. Bond, 1-42. Berkeley: University of California Press.

KLEINBERG, A. 1992. *Prophets in their own country: living saints and the making of sainthood in the later Middle Ages.* Chicago: University Press.

———— 2008. *Flesh made word: saints' stories and the Western imagination.* Cambridge, Mass.: Harvard University Press.

KRUEGER, D. 2004. *Writing and holiness: the practice of authorship in the early Christian East.* Philadelphia: University of Pennsylvania Press.

LE GOFF, J. 1988. *The medieval imagination* (trans. A. Goldhammer). Chicago: University Press.

LYONS, J.D. 1989. *Exemplum: the rhetoric of example in early modern France and Italy.* Princeton: University Press.

MACKLIN, J. 2005. Saints and near-saints in transition: the sacred, the secular, and the popular. In *The making of saints: contesting sacred ground* (ed.) J.F. Hopgood, 1-22. Tuscaloosa: University of Alabama Press.

MORGAN, D. 1998. *Visual piety: a history and theory of popular religious images.* Berkeley: University of California Press.

MOSHER, J.A. 1911. *The exemplum in the early religious and didactic literature of England.* New York: Columbia University Press.

ORSI, R. 2005. *Between heaven and earth: the religious worlds people make and the scholars who study them.* Princeton: University Press.

RIHBANI, A.M. 2003 [1922]. *The Syrian Christ.* Pontiac, Québec: Apamea.

ROBBINS, J. 2001. God is nothing but talk: modernity, language, and prayer in a Papua New Guinea society. *American Anthropologist* **103**, 901-12.

———— 2007. Continuity thinking and the problem of Christian culture: belief, time, and the anthropology of Christianity. *Current Anthropology* **48**, 5-38.

SCANLON, L. 1994. *Narrative, authority, and power: the medieval exemplum and the Chaucerian tradition.* Cambridge: University Press.

SCHMITT, C. 1996 [1923]. *Roman Catholicism and political form.* Westport, Conn.: Greenwood.

TOMLINSON, M. 2014. *Ritual textuality: pattern and motion in performance.* Oxford: University Press.

WARNICK, B.R. 2008. *Imitation and education: a philosophical inquiry into learning by example.* Albany: State University of New York Press.

WEBER, M. 1992 [1904]. *The Protestant ethic and the spirit of capitalism* (trans. T. Parsons). London: Routledge.

WITTGENSTEIN, L. 1998 [1977]. *Culture and value: a selection from the posthumous remains* (ed. G.H. von Wright & H. Nyman). Oxford: Blackwell.

———— 2009 [1953]. *Philosophical investigations* (trans. G.E.M. Anscombe). Chichester: Wiley-Blackwell.

WOODWARD, K.L. 1990. *Making saints: how the Catholic Church determines who becomes a saint, who doesn't and why.* New York: Simon & Schuster.

Séries exemplaires et typologie chrétienne : prendre modèle sur la sainteté à Damas

Résumé

Dans le présent article, j'explore la manière dont les exemples sont utilisés dans les sermons parmi les fidèles de Notre-Dame de Soufanieh à Damas, en Syrie. Dans ces sermons, une logique de sériation particulière est employée pour présenter des modèles et exemples spécifiques comme prismes des vies à imiter. Ces vies sont mises en valeur par des entextualisations, transformant la vie d'une personne en textes dont les autres sont appelés à s'inspirer. L'auteur retrace ce processus de transformation de la vie en texte et du texte en vie dans la production d'exemples lors des sermons hebdomadaires du samedi à Soufanieh. Tout en étant directement liés à la vie vécue, ces sermons symbolisent aussi une classe de vie, celle de la *forma vitae*, des vies à suivre. L'auteur explore donc l'exemple en tant qu'*exemplum*, histoire morale particulière utilisée pour l'édification et l'enseignement, histoire qui place l'auditeur en son centre en intégrant à la réponse de celui-ci les événements miraculeux de Soufanieh. Les sermons servent ainsi à examiner la création d'exemples et de modèles de sainteté à Damas dans les années qui ont précédé la guerre civile en cours.

4

Double standards: examples and exceptions in scientific metrological practices in Brazil

ANTONIA WALFORD *Centre for Research on Socio-Cultural Change, Open University*

Drawing on fieldwork with metrologists from Brazil's Space Institute in the southeast of Brazil, this paper explores the science of measurement and calibration in terms of the relation between examples and exceptions. It argues that in order to understand how examples circulate in metrological practice in the form of versions of an absolute standard for a measurement, it is necessary to take into account how they appear as *exceptions* from that standard. The example and the exception emerge as forms of each other – neither opposed nor alike, but conveying the same information differently. The paper then turns to examine how this example of exemplification as exception can be methodologically engaged. If the introduction to this special issue proposes that 'their' examples are best thought of as 'our' examples, this paper ends with a discussion of how exactly metrological exemplification could come to be anthropological description.

There have been many fascinating historical studies concerning how certain electrical standard units, such as the volt or the ohm, were stabilized and standardized as universally accepted units of measurement. These studies tell tales of conflicts and compromises between countries, ideals, and institutions in the geopolitical efforts made to quantify nature (Alder 1995; O'Connell 1993; Porter 1995; Schaffer 1992). A particularly fierce debate in the nineteenth century focused on the best means of establishing these units so as to ensure they were 'absolute' (O'Connell 1993). Absolutism in measurement required the unit – in this case the ohm – to be directly linked to what, as the British Association for the Advancement of Science described it in 1873, 'may be treated as fundamental', such that it 'bears the stamp of the authority ... of nature' (Jenkin 1873: 60, cited in O'Connell 1993: 139). The British were convinced that for this reason, the best way to express electrical units was solely in terms of mass, space, and time, considered to be the most fundamental of measurements and therefore axiomatic. The stabilization of such derived units was the first step in being able to spread them throughout the world in material form – as specific lengths of coils of wire, in the case of the ohm. That is, their dissemination was dependent upon their materialization.

These absolute standards then travelled outwards, so the story goes, from singular definition decided upon by experts, to universal unit employed everywhere there is electricity. Disputes over this trajectory, and others like it, often turn on the difficulty of singularizing and stabilizing the definition of something of which there are already multiple instances. Before the metric system, Theodore Porter tells us, measurements of mass were 'a matter of negotiation' (1995: 24). There were multiple measures of what was called 'a bushel' for every farming purpose and occasion, before mass was standardized as being based on the metric 'kilo', and subsequently firmly ensconced in the International Bureau of Weights and Measures (BIPM) near Paris. Porter sees this large-scale, state- and economy-governed standardization of quantification as a definitive break: the instigation of 'measurement that aspired to be independent from local customs and local knowledge' (1995: 22). It is also generally agreed upon by historians and sociologists of science that these standard units *became* universal. That is, settling the matter of what the absolute standard consists in is only half the battle: a great deal of work goes into ensuring that these standards then gain and subsequently maintain their universality and general validity. As Joseph O'Connell writes, '[T]he highest authority in the land is powerless unless it can make its influence felt in all the nooks and crannies of the kingdom' (1993: 152). These standard examples, then, are powerful because they are disseminated, and concretized through use. In this case, setting an example only works if others follow suit.

This paper aims to contribute to this question of what it means to 'become universal'.[1] It aims to do so from an ethnographic perspective, and with an anthropological focus on the process of metrological exemplification. The way in which metrological standards intuitively might be thought of as becoming universal is by managing to reproduce themselves – that is, managing to 'exemplify' themselves many times over. It is the complicated relation between an absolute exemplar and its exemplifications that I will be concentrating on, as encountered in the work of the metrologists I accompanied for a period of time during fieldwork completed in 2010 in Brazil.

Meteorological metrology

The metrologists I accompanied during fieldwork are from the Laboratory for Meteorological Instrumentation[2] (LIM), part of Brazil's National Space Institute (INPE). LIM is responsible for the maintenance of the scientific instruments used to collect data on meteorological variables throughout Brazil. These instruments either are part of a network of long-term meteorological data-collecting stations spread across the country, or belong to specific and normally shorter-term projects linked to other institutions. Alongside providing mechanical maintenance, LIM is also in the process of establishing Brazil's first accredited calibration laboratory for scientific projects (henceforth 'CL'). Calibration is the process by which the error and uncertainty in an instrument are calculated by comparing them to the universal standard for the units it measures in. There are already several such laboratories for the industry sector in Brazil but none exist to cater for the very specific calibration demands of scientific instruments that work in derived units, and require the simulation of specific environmental conditions. During the time I was there, the CL was in the process of being set up in order to rectify this. It is run by husband and wife team Patrícia and Márcio, who left their jobs in another metrology lab in INPE to take on the challenge.

In order to explore what I am calling metrological exemplification, I will start by describing the notion of absolute standards, or 'primary standards' as they are also known, within contemporary metrology in general. There are two different types of absolute standard, known as artefact standards and intrinsic standards (O'Connell 1993: 152). Artefact standards exist as material instantiations of themselves, such as the kilo, which resides in the BIPM. Metrological practice consists in ensuring that any kilo measured can be traced back directly to this standard. This is called 'traceability' (*rastreabilidade* in Portuguese), and these traces exist, in the case of the metrologists whom I worked with, as little stamps of accreditation that are stuck onto any instrument that is traceable in this way. These stamps effectively say that the instrument is now part of 'a documented unbroken chain of calibrations', as the BIPM puts it.[3] You gain one of these stamps either by being visited by a 'touring' standard, which is periodically and often with great difficulty toured around the various smaller laboratories (as used to happen with 'the volt' in the United States), or by sending equipment to national or international metrological laboratories to have them calibrated to the standard (O'Connell 1993). Thus Brazil's National Metrology Institute (INMETRO) has its standards calibrated by the BIPM, and in turn using these standards will calibrate the equipment sent to them from other laboratories in Brazil. INMETRO also performs accreditation evaluations on laboratories aspiring to be able to perform calibrations themselves. The whole system therefore can be conceptualized as a hierarchical nested network, with the BIPM at the top, then national, then regional laboratories, all looking to the level above them to set the example.

The other form of metrological standard is the intrinsic standard. These standards are physical experiments that labs can perform themselves, to 'create the volt, second, ohm or various temperature points right on their premises' (O'Connell 1993: 153). The volt, metre, and ohm were formerly all artefact standards, but have been converted into intrinsic ones. As O'Connell suggests, this implies a major conceptual systemic shift, in the sense that direct, unmediated contact with the absolute is now available to all.[4]

As I was conducting fieldwork in a metrological laboratory that specializes in the calibration of meteorological instruments, the units in question are all derived units: that is, they are units, such as the radiometric unit w/m^2, that are a composite of what are taken to be the fundamental units, such as the metre. Nevertheless, despite not being base units themselves, the logic of traceability of these units (as a chain of marks of accreditation leading back to an absolute) is wherever possible still the same. For example, as radiation is a commonly measured meteorological variable, radiometric instruments are often sent to LIM from all over Brazil to be calibrated. In order to perform these calibrations, Patrícia and Márcio have to send *their* standard radiometric instruments (which measure a particular wavelength of sunlight, called a pyranometer) to the World Radiation Centre (WRC) in Davos, Switzerland to be calibrated every two years. The WRC is responsible for ensuring the rather ambitious 'world-wide homogeneity' of solar radiation measurements in accordance with a group of six instruments called the World Standard Group, which between them produce the World Radiometric Reference (WRR). On the WRC website, we are told:

> The World Radiometric Reference is the measurement standard representing the SI unit of irradiance. It was introduced in order to ensure world-wide homogeneity of solar radiation measurements and is in use since 1980 … Every five years, an International Pyrheliometer Comparison (IPC) is held at PMOD/WRC to transfer the WRR to the participating pyrheliometers in order to ensure world-wide homogeneity of solar radiation measurements.[5]

Journal of the Royal Anthropological Institute (N.S.), 64-77
© Royal Anthropological Institute 2015

Thus every five years, representatives of participating regional and national meteorological institutions gather in Davos so that the WRR can be 'transferred' to their radiometers, and taken back to their respective countries and disseminated to the local laboratories. As Brazil is not a participating country, the CL therefore sends its radiometers to the WRC in Davos every two years in order to be calibrated. Then, using these radiometers, it can calibrate the other radiometers from around Brazil that are sent to it for calibration. In this way, the 'new value', I was told, is *repassado* – passed on, or transferred. The CL in fact works with a variety of standard instruments, ranging from radiometers traceable to WRC, to standards that it itself is testing and for which no absolute standard yet exists.

The CL is also itself hoping to move up the hierarchy, and become an accredited metrology laboratory. At the moment, its metrologists admit that they are 'right down the bottom of the chain' and perform 'the best they can' to meet the small but growing demand for calibration of scientific meteorological instruments in Brazil. As I have mentioned, they do use instruments that have traceability, that is, that have been accredited by INMETRO or other institutions that belong to the Brazilian National Network of Calibration. But in some cases, even if the standard instrument they have is traceable, they do not have the entire system necessary to perform the calibration – for example, they do not have a wind tunnel which is used to calibrate anenometers (which measure wind speed and direction). And in other cases, the instrument they use is not a standard traceable one, but simply an instrument that has never been used and so its original calibration certificate from the manufacturers is still valid. In these cases, what is performed is known as 'verification' rather than 'calibration', and is what Márcio calls a 'way round' (*saida*) the problem of the lack of infrastructure at the CL. Verification, he told me, would not be permitted in an accredited laboratory. To become accredited requires the lab to undergo a thorough process of evaluation by INMETRO, which consists in conforming to very strict criteria concerning not only calibration standards and the traceability of instruments, but also documentation and infrastructure standards, number of employees to meet demand, filing systems, and so on. In order not to get into any 'bad habits', Patrícia and Márcio already try to follow some of the norms of the International Organization for Standards (ISO), such as the one that governs how and what information is displayed on calibration certificates, and how the calibration is to proceed. But in order to count towards accreditation, any ISO norm followed needs to be completely standardized and always adhered to, and for most of the ISO norms, this is still beyond the capacities of the CL. In a certain sense, then, to become part of a metrological network of calibration requires that the laboratory itself be 'calibrated' to a standard performance.

Exemplar examples

From the description thus far, absolute standards can be seen as metrological 'exemplars', in as much as they are to a certain extent ideal. However, absolute metrological standards also have the interesting capacity to be universal and singular at the same time. There is certainly only one of each – this is, as I have briefly sketched out, a state of affairs that has been historically highly fraught. But at the same time, the logic of the metrological exemplar only holds if it is also universal – that is, that every metre everywhere is identical to the absolute standard metre. Thus this is not only a question of being a member of the same class, but being exactly interchangeable within that class. Such logic configures the putative relation between what is singular and what is universal in an interesting fashion, which I shall now demonstrate.

So far, I have tried to show the work involved in ensuring contiguity between an absolute standard and its instantiations – what I have called a process of exemplification, which proceeds via a chain of 'traceability'. The idea of exemplification that I have sketched out is therefore that there is an absolute standard unit, and there are many representations,[6] or instances, of that unit. So exemplification here takes place along the whole hierarchical chain, outwards from the absolute standard to every instantiation of the unit in question. This process of exemplification is potentially infinite, because at the end of this chain there is 'measurement'. The radiometric unit that originates in Davos is *repassado* to the various smaller laboratories, which via calibration then pass it on to all the instruments they calibrate, which are then placed in the middle of, for example, the Amazon forest or the Siberian tundra and churn out w/m^2 at a considerable rate, as data. In order for these w/m^2 to be comparable, and for the scientific data to therefore also be comparable,[7] they have to be considered as *good examples* of the international absolute standard.

If one considers the chain from this perspective, moving from a singular absolute standard to many exemplifications of that standard implies a uni-directionality, from singular to universal. The chain of traceability has at one end the static, localized, singular absolute standard, which becomes multiple instances of that standard in regional laboratories, and shades off at the other end into potentially infinite measurements being made in various different places around the world. However, the relation between these two qualities goes beyond this. As I have mentioned, the logic of this chain of standardization rests inherently on the absolute standard being interchangeable with its instantiations. This means that the standard is therefore simultaneously both everywhere and also in only one specific place. If considered as a singular entity, this can only be a singularity that resides in a proliferation of instantiations of itself; if considered as universal, it is universal and dispersed only because there is indisputably only one of it in the world. The idea of something singular 'becoming' universal therefore is complicated by the fact that universality here resides in singularity, and vice versa. The chain is also a circle, in this sense. This hints at the fact that the absolute standard, or exemplar, is simultaneously in fact also an example, as I shall now explore.

Sitting in the humming, air-conditioned calibration laboratory one day during a temperature calibration, I asked Patrícia if anyone calibrates the standard. No one does, she told me. Then she paused for thought, and explained that, actually, the standard is 'normally the materialized form of the thing'. Her comment harks back to a notion I introduced at the beginning of the paper – that absolute standards have to be 'materialized' somehow. The notion of a 'material form of a thing' implies that the 'thing' itself – the standard unit – is still, as such, *immaterial* – that is, not physically present. The absolute standard of the metrological chain is always itself, in a certain sense, also an instantiation – even as it is also an absolute, and therefore impossible to calibrate. The chain of traceability could thus be seen as having an infinite regress on both ends in different ways. One is endless repetition (measurements), the other is eternal displacement (the thing beyond its own materialization). Thus the singular standard is the universal reference at the same time as being itself part of its own universal expression.

However, this is not simply a question of the vanishing point of an absolute as inherent in a particular formulation of universality. In fact, as impressed upon me on several occasions by both Patrícia and Márcio, 'nothing is absolute'. Why this is so becomes apparent only when the focus shifts from the units themselves to what it is exactly that links these units, or, rather, *how* they are linked. The reason that nothing is absolute is that there is error and uncertainty, as Márcio put it, 'embedded' in every link of the chain, or every attempt to exemplify. If exemplars are also examples, I will now endeavour to explain how examples are also kinds of exceptions.

Calibration

The links in the metrological chain of traceability are achieved through the process of calibration. The calibration of any sensor at the CL requires at least: the standard you will be comparing it to; some sort of computer to register the data (normally a very simple computer called a datalogger); and the sensor in question. It also requires some way of controlling, or ensuring variation in, the phenomenon that the sensor measures. Patrícia and Márcio's laboratory is housed in a labyrinth of rooms at LIM, with a different set of calibrations being worked on in each. The main room, which is startlingly clean and cold, is dominated by a large gleaming contraption, a thermal chamber, which is connected to an array of computers. Whilst several technicians busy themselves around the chamber, Patrícia and Márcio oversee proceedings, every so often stopping to consult the meteorological tomes that are piled up in a little room behind a glass screen. To perform a temperature calibration, the thermometer to be calibrated is put in the thermal chamber along with the standard thermometer. Different parts of the chamber can be heated to different temperatures, depending on the range of your target environment (measuring in the Arctic does not have the same range as measuring in the Amazon – so you can calibrate just ranges of temperatures, rather than all temperatures), and the readings of the two thermometers are compared. But at every stage, uncertainty and error enter into the system.

First of all, there are the errors potentially introduced through physical phenomena, such as that of hysteresis. Hysteresis is a non-linear effect that means that the way that a thermometer heats up is not the way that it cools down. Thus if the ambient temperature increases by 1.05°C, the thermometer might regsiter an increase of 1°C; but when the ambient temperature drops by 1.05°C, the same thermometer records a drop of 1.1°C.[8] This means that the thermometers must be cooled back down to zero before being heated again to the different temperature points. If you were to go straight from 5°C to 10°C, you would end up with a different set of temperatures on the way up and on the way down. Not controlling this effect can introduce error into the system. The temperature and the humidity at which the standard you are using was calibrated must also be taken into account – in some cases, if the calibration in question is performed at a different temperature and relative humidity than the one that the standard was calibrated in, that must also be included as 'embedding local error' (*embutindo erro local*). The longitude and latitude are also included in the radiation calibration certificates from the WRC, because these too can affect the measurements made. 'Everything is going to interfere', Patrícia told me.

Secondly, there are some sources of error that are only discovered through experience. Pluviometers (which measure rainfall intensity and volume), for example, work via a system called the 'tipping bucket'. When the little buckets in them are full to a known volume, the weight of the water causes them to tip and touch a metal pad below them. This completes a circuit that causes a current to run through the sensor, registering data. But in different intensities of rainfall, this can fail to work sufficiently: either the rain is too intense for the bucket to register enough 'tips', or the rain is so light that it never quite manages to fill the buckets. That is to say, this type of pluviometer works with one level of uncertainty in heavy rainfall, and another one in light rainfall – and presumably in all the sorts of rainfall in between (see, e.g., Braga & Fernandes 2007). Thus when one calibrates a tipping bucket pluviometer, one has to be sure to re-create all the environmental conditions, simulating intensity of the rainfall as well as volume of water. As Patrícia pointed out as we examined a pluviometer being calibrated, 'Mechanics, electronics, physics, they all vary, there's a deterioration'.

Finally, and for the purposes of my argument most importantly, there is the question of uncertainty. The thermal chamber has a certain level of uncertainty – it can only be precise concerning the degrees to which it heats itself to a certain order of magnitude; likewise the standard thermometer has an inbuilt uncertainty. These uncertainties are ineluctable, and accompany the chamber and the thermometer as *evidence* that they have been previously calibrated. The datalogger also has a degree of uncertainty owing to the conversion of analogue signals into digital; in fact Patrícia and Márcio had to join forces with their old metrological laboratory to find some way to calibrate their own dataloggers, as they could not find anyone else in Brazil who could do so. And even taking all this into account, calibration is only valid for finite periods of time. Patrícia presented a temporal analogy: 'Calibration is a momentary thing – like taking a photo'. Representations here have a habit over time of drifting away from that which they are meant to be representing.

Exemplification, approximation, and uncertainty

What does this, then, add to our image of exemplification? It means that an example is alike, but also inescapably different from that which it is meant to exemplify. What characterizes the chain of traceability with infinite regress on both ends is that its links are made as much of difference as similarity, and metrological examples are exemplary as much because they differ from each other as because they reproduce each other. 'Nothing is pure', as Márcio says; 'the minute you start measuring, that's it, there's no way round it'. And this holds for every link in the chain. If the standard is the materialized form of the thing, what lies in-between the thing (unit) and its materialized form is the necessary and inescapable uncertainty that accompanies *all* metrological activity. As the head of LIM emphatically put it, 'You're always going to have a certain error which is uncertainty, the uncertainty of calibration, you can't escape it'.

This uncertainty, lying between the unit and its materialization, has the property of being both in the measurement process and in the world being measured. In metrological professional vocabulary this is captured neatly by the phrase 'conventional true value of a quantity'. This is 'a value of a quantity which, for a given purpose, may be substituted for the true value', as that true value is by definition unknown (Mallard 1998: 571). That is, the true value, or absolute standard must exist – but it exists precisely as an unknown. Alexander Mallard refers to this as the 'social' and 'natural' character of precise measurement, a 'pragmatics of approximation' (1998: 594). Proposing a conventional true value is certainly a pragmatic way to approximate a true value always at one degree removed. However, I suggest that whereas the idea of approximation hints again at a unidirectional dynamic – moving closer to reality (i.e. being a good example) – certainly present in the way metrological logic functions, there are also, as I have tried to demonstrate, more complex understandings at play. I would like to argue that it is the difference that is the result of calibration – the uncertainty – that is intrinsic to the metrological practice of exemplification.

When instruments are sent to the CL to be calibrated, they are cleaned and any mechanical fault is dealt with.[9] Then they are calibrated, as I have described previously. The result of this calibration is a certificate of calibration, which has two different sets of values on it. One is 'error', and the other is 'uncertainty'. The two are related, but can be separately defined thus: uncertainty is the range within which the 'true value' is asserted to lie – so as we have seen, uncertainty is the error embedded in the process of calibration by the calibration system being used. This uncertainty means that the standard value has a range around it – or, rather, is itself a range. It is often calculated using standard deviation. For example, if you are calibrating the temperature point 15°C, and your thermometer reads 14.9, 14.6, 14.8, 14.5, each time you repeat the measurement, then you have a high standard deviation – or a high dispersal of the numbers from their own average, which is an indicator of uncertainty. If, on the other hand, it reads 14.9, 14.9, 14.9, 14.9, then it is systematically wrong, but has very little deviance and therefore a much lower uncertainty. Error is defined as simply this *difference* between the measured value and the true value – the extent to which the instrument being calibrated errs from the (uncertain) standard. You can try to remove the error from your system, by correcting for it mathematically, or, if you can isolate the cause, mechanically. The researchers who receive the instruments back from the CL then are expected to correct their own measurements according to the coefficients provided to them. They are also provided with the uncertainty percentage that is built in to their system, and the entire chain of calibrations of which it is a part – and this they cannot correct.

What, then, is being passed around in this case is not actually the standard or unit itself (the metrologists very rarely adjust the instruments they receive), but error and uncertainty: how much the standard is *not* the standard (uncertainty), and how much your instrument is *not* the standard (error). Metrological exemplification is in a certain sense a form of approximation, but one that is constituted by difference; it is in fact uncertainty that is the biggest concern for those metrologists I worked with – how to discover it, and how to disseminate it. As the head of LIM confided,

> My biggest worry in all of this is the following: you calibrate everything and so on, and reach the conclusion that your thermometer has an uncertainty of 0.2 degrees and you start collecting data. Only, the researcher [whose thermometer it is] who gets this data, does he use this information? He doesn't use it at all. If it says 25.3 degrees, he's going to use 25.3 degrees, he's not going to take that 0.2 into consideration. He's going to use it as if this value is exact ... So even if you calculate the uncertainty of the equipment, it's not going to be used in the subsequent proceedings.

The 'fundamental level' here is that of uncertainty, as Márcio explained:

> Look, for [electrical] frequency, the primary standard today is the oscillation of caesium – how the caesium atom oscillates – that's the standard today. But it's got an error already of 5×10^{-16} – and it's the standard. Because if you put a lot of caesiums together, this is the difference between them – there's no way of improving this, it's nature. The error comes from nature.

What 'traceability' means, in fact, is the capacity to know how much your examples are in fact *not like* your absolute, which is itself *not like* itself. I suggest, then, that a process of metrological exemplification is equally constituted by means of *exceptions*.

Examples and exceptions are intimately related, as are similarity and difference, and, as we have seen, the singular and the universal. Metrological exemplification, however, configures these relations in a particular way. This is not a relation of opposition or mutual exclusion. Absolute standards serve as singular universals, but are themselves constantly displaced, not only by their imbrication in each other, but also by the fact that their relation is necessarily one of uncertainty. With this as the premise, the work of the metrologists is to try to find this uncertainty, in order to perpetuate these standards universally. That is, to *approximate* the standard in terms of similarity, what is constantly being *repassado* is in fact *uncertainty and difference*. Thus similarity and difference here are best understood not as opposite, but rather as inside-out versions of each other – they are, as Annelise Riles puts it 'the same form seen twice' (2001: 69). The one does not exclude the other, but nor does it represent the other or explain the other; it evokes the same information from the other side, as it were.

Thus a metrological example might be thought of as an inside-out exception: similarity (exemplifying) is not the opposite of difference (exception) – but difference seen differently, and vice versa. This is why the form of the example for metrologists can in fact be an exception, without this being contradictory. This is not simply a question of error – how far or near a measurement is from a standard – or even that, in a zero-sum scenario, to say how 'wrong' something is is also to say how 'right' it is. As I have demonstrated, the scenario that metrology presents is not simply zero-sum approximation, but one of infinite regress. What metrological uncertainty in fact adds to this logic of exemplification is how much the metrologists by definition cannot know the value in question. 'Uncertainty' is at one and the same time a comment on the incompleteness of knowledge, and the assertion that knowledge is constituted exactly through this incompleteness. It is an index of how much the measure is 'not' what it 'is'.

Metrological exceptions and anthropological examples

Annelise Riles has already substantially developed the relational term 'inside-out' to describe 'the recursivity of a form that literally speaks about itself' (2001: 69). Her aim in that instance is to suggest an alternative way of describing the informal personal relations and the formal networking practice of her interlocutors in an NGO in Fiji, other than to suggest that one explains the other in conventional representational format, such that networks 'reflect' society or society creates networks – with one or the other always given explanatory, referential power. Rather, what she finds concerning the relation between these two forms is that 'the inside and the outside of the artifact are not text and context to each other in the modernist sense', because 'each serves as inside and outside of each other' (2001: 69). At the same time, this relation of 'inside-outness' characterizes anthropological knowledge-practices' relation to themselves as well as their fields. Riles suggests that Marilyn Strathern's work, for example, turns the postmodern concern to put the ethnographer 'in the picture' (in the field, as it were) 'inside-out' by making the 'ethnographic state of mind a frame or form' (Riles 2001: 19). The possibilities for replicating this relation at all levels is clear, evidencing the fractal dynamic that Strathern explicates in her book *Partial connections* (1991), which Riles draws on substantially.

I would like to take the elegance of the form that Riles presents as 'the same form seen twice', but suggest that there is another way it may be applied methodologically, under the specific ethnographic conditions of metrological practice in Brazil. That is to say, in what way can this same form be made to work differently in the ethnographic context that this paper presents? This is also to take up the challenge laid down by Strathern (2005) when she asks what can be *done* with such a methodological 'duplex', be it personal relations/formal networking, or something closer to the behemoths nature/culture, or the general/particular. Such a duplex, Strathern suggests, is the very 'tool' of anthropology: 'the relation' (2005: 90). One uncovers more and more relations through this tool, but it is *only* relations that one can uncover in this way (Strathern 2005: 91). The task here, then, is to understand exactly how the specific relation I am attempting to describe works as such a relational duplex, rather than just to discern its duplexity. I will attempt to do this by applying this description to itself in a particular way, hoping to demonstrate what a metrological theory of exception can in fact exemplify anthropologically. That is to say, what can a metrological relation between example and exception *do* through, and to, its own anthropological description? Heeding back to the introduction to this special issue, another way to say this might be to ask just how these metrological examples might work as anthropological ones.

Singular laboratories

Both Patrícia and Márcio were shocked when they came to work in scientific research. 'In metrology', Patrícia told me,

> everything is already really well defined, and everyone agrees on it; in a *meteorological* instrumentation lab, you have to know what the researcher wants to measure, where he will install it, the conditions it will operate under – when you put the instrument in the field there could be a million factors that will influence it, pressure changes, rain – so you end up having to know what the researcher wants to do with it, why he wants it calibrated.

I wondered why, and Patrícia replied:

> Well, the researcher is the one who dictates what the calibration will be, what range ... It depends on what he wants, what precision he wants, because you could calibrate it to an uncertainty of 0.1 for example, but if he's working in degrees, maybe he only needs an uncertainty of 0.5 ... This is another difference: in industry the user knows exactly the precision he needs. The researcher, when you ask him, hasn't the faintest idea – 'What do you mean, margin?' he'll ask. He expects you to make an adjustment and then return the instrument 'without errors' the next day. So often the researcher is desperate, he needs the instrument back by next week, and you have to explain all the norms of calibration to him ... Sometimes you send them the certificate of calibration and they send it back saying, 'What on earth do I do with this?!'

Neither of them was sure whether this was a problem one could call specific to Brazil, but Márcio was certain that 'here in Brazil in meteorology, no one calibrates anything – over in Europe, or the US – in NOAA,[10] for example, they have a cupboard full of calibrated equipment, so the researcher going to the field can just take one from there'.

Furthermore, the CL is the only laboratory in Brazil that is attempting to calibrate meteorological equipment, and for many of these instruments, standards do not even exist. Patrícia and Márcio's colleagues in industry metrological labs think they are 'crazy' to work with this mixed 'salad' of units; it is much more common for a lab to specialize in one unit only. But as theirs is the only lab in Brazil undertaking this task, they do not feel that they have much choice. Márcio gave me a tour of the equipment that they have ingeniously assembled in order to try to verify as best possible the instruments they receive. They teamed up with another metrological laboratory in order to create a pressure calibrator, and one for pluviometers, and are testing a system to calibrate the sensors which measure heat flux in the soil in a small sand pit in the corner of one of the offices. Márcio explained that the standard thermometer they have is very expensive, and has to be calibrated every year – and they simply do not have the money that the French, British, or North American Metrological Institutions have to spend on instruments like that. Nor do they have the money to set up a radiation calibration laboratory in a sunny part of the country in order to ensure the requisite number of consecutive sunny days to perform a radiation calibration. So they have been researching a way to simulate sunshine inside the laboratory – except that a lamp that exactly reproduces solar radiation has not been invented yet. Patrícia explained forlornly that the Institute for American Standards, in its 2005 and 2010 review, seemed to have removed the section concerning indoor radiometric calibration, as its research had not yielded enough results – so the metrologists at CL are researching this, as far as they know, by themselves. They have been requesting funding for a wind tunnel for several years in order to be able to calibrate anemometers, but are unconvinced that it will appear any time soon.

The CL is the only laboratory of its kind in Brazil. It has to innovate technologies. It cannot do what other metrological institutions can, it lacks their resources, personnel and experience, and it does not meet world-wide standards. It is not accredited, but it performs the job an accredited metrological laboratory would in some other countries. Its problems are to a certain extent circumscribed specifically by the climatic, economic, bureaucratic, and political characteristics of Brazil. It does not, in this sense, consider itself independent from that locale. If we imagine its relation to the wider class of which it is a part – the metrological hierarchy – in terms of *examples*, then it seems clear that the CL is not a good example. Patrícia and Márcio themselves tell me there is a long way to go yet. At the same time, it would be incorrect to suggest that the CL is somehow not a metrological laboratory, or even that it is a bad one, as it is particularly configured to deal with as-yet peripheral metrological units in a country that is itself configured in a specific way.

Investigating this metrological hierarchy, Mallard (1998) carefully portrays the heterogeneity apparent in the different collection of practices that can still, he suggests, all be called 'metrological'. Demonstrating the extent of this gamut, he compares three cases: conventional and institutionally enshrined metrology and the control of industry standards; the simultaneous innovation of instruments and standards in a particular scientific laboratory; and the articulation of distributed measurement of air pollution. He maintains that a 'systematic study of metrology should simultaneously show the generality of metrological practices and point to their distinct realizations in these different situations' (1998: 594). Mallard is here picking up on the relation between the universal and the singular in the different manifestations that metrology can take. This emerges again in his depiction of the form of the 'generic' industry instrument and the 'individual' scientific one (1998: 575). In conclusion, he extends this to a brief discussion of the 'natural' and the 'social' (1998: 594), such that he ends up by suggesting that the different metrological practices he describes are united in their different ways of articulating 'truth' with 'uncertainty', or, in more familiar social-scientific terms, the 'natural' with the 'social'. In light of my fieldwork, I would add that paying close attention to these specific articulations suggests that these practices are equally *differentiated* through their unity. It is not so much that specificity is opposed to generality, but that their practice creates particularity as it creates universality, and the role of metrology therefore is to sustain this complex duplicity. However, it does so by sustaining and circulating the 'outside', we might say, of a particular way of knowing (measuring) the world in the form of uncertainty – such that, as I have demonstrated, exemplification is in fact composed through successive exceptions. An anthropological attempt to describe this could therefore draw upon these same notions.

If we consider the CL in terms of *exceptions*, it might be said that it is in fact a good exception. The issue inheres in its ability to be both at the same time – bad example and good exception. And whereas the notion of a bad example already makes intuitive sense, the logic of metrological exemplification also allows us to ask the more interesting question of what it means to be a good exception. It means that exemplification is effected *through*, rather than despite, difference. Allowing the CL to be a good exception in descriptive terms would mean countenancing the ways in which it differs from the standard laboratory – INMETRO, for example – as constitutive rather than detractive of what it is. This conclusion has methodological repercussions beyond the scope of this paper, but one important point to make concerns the limits of such an exemplificatory practice. Drawing on ethnographic relations with metrologists to try to understand how they might relate to themselves is one move that can be put to work to counter descriptions that would reduce deviance to detraction.

Philosopher of science Isabelle Stengers draws attention, through the work of philosophers Gilles Deleuze and Félix Guattari, to the negative side of processes of standardization – practices which the metrologists I work with undoubtedly in one sense engage in. Metrology in this sense adheres to an oppressive logic of the 'standard' that has 'the power to define everybody else in terms of a deviation from what then becomes taken as normal' (Stengers 2010: 13). Stengers addresses this in terms of the differences between majorities and minorities. Majorities are the expression of normal standards, homogenized such that all members are interchangeable. Minorities, on the other hand, are not merely 'small' majorities but completely different entities, participation in which does not imply common features but a willingness to be connected, and in which divergence is maintained. The benefit of this view for the study of minority populations of knowledge-practices is that it implies that they can be analysed on their own, divergent terms – which is to say, they can be permitted, as much as possible, to maintain what differentiates and deviates them rather than what assimilates them to a standard description (cf. Viveiros de Castro 2004).

Stengers goes on to suggest, however, that she might use a theory of the minority counterintuitively to characterize what have been traditionally seen as normalizing majority practices, such as physics. She proposes therefore that physics can have minority tendencies towards the dissolution of norms and standards, rather than their perpetuation (2010: 14), because physicists are concerned with what makes them 'think, feel and hesitate' (2010: 15), not with the cohesion of normalcy, even though these two may overlap at times.

The picture of exemplification as I have described it would suggest something else in the case of metrology: rather than giving rise to its opposite, standardization here perpetuates its own 'inside-out' inversions. I have explored how there is inherent in what the metrologists do a sort of duplicity: from the perspective of the universal and the singular, standards are absolute and the metrologists' role is to perpetuate good examples of those standards – though by propagating a universal that is also part of its own expression; but from the perspective of the mechanism by which this might take place, there is 'no such thing' as absolute, and the metrologists' job is to characterize, quantify, and disseminate exceptions from an absolute that is always, anyway, at one step removed. This duality, however, is not composed of opposing dynamics, whereby in pursuing one, the other is dissolved; in metrology, difference and similarity are in fact the same form seen twice. This 'relational duplex' that metrology offers can then be used to think through the double relation of the metrologists at CL/CL to their/its own double standards. CL is perhaps an exceptional example, in the same way as every instantiation of a standard is. Further pushing this form (perhaps too far) by returning to the relation between anthropology's and its interlocutors' exemplary practices, it might be asked to what extent anthropological exemplary practice should be an example of, rather than an exception to, the exemplary practices of those it engages with. In the case of this particular ethnographic exercise, one might say that the emphasis has been on the exception – which perhaps makes it a good example.

NOTES

My thanks go to Lars Højer and Andreas Bandak for giving me the opportunity to participate in the workshop behind this special issue, and for then tirelessly commenting on my contribution. My lasting thanks must also be extended to the Laboratório de Instrumentação Meteorológica at CPTEC/INPE, and particularly the metrologists Patrícia and Márcio, who not only allowed me into their laboratory but also read and corrected an earlier version of the paper. Casper Bruun Jensen and Morten Axel Pedersen read an early draft and provided invaluable commentary, and the three anonymous reviewers strengthened the paper's argument considerably. Of course, any errors nevertheless remain my own. I am very grateful to the IT University of Copenhagen, who funded the research on which this paper is based.

[1] There is a similar and ample discussion concerning this theme in Science and Technology Studies. See, for example, Bruno Latour's work on the maintenance of black boxes in science (Latour 1987; also Bowker & Star 1999).

[2] 'Meteorology' is the study of the weather; 'metrology' is the science of measurement.

[3] A definition taken from the BIPM vocabulary of metrological terms, which I was directed to by my interlocutors: *http://www.bipm.org/en/bipm/calibrations/traceability.html* (accessed 9 January 2015).

[4] O'Connell (1993) likens it to a Calvinist reformation, especially as one does not 'confess' or 'redeem' (i.e. calibrate) intrinsic standards, as they are not thought to drift.

[5] *http://www.pmodwrc.ch/pmod.php?topic=wrc* (accessed 9 January 2015). 'SI' is the International System of Units, maintained by BIPM, and consists of the seven 'base' units: the ampere, the metre, the kilogram, the second, the kelvin, the candela, and the mol.

[6] In the semantic and symbolic sense that the social sciences use the word, not in the sense employed in the literature on electrical standards (see O'Connell 1993: 167).

[7] For you to be able to claim, for example, that 33 per cent more long-wave radiation is absorbed by the Amazon forest than by the Siberian tundra – a typical, but in this case invented, example.

[8] *http://wattsupwiththat.com/2011/01/22/the-metrology-of-thermometers/* (accessed 12 January 2015).

[9] There are also cases in which the instrument is calibrated first in order to be able to correct field data, and then cleaned and re-calibrated.

[10] The US National Oceanic and Atmospheric Administration.

REFERENCES

ALDER, K. 1995. A revolution to measure. In *The values of precision* (ed.) M.N. Wise, 39-71. Princeton: University Press.

BOWKER, G.C. & L. STAR 1999. *Sorting things out: classification and its consequences.* Cambridge, Mass.: MIT Press.

BRAGA, S.M. & C.V.S. FERNANDES 2007. Perfórmance de sensores de precipitação do tipo 'tipping bucket' (Báscula) – um alerta para a ocorrência de erros. *Revista Brasileira de Recursos Hídricos* **12**, 197-204.

JENKIN, F. (ed.) 1873. *Reports of the Committee on Standards of Electrical Resistance appointed by the British Association for the Advancement of Science.* London: E. & F.N. Spon.

LATOUR, B. 1987. *Science in action: how to follow scientists and engineers through society.* Cambridge, Mass.: Harvard University Press.

MALLARD, A. 1998. Compare, standardize, settle agreement: on some usual metrological problems. *Social Studies of Science* **28**, 571-601.

O'CONNELL, J. 1993. Metrology: the creation of universality by the circulation of particulars. *Social Studies of Science* **23**, 129-73.

PORTER, T. 1995. *Trust in numbers: the pursuit of objectivity in science and social life.* Princeton: University Press.

RILES, A. 2001. *The network inside out.* Ann Arbor: University of Michigan Press.

SCHAFFER, S. 1992. Late Victorian metrology and its instrumentation: a manufactory of ohms. In *Invisible connections: instruments, institutions, and science* (eds) R. Bud & S.E. Cozzens, 23-56. Bellingham, Wash.: SPIE.

STENGERS, I. 2010. Including non-humans in political theory: opening Pandora's box? In *Political matter: technoscience, democracy and public life* (eds) B. Braun & S.J. Whatmore, 3-34. Minneapolis: University of Minnesota Press.

STRATHERN, M. 1991. *Partial connections.* Lanham, Md: Rowman & Littlefield Publishers.

——— 2005. *Kinship, law and the unexpected: relatives are always a surprise.* Cambridge: University Press.

VIVEIROS DE CASTRO, E. 2004. Perspectival anthropology and the method of controlled equivocation. *Tipití* **2**, 3-22.

Deux poids, deux mesures : exemples et exceptions dans les pratiques métrologiques scientifiques au Brésil

Résumé

À partir d'un travail de terrain avec les métrologistes de l'Institut national de recherche spatiale brésilien, dans le sud-est du Brésil, l'auteure explore la science de la mesure et de l'étalonnage en termes de relations entre exemples et exceptions. Elle avance que pour comprendre la manière dont les exemples circulent dans la pratique métrologique, sous la forme de versions d'une norme absolue pour une mesure, il faut prendre en compte la manière dont ils apparaissent comme des *exceptions* à la norme. L'exemple et l'exception s'avèrent des formes l'un de l'autre, ni opposées ni semblables mais véhiculant différemment la même information. L'article examine ensuite la manière dont cet exemple de création d'exemples en tant qu'exceptions peut être abordé du point de vue méthodologique. Si l'introduction à ce numéro spécial avance que la meilleure façon de penser « leurs » exemples est comme « nos » exemples, le présent article s'achève par une discussion de la manière dont la création d'exemples en métrologie pourrait s'avérer une description anthropologique.

5

Revolution is the way you eat: exemplification among left radical activists in Denmark and in anthropology

STINE KRØIJER *University of Copenhagen*

In anthropology, examples have always been an integral part of the investigation of the social life of people. Sometimes they simply work as a poor illustration of an author's general or existing theoretical ideas, but on other occasions they are conducive to setting new thoughts in motion. This paper explores the role of the example among left radical activists in the context of the Climate Summit (COP 15) protests in Copenhagen and a trip to forage for discarded food in a supermarket container in order to feed activists. I argue that examples make up a theory of change that evades problematic distinctions between the particular and universal, and set new actions in motion on a horizontal plane without relying on a predefined plan or end-point. The paper points to the ways this may inform the use of examples within the anthropological discipline.

This paper explores a political milieu in which examples play a prominent political role. I am thinking of left radical activists in Northern Europe – known to the public owing to their spectacular protests against political summits of world leaders and against the austerity measures launched in the context of the present economic crisis. For activists, the example serves as the overriding theory of change. 'Left radical' is an umbrella term used by activists in Northern Europe to refer to people on the extra-parliamentarian left of an anarchist, autonomist, and anti-capitalist bent.[1] Radical in the *emic* sense refers to someone who advocates radical change or, in other words, for a change from the roots of capitalist society. How this is envisioned and practised is, nevertheless, strikingly different from most previous, Marxist-inspired revolutionary movements in Europe – and this is where the role of the example comes into the picture.

The main argument of the paper is that exemplification is a key feature of political practice among activists, and that exemplification in anthropology may have something to learn from this. As outlined in the introduction to this volume, an example is conventionally thought of as an expression or manifestation of a larger whole or a general rule. In *Webster's dictionary*, definitions underline both the static and the dynamic character of examples: 'one (as an item or incident) that is representative of a group or type' and 'one that serves as a pattern to be imitated'. In *The coming community*,

Giorgio Agamben has offered a slight correction to this by defining the example, quite conventionally, as a manifestation of a class or type, and simultaneously as a singularity that stands for all others (1993: 12–13). In Agamben's understanding, the example escapes the antinomy between the particular and the universal, an antinomy that has also often been engrained in anthropological modes of theorizing the world. Lévi-Strauss (1963) collected a large number of myths in order to generalize about their underlying structure and give an insight into the universality of mind. Against this, but maintaining a similar distinction between the particular and the universal, both Clifford Geertz's version of symbolic and interpretative anthropology (Geertz 1973) and the situational analysis of the Manchester School (Gluckman 1958 [1940]; Kapferer 2006) advocated the detailed description of situations or events as a point of departure for generalizations about culture and society. Instead of taking examples as expressions of a general rule, I argue that the exemplification involved in activists' political actions has a double quality that has the potential for carving a new relation between the particular and the universal in anthropological thinking.

On the one hand, the actions of activists often work as a singular instantiation, and thereby as a fleeting exemplification, of an indeterminate future. Contrary to historical predecessors of the European revolutionary left, the activists described here generally refrain from defining ideological programmes and painting 'paradise pictures' of the future, and argue that this should be left open and indeterminate (Krøijer 2014; in press). As I shall discuss later, the fleeting performance of spectacular protests and political actions instead gives concrete form to the indeterminate (cf. Miyazaki 2004). The title of this paper, 'Revolution is the way you eat', which is taken from a rap song produced by a Danish anarchist music collective, refers to the way in which the simple acts of eating or collecting discarded food from supermarket containers are what I have called a 'figuration of the future' (Krøijer 2010; in press), insofar as a simple detail of daily living is both the seed and the brief manifestation of what is not yet. Figuration of the future describes how an indeterminate 'outside' or 'beyond' capitalism momentarily gains determinate form.[2]

On the other hand, protest actions of left radical activists serve as examples for other actions. This paper explores a series of instances of mass 'confrontational civil disobedience', and how these changed over time from their introduction in Denmark in 2002 to the Climate Summit (COP 15) in Copenhagen in 2009. I thus show how actions are both singular events that figurate the future, and part of a series of other actions that bring novelty into the world without relying on predefined end-points. As Brian Massumi puts it in *Parables of the virtual*, in which he builds on and extends Agamben's initial insights, 'every example harbours terrible powers of deviation and digression' (2002: 18) from which the unexpected may arise. In this view, the examples are not just expressions of a general rule or universal structure but are conductive to setting things in motion. In line with what has been concluded by Massumi, my point about activist politics is that there is nothing outside or beyond the example.

Taken together, this constitutes an activist theory of change that is largely devoid of ideological programmes and political manifestos. Attention to the activist concept of style can explain how certain actions come to serve as examples on a horizontal plane. Here I suggest that this theory has something to offer the anthropological conceptualization of the example. The paper describes a series of events from 2002 to 2009, only to delve into a detail that opens up a new example: a 'dumpster dive' – that is, a trip to collect discarded food from supermarket containers. Against this backdrop,

Journal of the Royal Anthropological Institute (N.S.), 78-95
© Royal Anthropological Institute 2015

the paper asks what happens if we place the activist theory of the example alongside anthropological theorization by way of examples?

Eduardo Viveiros de Castro has advocated for the conceptual, as well as political, self-determination of peoples (2003: 2) – a radical relativist stand partly turned on its head by insisting that this has to lead to a revision of anthropological concepts and theories. Martin Holbraad (2004) has continued this line of thought by arguing that anthropologists should imitate the 'native's' concepts and conceptions for theoretical purposes. To Holbraad and others, who are part of the 'ontological turn' in anthropology (Henare, Holbraad & Wastell 2007; Holbraad 2004; 2012; Holbraad, Pedersen & Viveiros de Castro 2014; Pedersen 2011; 2012), this has been a way to side-step the deadlock of the representational debate, and to renew anthropological theorizing.[3] Following this line of thought, I place activist theory *on a par* with anthropological traditions of exemplification, and I therefore maintain a distinction between the two for heuristic purposes. What will be revealed is how the activist way of exemplification stands 'at a right angle' (Viveiros de Castro 1998) to what we conventionally think of as the universal and the particular as they are both in the same move.

A series of confrontational civil disobedience actions

Almost six years ago, an acquaintance of mine, who was involved in launching the Danish activist network Globale Rødder (meaning both 'global roots' and 'global troublemakers'), tried to drive home to me the difference between left radical activists and the traditional Marxist left in Europe by comparing the former's view on the future with Islam's aniconism (prohibition against images). 'By avoiding painting pictures of the future, we want to avoid the idolatry and sectarianism that has characterized the Marxist left, and which inevitably follow from defining one's end-point', he explained at a meeting in a study circle where we were reading Michael Hardt and Antonio Negri's work *Empire* (2000), which describes the emergence of a new global regime without temporal boundaries. My acquaintance firmly believed that the future had to remain an open question, and that we therefore had to avoid painting pictures of an ideal society.

Although I subsequently forgot about this conversation, it came to my mind a few years later when I was doing fieldwork on forms of political action among activists because it clearly articulated a particular view of capitalism and the future that is prevalent within this group.[4] As I have described in detail elsewhere (Krøijer 2014), activists describe the present world as fundamentally unjust. War and starvation, exploitation and global inequality, as well as the natural devastation of the planet, are depicted as effects of corporate businesses' insatiable appetite for profits as well as political leaders' desire for power, both of which result in the excessive use of cohesive force to keep the world under their control. At the same time, activists describe capitalism as penetrating every aspect of our lives: how we eat, dwell, make love, and relate to one another. It is difficult, if not impossible, to overcome suddenly or completely. Instead, capitalism has to be confronted, challenged, and changed in everything one is doing, but is also perceived as constantly encroaching (Krøijer 2014: 64-5). While there is little hope for any sudden radical change or revolution, and thus little reason to define one's end-point, summit events are viewed as particular moments when the evil forces of capitalism convene and materialize in bodily form (as police officers and political leaders).

In light of the fact that activists perceive the future as indeterminate, and leave it that way consciously, their theory of change has come to rest heavily on staging ruptures and producing examples. In the following, I will describe a series of political actions and protests in Denmark, which Danish activists describe as events with an internal relationship – entailing that each served to push other events along.

The upsurge of summit protests and the so-called 'alter-globalization movement'[5] at the dawn of the twenty-first century became the space for experimentation with new forms of action. Globale Rødder was an activist network created in 2001 in Denmark in view of the country's status as host of an EU Summit the following year. The idea of the organizers, several of whom later participated in the above-mentioned study circle in order to make sense of their own practices, was to create a Danish expression of the radical strain of the alter-globalization movement inspired by Italian activists that went under the name of Tute Bianche.

Tute Bianche means 'white overalls', and the name was born as an ironic reference to the 'ghosts' of urban conflicts in Italy in the late 1990s (Bui 2001: 5).[6] Under the influence of the Italian autonomist movement (Hardt & Negri 2000; 2004; Juris 2008), activists started wearing chemical-proof white jumpsuits, elaborate forms of padding, foam armour, and helmets at demonstrations and direct actions, and described themselves as 'a ghost army' bent on developing a new language of direct action (Bui 2001; Juris 2008). When in the streets, the elaborate white clothing marked a visibly distinct style compared to the black bloc, a form of action developed by German left radical activists in the 1980s.[7] By virtue of their padded bodies, activists from the Tute Bianche entered into a spectacularly confrontational yet non-violent clash with the police in order to stage a conflict over the laws, institutions, and norms of the political and economic order.

During the 1980s, Danish activists, or squatters as they were called at the time, were preoccupied with establishing autonomous social centres and with squatting empty buildings ripe for condemnation in order to create alternative living spaces (Karpantschof & Mikkelsen 2009: 33–4; Mikkelsen & Karpantschof 2001: 615). By 1990, however, the Danish police had evicted almost all the squatted houses as part of an urban gentrification process. The evictions turned increasingly violent, and after years of intense conflict activists began looking to other projects and political issues. On 18 May 1993, activists blocked streets and declared 'their' neighbourhood 'an EU-free zone' in contempt of the Danish ratification of the Maastricht Treaty. The day ended with eleven activists wounded by live ammunition and around a hundred police with varying degrees of injury. Following this, the police revised the operational concept of the riot police (Vittrup 2002), and some groups of activists started reconsidering the expediency of entering into near-symmetrical confrontations with them.

Several Danish activists participated in the first summit protests on European soil, and, in Prague in 2000 (see Juris 2005; 2008), they encountered the Tute Bianche. The inspiration from these events led to the formation of Globale Rødder, and the protests around the EU summit in Copenhagen in 2002 became the first attempt to adapt the 'confrontational civil disobedience' of the Italian activists to a Danish context.

During the EU summit in Copenhagen in 2002, a division became evident within the left radical scene in Copenhagen. While there was agreement to oppose and confront the meeting of ministers at the Bella Centre summit venue, there were disagreements regarding the tactics and means of doing so. A Danish Anarchist Federation was formed, which favoured black bloc demonstrations. Globale Rødder, on the other hand, organized what was supposed to be a 'confrontational action of civil disobedience', with the participation of visiting Tute Bianche activists, among others, which resulted in a

Journal of the Royal Anthropological Institute (N.S.), 78-95
© Royal Anthropological Institute 2015

highly symbolic transgression of a barrier around the summit venue at the Bella Centre on the outskirts of Copenhagen.

It is possible to follow references to and variations on this form of 'confrontational civil disobedience' action over the next seven years. Globale Rødder was dissolved around 2003, but activists from the network were subsequently involved in a host of other initiatives on the extra-parliamentary left. Around 2007 and 2008, the first generation of activists from Globale Rødder was no longer involved in street protests, but the 'confrontational civil disobedience' was again taken up by younger activists, only a few of whom had participated in the 2002 action at the Bella Centre. This reinvention of the form of action occurred in the context of a fight over the eviction of an activist-run social centre known as Ungdomshuset (the Youth House), which was one of the few places left following the wave of evictions in the late 1980s.

Ungdomshuset was evicted, and the building torn down, but the protests, which also counted on the significant participation of left radical activists from abroad, continued to grow, together with a demand for a new social centre. Six months after the eviction, an action called G13 – named after the address at Grøndalsvænge Allé No. 13 where activists had announced that their new social centre was to be located – was organized with the significant participation of the younger generation of activists from Globale Rødder. The reinvention of form that G13 entailed was influenced by activists' participation in the protests against the G8 meeting in Heiligendamm in Germany, where a large mass action successfully blocked the entrances to the summit venue. The blockade in Heiligendamm consisted in five strands or so-called 'fingers', which acted independently of one another but under a shared 'action codex'. In large activist gatherings, a 'diversity of tactics' had been agreed upon in order to agglutinate groups on the extra-parliamentary left, because it allowed groups with different tactical preferences to work together in a common choreography of action. At the G13 action, instead of fingers, participants divided into four colour-coded blocs, each of which prepared its own tactics for reaching and squatting the house on the day of the action and, in this way, the single action managed to encompass activists of different tactical inclinations (i.e. different ways of entering into conflict with the police). The four blocs followed different routes after meeting the first police blockade and, at Grøndalsvænge, the action ended with activists from the yellow 'queer-feminist' bloc placing a pirate flag on the rooftop of the building, in spite of the police who had besieged the area since the previous day (see Krøijer 2008; and Krøijer & Sjørslev 2011 for an encompassing description). The participants considered the day a great success, even though they were soon arrested. Vigga,[8] who had participated in the planning of the yellow bloc, described the success as a bodily sense of strength:

> It was really cool to break through the fence and get onto the site, but it did not compare with the victories on the way there: to pass the police line, and the incredible strength and force in 'now we walk in chains together', and 'we stick together', and 'we do not give a damn that the police is here' … If I sometimes feel powerless then there is an enormous strength in taking back the street and setting the agenda … If I have to think of one moment where I felt that way strongly, then it was when we were on our way to Grøndalsvænge with a yellow bloc and managed to get around the police line; or the situation that emerged in Nørrebro the night after Ungeren [slang for Ungdomshuset] was evicted (cited in Krøijer & Sjørslev 2011: 99).

The next day the media criticized the police for using excessive force and, soon after, negotiations regarding a new house were opened. The organizers also found that the action had helped to mobilize and engage a large number of new activists, create a vibrant scene with many inventive activities, and overcome the internal conflicts concerning tactics and violence that had characterized the milieu for years.

To many participants, G13 became exemplary, apt for context-dependent innovation and renewal during subsequent actions, and around six months later, in the spring of 2008, a handful of activists started talking about organizing a similar action but with the objective of addressing what they saw as the increasing racism and xenophobia of Danish society. The new action, which entailed adapting the form to a different situation and agenda, became known as 'Luk Lejren' ('Shut Down the Camp') and was aimed at shutting down a refugee retention centre in the countryside north of Copenhagen. Instead of dividing into four blocs from the outset, the participants stuck together in a procession of demonstrators until they reached the gates of the retention centre. Here, two fingers broke off from the main demonstration, spread out across the open field, and sought to outrun or outsmart the police by slipping through the gaps that would open up in the police line, thereby taking up and adapting another element from the G8 blockades in Heiligendamm. This gave the action a more decentralized form, which allowed some of the participants to reach and cut down part of the fence around the retention centre, although, in doing so, they did not manage to do more than to shut the camp down for the day.

A few months before Shut Down the Camp took place, Danish activists became aware that Copenhagen had been chosen to host the Climate Summit (COP 15) in December 2009. Subsequently, a group of activists under the name of 'the climate collective' called for the first international planning meeting a year and a half ahead of the summit. At these international planning meetings, of which three were held in Copenhagen, visiting activists hammered out the choreography and concept of action. Apart from participating in a large peaceful demonstration co-organized with large sections of civil society, activists decided to organize another mass action of civil disobedience named Reclaim Power.

At one of these meetings, taking place in Freetown Christiania[9] and also hosting and feeding the approximately fifty foreign participants, long discussions as to the exact target of the action were developed, giving some insight into how forms of actions circulate and set new actions of protest in motion. A number of factors are taken into consideration in these discussions, namely the previous experiences of participants and what has been learned from other actions, knowledge of police tactics, the possibilities of the landscape, and the likely public reactions. At the meeting, a consensus was reached to try to topple the fence around the summit venue in order to create 'a third space between inside and outside' where a people's assembly on climate change could be held. This suggestion to create 'a third space', which came from a few participants from the Italian Ya Basta Network (former Tute Bianche), two of whom had also been in Copenhagen for the EU summit in 2002, was recognized by other participants as a 'new thing'.[10] The idea of a people's assembly – where direct democracy could be exercised in the vicinity of the formal Conference of the Parties – was selected as the aim after an array of other alternatives, such as seeking to enter the Bella Centre to disrupt the official meeting or seeking out alternative targets in the city, had been discussed in depth. Throughout the meeting, the debates remained on a tactical plane, concerned with the appropriateness and persuasiveness of various forms of action, while a joint analysis of the official climate change policy was never part of the agenda. It was also agreed that the Reclaim Power action would consist of three blocs, each following a different route and employing 'a variety of tactics' to reach and cross the fence around the summit venue at the Bella Centre in Copenhagen. The participants in the blue bloc planned to walk together and collectively push their bodies against the police line – without hitting, kicking, or throwing objects – and to help each other climb or tear down the fence (similar to the choreography of most summits, and to G13). Modelling themselves on bee behaviour, a green bloc applying a 'swarming tactic' and consisting of small groups of activists intended to move in concert but without a central leader so as to converge on the fence (similar to Shut Down the Camp and tactics during riots). And finally, a newly invented 'bike bloc' was organized by British activists who were planning to transform discarded bikes found in the street into imaginative two-deck bicycles, bicycles with loudspeakers to give the impression of an approaching crowd, and bicycles elaborately welded together that would make it possible to jump the fence or to block a two-lane road (Krøijer 2013: 46). In their planning, activists took elements from previous actions, layering examples on top of other examples, whereby they came to extrapolate from these without providing an exact imitation, and without relying on an overarching script or programme they could still produce 'surfaces of recognizable form' (Gaonkar & Povinelli 2003: 396).

Aske, a 24-year-old activist from Copenhagen, and one of my key interlocutors who had participated in both G13 and Shut Down the Camp, had become involved rather late in the planning for the Climate Summit. 'We have a Bella Centre complex', he argued after the meeting. 'After that wimpy action in 2002, we don't even believe ourselves that we will be able to topple that fence and make a forceful action'. Even though this feeling was shared by at least a handful of other Danish activists, however, most participants were young or came from other countries and had no association with the 2002 action organized by Globale Rødder, and put their backs into the planning of the Reclaim Power action.

Reclaim Power

On the morning of the action,[11] which was cold with a hint of snow in the air, the blue bloc left Tårnby train station close to the summit venue at 9 a.m. accompanied by a sound truck to provide speeches, chants, music, and, not least, guidance to the participants on how to proceed. The bloc counted some 4,000 at most, which was fewer than the 100,000 people who had turned out four days earlier in a common demonstration to call on politicians to take action on climate change. The Bella Centre was only a short distance away, but the participants were forced to walk slowly owing to the police vans on their flanks, which continued to close in on the demonstration. Way before the bloc had reached its goal, everybody was walking in a tight formation with arms locked together.

There was a moment of hesitation as the blue bloc reached the perimeter of the Bella Centre, which is surrounded by open fields. Nobody took the initiative to storm the police line that had taken up position in front of a row of vans and a tall fence. People were urged to move left of the sound truck, which was decorated with an oversized bolt cutter, materializing a collective intention to cut down the fence. Immediately prior to the collective push against the police line, Iza, an experienced activist trainer standing on the sound truck, made everybody repeat her words (quoted from my memory):

Iza:	First we will take three steps to the left . . .
Everybody:	First we will take three steps to the left . . .
Iza:	then we will count down from ten . . .
Everybody:	then we will count down from ten . . .

> *Iza*:   then we will push and push until we get over the fence!
> *Everybody*:   then we will push and push until we get over the fence!

During the Reclaim Power action, activists proceeded in accordance with Iza's, or rather their own, words. From the sound truck there was a countdown: '10, 9, 8 ... Push! Push!' everybody screamed. But the police stood their ground, barring access to the fence, thus producing a tight pack of Italian Ya Basta activists, British climate campers, and Swedish, German, and Danish left radical activists between the sound truck and the police line. There was a period of serious chaos, screaming and pushing, which lasted for around twenty minutes.

After the first three pushes there was a brief pause. Several participants had padded their bodies to endure the beating of the riot police, who had formed a ring around the fence. Many were squashed while trying to squeeze through the police line and, meanwhile, others were being pulled out of the crowd to get treatment for pepper spray from the accompanying street medics. The pushing assembled a collective body of people that began to roll in waves, and where the movement of one part instantly impinged on the rest. Some people reported afterwards that they had been unable to breathe or attained a 'joined breathing', simply because their movements and breathing had become indiscernible from those of the people around them.

Only a few activists from the bike bloc made it across a muddy stream into the summit area on air mattresses, and they were quickly arrested. Another group pressed themselves against the police line with a big inflatable rubber dinghy while chanting, 'This is not a riot; this is not a riot!' Riot police moved in from behind, and managed to get through to the sound truck, where the two Danish spokespersons were arrested. In the end, when it proved impossible to climb or topple the fence, and hence to meet a group of delegates coming from the inside, the protesters settled for holding the planned people's assembly on climate change right there in the snowy street (Krøijer 2013: 47–9).

A few days after the action, Aske and I were walking along the street looking for a pub. He had followed the front line of the action from the accompanying sound truck and vividly recalled the intensive pushing:

> It was actually amazing how close we were. They [the police] were overwhelmed by that first push, and we were so close to getting through. I could see it from the truck: it was just like one big body acting together. All this talk about forming a new movement: in these situations, you *are* the movement.

This experience of becoming 'one big body acting together' is not unusual at actions, and is often connected to the physical compression produced when clashing with the police (Krøijer 2010; 2011). When the form is effective, it coincides with the intense experience of strength and freedom of action, which Vigga was referring to above. The change in the experiential state of the body involves both its form – from singular bodies to a kind of collective body – and a change in its state of vitality (cf. Gell 1980). Bodily 'affect' is the term Brian Massumi has employed to describe this augmentation of the body's capacity to act (1987: xvi). Here, the collective affect of the body, simultaneously one and multiple, is – as I shall discuss later – however vaguely and momentarily, creating a figure that binds these actions together. The collective strength and freedom of action simultaneously is and figurates what is not yet.

By looking at protests over a stretch of time, it becomes possible to appreciate how the forms of actions travel, as examples for other actions, between groups and countries and between subject matters. According to activists' own theory, each action implies both a repetition and a deviation in relation to previous ones. This sometimes produces a sense of unproductive repetition of past failures owing to a lack of historical awareness or power of innovation, but at others times it is experienced as a creative renovation of forms of action, which imbues people with a sense of emerging direction.

Style and sideways innovation

'A number two is always a downer' (*en to'er er altid nedtur*), Aske explained to me in a discussion we had about the multiple smaller squatting actions following on from the G13 action in 2008. He was thereby implying that exact repetitions should be avoided as this would entail a kind of bodily depression or standstill, in contrast to the 'movement' and vitality that the collective body entails (Krøijer 2014). The expectation that no action should be completely like a past one points to something crucial in this 'native' theory of change because it implies that past examples should always push new examples along, or leak into them. They connect sidewards, as Massumi says (2002: 16–18), setting things in motion in unexpected directions. Among activists the demand for something 'new' is constant, but the question is obviously how does the new come about, apart from being propelled by this avoidance of exact replication?

In the previous sections, I have described how past protest events come to serve as examples for new actions. The forms of action circulate among activists across the globe – via face-to-face meetings, on the Internet, and through mainstream media reporting from protests. In anthropology, a discussion of this easily activates a classic discussion on the circulation of cultural forms in times of globalization (see Appadurai 1996; Gaonkar & Povinelli 2003; Lee & LiPuma 2002). Arjun Appadurai's (1990) argument about global flows, on the one hand, presupposes rather static units – the communities of interpretation or contexts – that adapt and transform the circulating forms. Gaonkar and Povinelli, on the other hand, argue for a focus on the changing power constellations of 'demanding environments', and how they come to produce 'surfaces of recognizable form' (2003: 396). In so doing they advocate an attention to 'transfiguration' instead of meaning-centred translation (2003: 394–5), which I take to mean a consideration of how forms are shaped by relations of power, change, and leak sideways into one another on a horizontal plane while still being recognizable as a distinct class of phenomena.

When looking at circulating forms of action among left radical activists, neither context nor forms of actions can be held steady and stable. Nevertheless, activists themselves make the connection between the discrete events, and hence come to constitute the actions as a class of phenomena (confrontational civil disobedience actions). To understand how this comes about when both contexts and forms of action are changing – among other reasons owing to the constant demand for something new – one needs to pay attention to the activists' concept of style.

At the large planning meetings taking place prior to actions, activists' process of analysis revolves around the notion of style. Previous experiences are brought up and analysed and a new 'concept of action' is outlined and agreed upon via consensus. In the process, activists make assessments about what is considered 'good' and 'bad' style (*god og dårlig stil*). The concept of style embodies concerns over what constitute appropriate actions for the situation at hand, what forms will persuade fellow activists (and the police) to take part in events, and, not least, what forms will have the best effect in terms of producing the sense of strength and freedom of action described above. In this process, the plans for new actions are evaluated against a number of past examples, but context-specific knowledge, for instance about the urban terrain and police tactics, is also brought into the picture. Activists' collective analysis may give rise to new forms of action such as the people's assembly and the bike bloc, which became crucial elements in the Reclaim Power action. A concept of action 'with a good style' is said to demand a relatively clear idea as well as an inventive and appropriate form that can be communicated to fellow activists. The form must not be too rigid but must accommodate the diversity of tactics discussed above, and innovation is praised. In sum, activists do not scale single actions against an abstract scale external to the actions such as a fixed protest template (a universal form), a clear idea of an ideal society (an end-point), or an ideological programme as found in party politics or traditional social movements.[12] What activists talk and think of as 'good style' is internal to the phenomenon itself, which distinguishes their theory from traditional anthropological theories of circulation.

A successful action produces an organic transformation of activist practices (multiple bodies becoming one), and a fleeting sense of profound change in the moment of action (strength, freedom). This leads me to the second element in activists' theory of change, namely the way that actions replicate within. In theoretical terms this refers to how examples extend inwards to other incipient examples (Massumi 2002: 16–17), thereby 'replicating across scales' (Wagner 1991: 166). The following example – a trip to collect discarded food from supermarket containers during the preparation meeting for the Reclaim Power action in the context of the COP 15 in Copenhagen – both shows how a detail opened up is as complex and as exemplary to activists as the action from which it emerged, and draws attention to a figure that replicates itself though all traditional shifts of scale.

A dumpster dive

During the international preparation meeting for the climate summit in Copenhagen, meals were prepared three times a day to feed the visiting activists. In the following, I describe a trip during those days to forage for food in supermarket containers:

I meet up with a group of seven people a little after 9 p.m., nobody I knew well except for Naya, whom I had met during the meeting. She is 27 years old, a dedicated shoplifter, dumpster diver, and vegan, and has lived almost all her life in Christiania. It is freezing cold and I am full of foreboding. I have been allowed to participate in a trip to forage for food in supermarket containers – food that is to be served as a free meal at a meeting preparing for the Climate Summit. Naya has said it will be okay for me to come along as long as I don't mention names or our exact whereabouts. I have been told to bring a flashlight, preferably a headlamp, and gloves if I do not feel like touching the garbage.

The plan is to split up into groups so as not to attract too much attention, and go to different supermarkets to 'recover' food to serve at the meeting the following day. I cycle with Naya and another young woman to a supermarket in Frederiksberg, a wealthier and conservative municipality within Copenhagen. The supermarket is located along a road with several lanes coming from the city centre, although at this time of night only few cars speed by. My head is full of questions, but I wonder if we can speak. 'They tend to throw out nice stuff', Naya says, 'and the container cannot be locked'. I ask if it is illegal to dumpster dive. 'Not really', she replies. 'When it's thrown away, it's not their property any more, unless the container's locked, of course'. 'Can we talk or is it best not to be detected?' I ask. 'It's probably best to whisper', says a young woman with a crew-cut, who I learn is called Anja and is a 'radical feminist'.

Journal of the Royal Anthropological Institute (N.S.), 78-95
© Royal Anthropological Institute 2015

We arrive. We park our bikes around the corner from the supermarket, which has now closed, and walk down a small alley. After some 20 metres, the alley runs into a backyard and I realize that the light is still on in many apartments overlooking the back entrance to the supermarket. Luckily, it seems to be too cold for people to be outside at this time of night. I can see that Anja and Naya have been here before from the way they walk directly towards a large blue container located near the supermarket entrance. Anja slips her gloves on, lifts herself up to the edge, and jumps in. 'You are welcome to stay here', Naya whispers. My face must have revealed that I am not too comfortable about the whole thing; I keep imagining how my feet will sink into day-old minced meat. I feel acutely that this is against everything I have ever learned but, nevertheless, follow her into the container.

I am on firm ground. The sweet smell of decay hits my face and I try to block my sense of smell. A small heap of vegetables is visible at the farther side of the container but, apart from this, I can see mostly grey plastic. 'How do you know what to take?' I ask. Naya explains:

> It's not too difficult really. Look at the bread and vegetables: if it's not visibly rotten or mouldy, you can eat it. We don't touch the meat or the milk products, but that's because we are vegans, you know. I wouldn't recommend taking home meat, but it's not hard to detect if the milk products are too old. It's just like in the refrigerator at home.

Anja abruptly adds: 'The best way to know what to eat is to take a sniff of it'. After fumbling about for a while, we find a common rhythm. They dig and I hold a green box to carry home the vegetables while I carefully avoid touching the sludge on the sides of the container.

For a while Anja and Naya sink into their own little world and the only sound is that of plastic being ripped. They are quite systematic and consumed by their endeavour: every single plastic bag is ransacked, and the small heaps of garbage are gone over with a trained motion of the hand. I try to participate but continually pause in order to listen for sounds from the outside. Nobody disturbs us. Naya digs out several bags of pasta from a plastic bag at the bottom of the container, and Anja laughs and presents them to me. 'I am amazed at how much is thrown away', I say. 'Yes', Anja replies in a much friendlier voice now. 'We've been lucky today. There are often huge amounts of nice food on Saturdays. There's nothing wrong with it. It's kind of gross actually; they prefer to trash it than to give it to somebody in need'. She pauses. 'But it's funny to know that you can live off the stuff that other people throw away'. I start digging too and am soon carried away by a feeling that it actually makes a difference.

I lose my sense of time, but after what seems like 15 or 20 minutes, we leave. We quickly load the green boxes onto Naya's platform bike, and throw some empty rubbish bags back in the container. Naya's bike is loaded with tomatoes, peppers, squashes, onions, apples, and a few other fruits and vegetables. We also found pasta, two cartons of soya milk, tea, chips, and biscuits. 'We were lucky with the tea. You seldom find that', Naya says. 'It must be beginner's luck', I reply with a smile, relieved that nobody detected us halfway through. 'What do you do if somebody turns up?' I ask.

> A lot of people don't mind; we leave the place tidy. Sometimes I just leave if people get angry, and come back later. It's bad style (*dårlig stil*) to make a mess. But once I got into a discussion with a man who shouted that we should get ourselves a job. I tried to explain to him how stupid it is to throw out a box of apples just because one has a brown spot.

Journal of the Royal Anthropological Institute (N.S.), 78-95
© Royal Anthropological Institute 2015

Silence falls on us again. It is freezing cold, and Anja and Naya take turns with one pair of gloves as we bike back to the kitchen with our findings. The other two groups have not arrived yet. 'We need to buy oil tomorrow unless the others have found some. If they turn up at all, that is', Anja says in a sulky voice. 'Anyway, we can make a pickle of the peppers'. We are all exhausted, but carefully wash and wipe dry all the vegetables while we drink tea in the large industrial kitchen filled with pots, pans, and piles of very diverse plates. Anja and Naya are not really inclined to talk of the experience, though I try to understand why they think it is worthwhile going dumpstering instead of putting their energy into organizing the summit protest. I am offered various explanations: Naya tells me that 'dumpstering is as important as the protest' and that it gives her a sense of 'being able to do something' and 'the strength to continue'. Anja lets me know that this is how it is done at international meetings, where money is seldom available to pay for food.

The next day our findings are served as delicious vegan dishes. Large portions of pickled peppers, pasta, and a lentil dish with vegetables are handed out to a long queue of people from behind a serving table. Next to the pile of plates is a little plastic cup for donations, but collections are meagre and the organizers end up paying a part of the expenses for the meeting out of their own pockets.

The example as theory of change

Every night, Danish supermarkets fill their rubbish bins with food past its sell-by date, and every night an increasing number of activists and young people turn up to collect the discarded unspoiled food. The practice of dumpster diving seems to have grown since the mid-1990s. Many young left radical activists have tried dumpster diving, although only a minority collect all or most of their food from the bins of supermarkets, bakeries, and restaurants. Activists explain that in this way they are able to liberate themselves from capitalism (albeit only momentarily).

Exemplification is the only plausible way to do radical politics when capitalism, as discussed above, is perceived as a pervading circumstance of life. On the traditional Marxist left in Western Europe, the revolution has often been thought of as a turning-point in time at which one system of rule is replaced with another. The moment of revolution rests on the idea of a linear accumulation of people and forces until the awaiting workers can finally 'storm the Winter Palace' (Maeckelbergh 2009). Eating as a revolution does not fit into this picture, and this points to the fact that both the meaning of and way of practising radical politics have changed on the European extra-parliamentary left. Rather than waiting, or organizing for, a future turning-point, activists seek to 'build the new within the shell of the old' (Graeber 2009: 203; see also Gibson-Graham 1993), as an anarchist catchphrase goes. This is epitomized in 'revolution is the way you eat', which implies radically changing the world in its unfolding.[13] Ideally, however, the practice would need to expand for dumpster diving to be a plausible theory of change. Both dumpster diving and protesting rest on the ability to persuade others to come along, and thereby on the ability to set examples for the actions of oneself and others. The persuasive power depends in part on the stories circulating about 'hunters' luck' and bragging about where and how to make a 'good find'. It depends also, as Naya phrased it, on maintaining a 'good style' (*god stil*): that is, on developing an appropriate form in the course of action.

During our conversation in the kitchen, Naya makes an analogy between dumpster diving and protesting, stating that one is as important as the other. In Naya's explanation, dumpstering generates a sense of 'strength' and 'self-reliance', which mirrors Vigga and other activists' concern for 'strength' and freedom of movement in the context of protesting. The comparison points to a very particular equivalence where each event stands for everything else (in terms of the potential for changing capitalism). This makes a figure replicate across scale: both kinds of action are, according to activists, characterized by embodying the solution to the problem they are addressing. In my terms, this fleeting sense of bodily strength, or intensity, as Massumi puts it, and of materializing the solution, is a figuration. It entails a bodily *figuration* of an otherwise indeterminate future (Krøijer 2010; 2013; in press). In both kinds of action, there is a fusion of what are conventionally seen as means and ends, which underlines that there is a qualitatively different temporal figure involved in activist politics. The future folds into the present and becomes a co-present bodily perspective which is epitomized in the 'becoming one big body acting together' described by Aske in connection to the Reclaim Power action. It is not a model of or for the revolution to come; the moment of intensity in the dumpster simply *is* radical change unfolding. There is, then, no obvious distinction between action and ideology or theory as is usually the case in political movements. So what dumpster diving as 'example' does is not only to imbue activists with a sense of agency; it also performs work on time, meaning that the example and what is exemplified become one and the same.

What can we learn from the activist theory of change, if placing activist 'theory' of change on a par with anthropological theory? Or, put differently, how has anthropology generalized by way of examples, and how can activists' way of living change through exemplification inform this?

Generalization in anthropology involves movements of comparison and scaling – we need only think of the way Lévi-Strauss (1963) compared hundreds of myths, or how the Manchester School despised the 'myopia of the local' (Kapferer 2006; 2010) and argued for a rigorous comparison within the same regional context. The situational analysis of the Manchester School, championed by Max Gluckman in *Analysis of a social situation in modern Zululand* (1958 [1940]), promoted a meticulous registration of an excess of detail in order to counter a tendency, which Gluckman associated with Sir James Frazer, of simply using the case or example as a curious or apt illustration of an existing theoretical point. However, the regional comparison, one of the prime methods of the Manchester School for reaching higher levels of generalization, also involves turning cases into an expression of general rules. As opposed to Lévi-Strauss's effort to make generalizations through the comparison of an impressive number of myths, Clifford Geertz (1973) opted for in-depth description as the road to reaching deeper insights into human culture. In this view, anthropology is a kind of science whose task it is to generalize about patterns of meaning. In the case of Geertz, and of Gluckman for that matter, exemplification should be far more than illustrations of existing theoretical points. They were seen as analytical as much as empirical constructs, but the scaling involved in generalizing from examples continued to be fairly traditional, resting on a clear distinction between the particular and the universal.

Marilyn Strathern has something interesting to offer to this debate in *Partial connections*. In her interpretation, scale articulates how anthropologists shift 'from one perspective on a phenomenon to another' (Strathern 2004 [1991]: xiv). She employs the metaphor of the map and the tree to describe the two ways that anthropologists scale their objects: the map implies a move of either 'zooming in' to get more detail, or 'zooming out' to gain increased overview of multiple phenomena. Zooming out, studying a hundred myths instead of just one, often entails the idea that the analysis becomes increasingly complex (Holbraad & Pedersen 2009: 373). The other way of scaling is like a tree, implying a move to keep the content under study stable, although it is looked at from the perspective of different domains (or branches of a disciplinary tree) (Strathern 2004 [1991]: xiv), for example from an economic or religious perspective. These two ways of scaling establish a certain distance that allows the 'things' to be kept separate both from each other, and from the scale that the comparison is either implicitly or explicitly plotting against (Holbraad & Pedersen 2009: 374).

The use of examples in anthropology, as also evident from my discussion of globalization and cultural circulation, is often part of a movement of 'zooming out' in order to reach a higher level of generalization. But activist exemplification shows that the distinction between the universal and the particular cannot always be upheld. A figure replicates across scale independent of an analytics of zooming in or zooming out, as in the examples of the Reclaim Power action and the dumpster dive during the preparation meeting. What I have called figuration of the future entails something similar to what Massumi (2002: 18) has described as the 'all in one' and 'one in all' quality of exemplification. As the figuration repeats itself, means and end cease to be a relevant distinction. There is nothing outside the example, which also means that activist exemplification opens up the possibility of being particular and universal in the same movement.

Anthropologists have at different points in time experimented with developing concepts carrying an 'etymological signature' (Viveiros de Castro 2003), such as *kula* or *mana*; concepts that have the quality of being particular and universal at the same time. In the view of Eduardo Viveiros de Castro and others (e.g. Holbraad 2004), native concepts can challenge the way we think and make concepts within the discipline.[14] Here I have tried to take this a step further by making activist exemplification a model for my anthropology of the example. Unlike the concept of style (*stil*), the concept of figuration is a lexical invention that embodies a native theory of change that destabilizes the ontology of linear time still underpinning most anthropology (Hodges 2008; Munn 1992; Robbins 2007) as well as prevalent models of radical change.

My experiment has involved producing a text where the examples – as an analogy to activist exemplification – show how incipient examples (the dumpster dive) are embedded within other examples and reconfigure problematic oppositions such as the particular and the universal. Activist exemplification concerns how to find a solution to the apparent changelessness of the world, and the answer is that the world is changed by way of examples. A good 'activist' example is able to produce a strong bodily affect, an intense vital force, thereby generating a truly radical context. The expression 'revolution is the way you eat' points to how an everyday action such as eating, foraging, or making love is potentially as radical as major protest events or revolutions. These moments falling outside conventional representation are as important to the movement as they should be in anthropological writing. A good example must take on a persuasive form (have a good style), and by being put in conjunction with other actions or examples it may avoid being an exact repetition, thereby enabling anthropological theory to 'differ from itself' (Holbraad *et al.* 2014). Examples should extend sideways as well as inwards and outwards without adhering to a predefined plan or (ideological) programme, without respecting conventional perceptions of scale, in order to set new thoughts in motion.

Journal of the Royal Anthropological Institute (N.S.), 78-95
© Royal Anthropological Institute 2015

NOTES

   I thank the anonymous peer reviewers for *JRAI* as well as the editors of this special issue for their useful comments on the earlier versions of this paper. I also thank Morten Axel Pedersen and Elizabeth Povinelli for comments and inspiration.

[1] After the protests against the World Trade Organization summit in Seattle in 1999, the same tendencies have also been described as a radical strain of the alter-globalization movement (Graeber 2002, 2009; Juris 2008; Maeckelbergh 2009; Sullivan 2005), and, in the context of growing economic crisis, groups of a similar inclination have manifested themselves as 'Los Indignados' (the Indignant movement) and as the Occupy movement (Castañeda 2012; Della Porta & Andretta 2013; Juris 2012; Razsa & Kurnik 2012).

[2] Owing to the indeterminacy of the future, this cannot be reduced to a prefigurative practice (see Maeckelbergh 2009; 2011), which relies on knowing the end-point of one's political endeavours.

[3] The experiments with anthropological theorizing inherent in the ontological turn usually imply that the conceptual affordances of the ethnography are used to question and rethink the theoretical foundations of anthropological knowledge (Pedersen 2012). This attempt to 'take seriously' interlocutors' concepts and conceptions has produced vivid debate (Candea 2011*a*; 2011*b*; Heywood 2012; Holbraad 2012; Pedersen 2012; Viveiros de Castro 1998, 2003). My move comes close to that performed by Matei Candea (2011*b*) in his analysis of how the political and the non-political play out in Corsica, and the implications this might have for anthropological theorizations of politics. Taking seriously activists' concept of style and their theory of change in a context where capitalism is experienced as a pervasive circumstance of life is a way to overcome the problematic opposition of the particular and the general that has characterized much anthropology.

[4] Left radical activists are not a group in the conventional sense. They are organized in a network structure with so-called 'affinity groups', that is, groups of friends doing politics together, as the basic organizational unit (Graeber 2009: 288). Affinity groups are brought together during the planning of larger actions, or across several actions, under provisional organizational identities.

[5] In 1999, mass actions in Seattle, where approximately 50,000 people blocked the summit of the World Trade Organization (WTO), marked the beginning of a storm of protests against the meetings of global political and financial institutions such as the WTO, the EU, the G8, the World Bank, and the International Monetary Fund. The dynamo of the protest was a 'movement of movements', that is, a swarm of groups, organizations, and *ad hoc* networks with different political motives, projects, and forms of organizing (Graeber 2002; Katsiaficas 2006; Maeckelbergh 2009). This movement of movements was known as the anti-globalization movement during the protests in Seattle (Graeber 2002: 63). Other frequently used names are 'the global justice movement' and the 'alter-globalization movement' (Eschle 2005: 31; Rupert 2005: 36-7), each name highlighting different characteristics of the movement as well as the political or theoretical inclination of the writer.

[6] In the context of the eviction of a squatted social centre in Milan, Italy, the mayor of the city publicly announced, 'From now on squatters will be no more than ghosts wandering about in the city!'

[7] Black bloc is a form of action where people attending a protest wear black clothes, cover their face with masks or bandanas, and form a tight block by locking arms. This is done to avoid identification, the arrest of single persons, and to give the demonstration a militant expression (Graeber 2009; Katsiaficas 2006). Frequently, black bloc demonstrations entail vandalizing the symbols of capitalism, and sometimes lead to riots or violent clashes with the police.

[8] I use pseudonyms.

[9] Freetown Christiania is an area of former military barracks close to the centre of Copenhagen. It was squatted in 1971 and transformed into a 'free city' governed through direct democracy. Today, Christiania has approximately a thousand inhabitants and is the self-governed space in Copenhagen which has most consistently developed its own economy, activist infrastructure, and system of democratic decision-making.

[10] This new form of protest resonated with a discussion among European activists at the time about creating a presence in public space of a longer duration as an alternative to the momentary appearance characteristic of the usual summit protests (Krøijer in press). In hindsight, the assembly on climate change on the street outside the summit venue in Copenhagen, where activists who were later to be part of Occupy Wall Street were active participants, can be seen as an early expression of the new trend of more permanent activist encampments in public space.

[11] I have described this action elsewhere (see Krøijer 2013: 47-9; in press) in order to explore activist security practices and the temporalities of activist politics. My re-use of this case as part of different arguments illustrates how an ethnographic example can help to set new thoughts in motion.

[12] Hitherto, the concept of style has been associated with the renowned work of the Birmingham School (Hall & Jefferson 2006 [1975]). In the Birmingham School, style referred to the appropriation and

Journal of the Royal Anthropological Institute (N.S.), 78-95
© Royal Anthropological Institute 2015

transformation of symbolic meaning attached to dress, music, bodily postures, and language, and was tied to the construction of an oppositional identity (Clarke, Hall, Jefferson & Roberts 2006 [1975]: 40-5). Style was associated with leisure time, and countercultural experiments were expected by researchers to be co-opted and reincorporated into mainstream culture (Hebdige 2006 [1975]: 77). Several anthropologists have applied this concept in their study of anarchist, left radical, and alter-globalist activists (Juris 2008: 181-2; see also Clark 2004; Krogstad 1986), with the result that their actions are judged to have no 'real' transformatory potential. The concept of style outlined here measures the appropriateness, persuasiveness, and effectiveness of form in a sideways manner, and thereby has more in common with Marilyn Strathern's concept of aesthetics (Strathern 1988; 2004 [1991]) and the attempts to overcome the form/content dichotomy in politics (Riles 1998).

[13] Deleuze and Guattari have described this as the otherwise in the plane of immanence (1987: 266-7).

[14] In line with this idea, activists' concept of style can enable us to rethink the form/content distinction inherent in much political theory, and to understand how new forms of action develop without resting on a determinate end-point or ideological programme. Massumi's take on the relationship between theory and example is slightly different. Even if his goal is also to challenge the concepts by which we think, he takes his point of departure in theoretical concepts, and drags them into dialogue with the example by liberating the concept from its theoretical system.

REFERENCES

AGAMBEN, G. 1993. *The coming community* (trans. M. Hardt). Minneapolis: University of Minnesota Press.

APPADURAI, A. 1990. Disjuncture and difference in the global cultural economy. *Public Culture* **2: 2**, 1-24.

——— 1996. *Modernity at large: cultural dimensions of globalization*. Minneapolis: University of Minnesota Press.

BUI, R. [Wu Ming 1]. 2001. Tute Bianche: the practical side of myth-making (in catastrophic times) (available on-line: *http://www.wumingfoundation.com/english/giap/giapdigest11.html*, accessed 14 January 2015).

CANDEA, M. 2011*a*. Endo/exo. *Common Knowledge* **17**, 146-50.

——— 2011*b*. Our division of the universe: making a space for the non-political in the anthropology of politics. *Current Anthropology* **52**, 309-34.

CASTAÑEDA, E. 2012. The *Indignados* of Spain: a precedent to Occupy Wall Street. *Social Movement Studies* **11**, 309-19.

CLARK, D. 2004. The raw and the rotten: punk cuisine. *Ethnology* **43**, 19-31.

CLARKE, J., S. HALL, T. JEFFERSON & B. ROBERTS 2006 [1975]. Subcultures, culture, class. In *Resistance through rituals: youth subcultures in post-war Britain* (eds) S. Hall & T. Jefferson, 1-59. London: Routledge.

DELEUZE, G. & F. GUATTARI 1987. *A thousand plateaus: capitalism and schizophrenia* (trans. B. Massumi). Minneapolis: University of Minnesota Press.

DELLA PORTA, D. & M. ANDRETTA 2013. Protesting for justice and democracy: Italian Indignados? *Contemporary Italian Politics* **5**, 23-37.

ESCHLE, C. 2005. Skeleton women: feminism and the antiglobalisation movement. *Signs* **30**, 1741-69.

GAONKAR, D.P. & E.A. POVINELLI 2003. Technologies of public forms: circulation, transfiguration, recognition. *Public Culture* **15**, 385-97.

GEERTZ, C. 1973. *The interpretation of cultures: selected essays*. New York: Basic Books.

GELL, A. 1980. The gods at play: vertigo and possession in Muria religion. *Man* (N.S.) **15**, 219-48.

GIBSON-GRAHAM, J.-K. 1993. Waiting for the revolution, or how to smash capitalism while working at home in your spare time. *Rethinking Marxism* **6: 2**, 10-24.

GLUCKMAN, M. 1958 [1940]. *Analysis of a social situation in modern Zululand*. Manchester: University Press for the Rhodes-Livingstone Institute.

GRAEBER, D. 2002. The new Anarchists. *New Left Review* **13**, 61-73.

——— 2009. *Direct action: an ethnography*. Edinburgh: AK Press.

HALL, S. & T. JEFFERSON (eds) 2006 [1975]. *Resistance through rituals: youth subcultures in post-war Britain*. London: Routledge.

HARDT, M. & A. NEGRI 2000. *Empire*. Cambridge, Mass.: Harvard University Press.

——— & ——— 2004. *Multitude: war and democracy in the age of empire*. Cambridge, Mass.: Harvard University Press.

HEBDIGE, D. 2006 [1975]. The meaning of mod. In *Resistance through rituals: youth subcultures in post-war Britain* (eds) S. Hall & T. Jefferson, 71-9. London: Routledge.

HENARE, A., M. HOLBRAAD & S. WASTELL 2007. Introduction: thinking through things. In *Thinking through things: theorizing artefacts ethnographically* (eds) A. Henare, M. Holbraad & S. Wastell, 1-31. London: Routledge.

HEYWOOD, P. 2012. Anthropology and what there is: reflections on 'ontology'. *Cambridge Anthropology* **30**: 1, 143-51.

HODGES, M. 2008. Rethinking time's arrow: Bergson, Deleuze and the anthropology of time. *Anthropological Theory* **8**, 399-429.

HOLBRAAD, M. 2004. Defining anthropological truth. Paper for Truth conference, Cambridge, 24 September (available on-line: *http://nansi.abaetenet.net/abaetextos/defining-anthropological-truth*, accessed 14 January 2015).

————— 2012. *Truth in motion: the recursive anthropology of Cuban divination.* Chicago: University Press.

————— & M.A. PEDERSEN 2009. Planet M: the intense abstraction of Marilyn Strathern. *Anthropological Theory* **9**, 371-94.

—————, ————— & E. VIVEIROS DE CASTRO 2014. The politics of ontology: anthropological positions. *Fieldsights – Theorizing the Contemporary, Cultural Anthropology Online*, 13 January (available on-line: *http://culanth.org/fieldsights/462-the-politics-of-ontology-anthropological-positions*, accessed 14 January 2015).

JURIS, J.S. 2005. Violence performed and imagined: militant action, the black bloc and the mass media in Genoa. *Critique of Anthropology* **25**, 413-32.

————— 2008. *Networking futures: the movements against corporate globalization.* Durham, N.C.: Duke University Press.

————— 2012. Reflections on #Occupy Everywhere: social media, public space, and emerging logics of aggregation. *American Ethnologist* **39**, 259-79.

KAPFERER, B. 2006. Situations, crisis and the anthropology of the concrete: the contributions of Max Gluckman. In *The Manchester School: practice and ethnographic praxis in anthropology* (eds) T.M.S. Evans & D. Handelman, 118-56. Oxford: Berghahn.

————— 2010. Introduction: in the event – toward an anthropology of generic moments. *Social Analysis* **54**: 3, 1-27.

KARPANTSCHOF, R. & F. MIKKELSEN 2009. Kampen om byens rum: Ungdomshuset, Christiania og husbesættelser i København 1965–2008. In *Kampen om Ungdomshuset: studier i et oprør* (eds) R. Karpantschof & M. Lindblom, 19-40. Copenhagen: Frydlund og Monsun.

KATSIAFICAS, G. 2006. *The subversion of politics: European autonomous social movements and the decolonization of everyday life.* Oakland, Calif.: AK Press.

KROGSTAD, A. 1986. Punk symbols on a concrete background: from external provocation to internal moralism. *Tidsskrift for Samfunnsforskning* **27**, 499-527.

KRØIJER, S. 2008. Direkte aktion: utopisk nutid blandt venstre-radikale unge. *Jordens Folk* **4**, 56-62.

————— 2010. Figurations of the future: on the form and temporality of protests among left radical activists in Europe. *Social Analysis* **54**: 3, 139-52.

————— 2013. Security is a collective body: intersecting temporalities of security around the Climate Summit in Copenhagen. In *Times of security: ethnographies of fear, protest and the future* (eds) M. Holbraad & M.A. Pedersen, 33-56. New York: Routledge.

————— 2014. Aske's dead time: an exploration of the qualities of time among left radical activists in Denmark. In *Ethnographies of youth and temporality: time objectified* (eds) A.L. Dalsgård, M.D. Frederiksen, S. Højlund & L. Meinert, 57-80. Philadelphia: Temple University Press.

————— in press. *Figurations of the future: forms and temporalities of left radical activism in Northern Europe.* Oxford: Berghahn.

————— & I. SJØRSLEV 2011. Autonomy and the spaciousness of the social: the conflict between Ungdomshuset and Faderhuset in Denmark. *Social Analysis* **55**: 2, 84-105.

LEE, B. & E. LIPUMA 2002. Cultures of circulation: the imaginations of modernity. *Public Culture* **14**, 191-213.

LÉVI-STRAUSS, C. 1963. The structural study of myth. In *Structural anthropology* (trans. C. Jacobson & B.G. Schoepf), 201-12. New York: Basic Books.

MAECKELBERGH, M. 2009. *The will of the many: how the alterglobalization movement is changing the face of democracy.* New York: Pluto.

————— 2011. Doing is believing: prefiguration as strategic practice in the alterglobalization movement. *Social Movement Studies* **10**, 1-20.

MASSUMI, B. 1987. Notes on the translation and acknowledgements. In *A thousand plateaus: capitalism and schizophrenia*, G. Deleuze & F. Guattari (trans. B. Massumi), xvi-xx. Minneapolis: University of Minnesota Press.

———— 2002. *Parables of the virtual: movement, affect, sensation.* Durham, N.C.: Duke University Press.

MIKKELSEN, F. & R. KARPANTSCHOF 2001. Youth as a political movement: development of the squatters and autonomous movement in Copenhagen 1981–1995. *International Journal of Urban and Regional Research* **25**, 609-28.

MIYAZAKI, H. 2004. *The method of hope: anthropology, philosophy, and Fijian knowledge.* Stanford: University Press.

MUNN, N.D. 1992. The cultural anthropology of time: a critical essay. *Annual Review of Anthropology* **21**, 93-123.

PEDERSEN, M.A. 2011. *Not quite shamans: spirit worlds and political lives in northern Mongolia.* Ithaca, N.Y.: Cornell University Press.

———— 2012. Common nonsense: a review of certain recent reviews of the 'ontological turn'. *Anthropology of This Century* **5** (available on-line: *http://aotcpress.com/articles/common_nonsense/*, accessed 14 January 2015).

RAZSA, M. & A. KURNIK 2012. The Occupy movement in Žižek's hometown: direct democracy and a politics of becoming. *American Ethnologist* **39**, 238-58.

RILES, A. 1998. Infinity within the brackets. *American Ethnologist* **25**, 378-98.

ROBBINS, J. 2007. Continuity thinking and the problem of Christian culture: belief, time, and the anthropology of Christianity. *Current Anthropology* **48**, 5-37.

RUPERT, M. 2005. In the belly of the beast: resisting globalisation and war in a neo-imperial moment. In *Critical theories, international relations, and 'the anti-globalisation movement': the politics of global resistance* (eds) C. Eschle and B. Maiguashca, 36-52. London: Routledge.

STRATHERN, M. 1988. *The gender of the gift.* Berkeley: University of California Press.

———— 2004 [1991]. *Partial connections.* Lanham, Md: AltaMira Press.

SULLIVAN, S. 2005. 'We are heartbroken and furious!': Violence and the (anti-)globalisation movement(s). In *Critical theories, international relations, and 'the anti-globalisation movement': the politics of global resistance* (eds) C. Eschle & B. Maiguashca, 174-94. London: Routledge.

VITTRUP, K. 2002. *Operation.* Copenhagen: Københavns Politi.

VIVEIROS DE CASTRO, E. 1998. Cosmological deixis and Amerindian perspectivism. *Journal of the Royal Anthropological Institute* (N.S.) **4**, 469-88.

———— 2003. AND. After-dinner speech at 'Anthropology and Science', the 5th Decennial Conference of the Association of Social Anthropologists of Great Britain and Commonwealth, 14 July. *Manchester Papers in Social Anthropology* **7** (available on-line: *http://nansi.abaetenet.net/abaetextos/anthropology-and-science-e-viveiros-de-castro*, accessed 14 January 2015).

WAGNER, R. 1991. The fractal person. In *Big men and great men: personifications of power in Melanesia* (eds) M. Godelier & M. Strathern, 159-73. Cambridge: University Press.

La révolution dans l'assiette : création d'exemples parmi les activistes d'extrême-gauche danois et en anthropologie

Résumé

En anthropologie, les exemples ont toujours fait partie intégrante de l'étude de la vie sociale. Parfois réduits à de minces illustrations des idées générales ou des théories d'un auteur, ils peuvent aussi contribuer à la naissance de nouvelles idées. L'article explore le rôle de l'exemple parmi des activistes d'extrême-gauche dans le cadre des manifestations accompagnant le Sommet sur le climat (COP 15) à Copenhague et d'une maraude à la recherche de produits alimentaires jetés dans la poubelle d'un supermarché pour nourrir ces activistes. L'auteure avance que les exemples constituent une théorie du changement qui élude les distinctions problématiques entre le particulier et l'universel et met en marche de nouvelles actions dans un plan horizontal sans s'appuyer sur un plan ou un but prédéfini. Elle esquisse les manières dont on pourrait ainsi éclairer l'utilisation d'exemples dans la discipline anthropologique.

6

The failed image and the possessed: examples of invisibility in visual anthropology and Islam

CHRISTIAN SUHR *Aarhus University*

This paper asks whether an exploration of responses to visual media in neo-orthodox Islam could provide new answers to the recurrent queries regarding the value of images in visual anthropology. It proposes that the photographic image shares a curious resemblance to the bodies of people possessed by invisible spirits called jinn. The image as a failed example or model of reality works like the possessed body as an amplifier of invisibility pointing towards that which cannot be seen, depicted visually, or represented in writing. This suggests a negative epistemology in which images obtain their value not from the adequacy of their correspondence to perceived reality, but rather from the ways they fail to exemplify that which they appear to depict.

Let us consider an image from a YouTube video entitled '7000 year old jinn inside man', (Fig. 1).[1] Several features about this image may strike us as peculiar. A man with a thick black beard dressed in a white *jalabiya* and a turban sits to the right of the image frame. The dress and physical appearance suggest that this could be a Muslim of some dedication – a shaykh perhaps, a person with religious training and authority. While looking out towards the lower left corner, presumably speaking to a person who sits outside the frame, the shaykh points his finger directly at the face of another man sitting behind him to the left side of the image frame. This man is dressed in dark trousers and a white shirt. He is wearing a white cap of the sort many Muslims use for praying – a *taqiyya*. His eyes are covered by large sunglasses but he appears to stare directly back at the shaykh, pointing at his face. A green speech bubble translates the shaykh's words. He is telling us that the person he is pointing at is in fact a jinn and that 'the jinn has just told us that jinn are able to possess humans'.

The image presents us with an example in at least two senses. The person wearing the black sunglasses is allegedly a case example of jinn possession – an instantiation of the type of event in which invisible agencies take residence in the visible world. The example, in this sense, works as an illustration of a range of phenomena that can be grouped within the category of spirit possession.

Journal of the Royal Anthropological Institute (N.S.), 96-112
© Royal Anthropological Institute 2015

Figure 1. Still of screen image from the video '7000 year old jinn inside man', as featured in the ethnographic documentary *Descending with angels* (Suhr 2013*b*).

The image itself, however, is also an example in a different sense, namely in the sense of providing visual evidence for the existence of the case example – evidence of the fact that the case example as an event actually happened. The image is quite literally an imprint of the visible light and shadows that, at a specific moment, constituted this peculiar scene and were cast into and captured by the microchip of a camcorder. Through various digital translations, this mixture of light and shadow is now recast and presented to us as a substrate or sample of reality, an indexical proof of the existence of this body, which exemplifies for us how a human may become possessed by jinn.

According to the Qur'an and the practices and sayings of the Prophet (*sunnah*), jinn exist alongside the world of humans, but the two worlds are separated by a veil (*ḥijāb*, Qur'an 41:5). Considerable debate persists among Islamic scholars about the possibility of jinn entering the world of humans and the extent to which they are able to do this. Within vernacular traditions, cases abound in which humans enter into alliances with these invisible creatures, even to the degree of marriage and sexual reproduction (Boddy 1989; Drieskens 2008; Pandolfo 1997; Taymiyah 2007 [1409]). This stands in clear contrast to the current movements of neo-orthodox Islam often identified as Salafism, in which a call is made for a return to what is considered to be the true practice of the Prophet and his immediate companions (see, e.g., Sedgwick 2010). Many Muslims within these movements aim for a complete detachment from the world of jinn, as they argue that any interaction between the worlds of humans and jinn is essentially a violation of the divinely ordained decree of separation. Consequently, jinn who enter into the bodies of humans must be evil and have to be either exorcized or exterminated (Philips 2007).

The case example brought to us by YouTube in the form of a man wearing dark sunglasses may not immediately, by its physical outline, indicate much in the way of a hostile takeover of a human body by a malicious invisible creature. As one YouTube commenter pointed out: 'I believe in jinn ... but the video is a lie a big one!!!!' Another commenter argued that '[jinn] r way 2 smart 2 let them selves be recorded ... trust me 98% of the online recordings r fake ... this is all just made up, not real'.

Somehow the verbal postulate claiming that this man is a jinn seems not fully supported by the visible evidence. In fact it is hard to imagine what amount and form of visible evidence would suffice to prove the existence of something invisible. As illustrated by the lengthy debate on YouTube, the case example of jinn possession is simply not enough to convince many viewers – Muslims as well as non-Muslims. The photographic exemplification fails to provide us with an undeniable experience of this alien creature hosting itself within human flesh. In this sense, both the possessed body and the image of the body fail in their attempt to show what they were intended to exemplify.

In anthropology, similar debates have occurred over the questionable value of photographic images and film in providing a window into unseen realities (Henley 2006; Kiener 2008; MacDougall 1998; Marcus 1994; Suhr & Willerslev 2012; 2013; Weiner 1997). One anthropologist who openly acknowledges severe problems in attempting to apply visual media to show the invisible is Kirsten Hastrup (1992). During fieldwork in Iceland, Hastrup once attempted to photograph an Icelandic agricultural show of rams. Soon she realized that the show of rams was a secret ritual competition for male potency focused on measuring the size and weight of the ram's testicles. Later, when she developed the photographs – ill focused, badly lit, lopsided, featuring the backs of men and rams – she was rather disappointed: 'The texture of maleness and sex had been an intense sensory experience, but it was invisible. The reality of the total social event had been transformed into a two-dimensional image, a souvenir' (Hastrup 1992: 9).

Like our YouTube exorcism, Hastrup's failed photography seemed to point at the lack of invisibility in the visually mediated recasting of reality: look, here was the invisible, why can't we see it? Both the shaykh and Hastrup demand of the image that it shows the invisible, understood as an extraordinary realm of ritualistic, sexually charged, or magical atmosphere. Yet the problem is that the invisible simply cannot be contained within the image. Somehow the overwhelming abundance of visual detail provided by the image makes it difficult to grasp the traces of invisible phenomena designated by concepts such as 'spirit possession' or 'competition for male potency'.

Why do both pious Muslims and anthropologists spend their time with images, if the knowledge they produce, as Hastrup (1992: 17) concludes, inevitably remains 'iconographic' and 'thin' and hence irrelevant to any serious exploration of the unseen dimensions of human reality? In the following pages I discuss the problems of visually exemplifying phenomena such as jinn possession in neo-orthodox Islam and relate this to ongoing debates about the value of images in visual anthropology. I begin by taking a close look at the reception of this particular YouTube exorcism among a small group of young Muslims in Denmark.

Young Muslim men watching exorcism

Seven young men in their late teens or early twenties sit gathered around a sofa table with cookies, coffee, and tea in an apartment in the large social housing complex officially identified as the 'ghetto' of Gellerup, in Aarhus, Denmark. '7000 year old jinn inside man' has been put on the large plasma screen hanging on the wall.

I became interested in this group of young Muslims when they started cleaning up the garden, the party room, and the 'torture chamber' of a former Hells Angels fortress on the outskirts of Aarhus in August 2010. The current owner, a former leader of the so-called 'immigrant gang' Black Cobra, had offered the place to the group. They wanted to build a small mosque as a refuge from the demands of parents and the corrupting influences of Danish society. The young men were children of refugees or immigrants who moved to Denmark from Iraq, Lebanon, Afghanistan, Somalia, and Turkey. Several participants in the project had previously been engaged in small-scale crime, drug dealing, hash smoking, or alcohol abuse. Most of them had experienced a hard time growing up in the Danish school system. For them, neo-orthodox Salafi Islam was a way of escaping from all of this, purifying their hearts, and getting their lives back on track.

I was looking forward to making an ethnographic film about their ambitious project of transforming the Hells Angels fortress into a centre for pious Muslim youth. After five or six weeks, however, the project came to an end. Members of a neighbouring mosque had convinced the young men that it would be better to pursue their activities in an already established institution. A rift appeared between those in the group who felt that the local mosques were too limiting and politically corrupt, and those who agreed that, as young people, they still needed the advice of older generations.

In 2011, several members of the group decided to leave Denmark to study Arabic in the Middle East. It was on one such evening as they were gathered to say goodbye to a friend that the talk turned to possession by jinn. The young men had recently witnessed several severe cases of possession, including the possession of their friend Feisal by more than twenty-six jinn of multiple origins and religious convictions, and the possession of a young Somali boy by the Danish female jinn Dorthe, her husband, and their dog Hugin. These harrowing scenes were a favourite topic for discussion. Frequently, they would try to make sense of them by comparing their own experiences with videos on YouTube. This evening I was allowed to record their discussion. Their hope was through direct visual exemplification to convince viewers of my ethnographic film of the truth of the existence of jinn (Suhr 2013a; 2013b).

First, we watched a video of a group of 'false' shaykhs who were allegedly inserting jinn directly into their patients through the tips of their fingers. Then we saw some people identified as 'Sufis', both women and men together, apparently also possessed by jinn, dancing wildly and head-banging with their robes, long beards, and hair flapping around. According to the young men, practitioners of Sufism imagine that such obscure body movements bring them into oneness with God. The display was at once amusing and frightening: 'A ʿūdhu bi-l-Lah, God protect us from the Sufis . . . Do you want some more coffee?'

Finally, Adrees asks the others to put on the video of the '7000 year old jinn'. The loud, determined voice of the YouTube exorcist fills the room:

'What is your religion – are you Muslim, Christian, or Jewish?'

The arms of the possessed body move awkwardly. The head tweaks to the side. The jinn stammers out its answer to the shaykh:

'Jewish'.

The shaykh continues his inquisition. It is in Arabic. Mubarak, who came to Denmark with his parents as a refugee from Somalia, does not speak the language. He asks Imad, who is half-Lebanese, to translate.

'[The shaykh] says: Tell us how old you are – don't lie. She says, she doesn't lie. 7000 years old'.

Adrees summarizes the statements of the jinn for the camera:

'It's a female jinn called Varia. She claims that she's 7,000 years old. She's from Congo'.

Journal of the Royal Anthropological Institute (N.S.), 96-112
© Royal Anthropological Institute 2015

Now the jinn switches to Kurdish. Imad asks Karzan, whose parents arrived in Denmark from the Kurdish part of Turkey, to translate:

Karzan is gasping at the scene: 'The jinn saw this man and she liked him. She liked him so she decided to enter him. She fell in love with this guy'.

'Does the jinn speak Kurdish?' Adrees asks. Adrees was born in Afghanistan and came to Denmark with his brother and parents as refugees. He understands some classical Arabic but not Kurdish.

Chya, who sits next to Karzan and who also speaks Kurdish, confirms:

'Yes, they both speak Kurdish'.

Adrees talks to the camera again: 'This is an example: a black woman from Congo who speaks Kurdish'.

Referring to the possessed body, Imad adds: 'But he also speaks Arabic. He speaks Arabic to the camera'.

'Who is the shaykh, where is he from?' Adrees asks.

Chya replies: 'You can see he's a shaykh. At least he has left his beard'.

Imad: 'Either Kurd or Arab'.

Mubarak is getting annoyed by all the interruptions: 'Just play it'.

Adrees: 'We don't know where he's from'.

The video starts again.

Chya translates: 'Now the jinn is explaining why she possessed the man: He was very beautiful so I chose him'.

Karzan continues the translation: 'The shaykh says, the jinn is lying: You're lying, you don't like him. She says: No, no, I'm not lying'.

Some of the guys in the group start to laugh. Now the voice of the shaykh is translated in green speech bubbles. He is speaking to the jinn:

'There are some people out there that do not believe that jinn can possess humans. Can a jinn possess a human?'

'Yes, yes', the jinn confirms that this is possible.

The shaykh turns his attention to a person outside the image frame and then looks directly at the camera:

'Listen scholars, and those of you who call yourselves scholars. The jinn says that it can enter a human and possess it. Witness with your own eyes on [video]'.

Adrees asks: 'Who is a Jew?'

'The jinn', Imad replies.

Adrees is still confused: 'I thought it was from Congo?'

Imad laughs: 'Yes, but it's a Jew. It's a Jew from Congo. Congo is its nationality'.

Mubarak asks again to have the words of the jinn translated. It has started to speak in Kurdish again. Its movements are becoming increasingly odd.

Chya: 'The shaykh in the video says: I know you're not afraid of me. What is it you're afraid of?'

Karzan takes over: 'He says: They tell me to leave. The angels are big. He asks: Are they larger than you? He answers: Yes, they're much larger than me'.

Imad has started to laugh again. Karzan continues:

'Can't we use this as evidence? She says that the angels are big and that they are present in this room. They yell and demand that it leave. So this is evidence that . . .'.

Khalil, who has remained silent until now, interrupts: 'Evidence of what?'

'That angels exist', Karzan replies.

Mubarak is not convinced by Karzan: 'But he says himself that jinn lie a lot'.

The discussion continues for a while. What was intended as a serious presentation of evidence of the divine truth that jinn exist is turning into a scrutiny of falsity and make-believe. The fact that I am present with a camera seems to add to a degree of tension.

The good, the bad, and the failed example

In academic discourse the word 'example' is sometimes used to mean an attempt at illustration. The validity of the example is often conceived to rest in its correspondence with reality – the degree to which it mirrors and is representative of reality (cf. introduction to this volume; C. Taylor 1990: 101). When this group of young Muslims discusses the possibility of using the video example as evidence of the existence of jinn and angels, it is in terms of such a correspondence – the degree to which the image and the body of the possessed faithfully mimic reality. This notion of example as illustrative or representative of reality stands in contrast to the original, but still widely used, connotation of the example as model not only *of* but also *for* the conduct of social life. An example in this older sense is not just illustrative but also morally normative by being exceptional in some way. It stands out by embodying in pure form that of which it is exemplary (cf. introduction to this volume). In the Qur'an, the word *uswa* is used to describe the good example of the Prophet. Here *uswa* carries the connotation of example as a pattern to follow – or role model – *uswatun ḥasanātun*, a beautiful pattern (Qur'an 33:21).

In the neo-orthodox Islamic work of faith, considerable attention is given to how one may best follow the example of the Prophet. His mode of behaviour, manner of speech, physical appearance, and high morals are described as the finest and most perfect that has and ever will be achieved by a human. The Prophet is the embodiment of 'the good example' in the sense of being a condensation of all possible ethical values that a human being can achieve (cf. Robbins, this volume) – the 'seal' and completion of divine prophethood. The task for the Muslim is therefore to emulate this model as best possible in all areas of life – ranging from the most trivial of everyday tasks, such as how to get up in the morning, the order in which one puts on one's shoes, and how one enters and exits a bathroom, to the important ritual procedures at birth, marriage, death, and so on.

Yet since the Prophet constitutes the asymptote of perfection, no other human can ever achieve his degree of completeness. Desires, delusional thinking, and evil forces compete tirelessly to drag ordinary humans away from this ideal example. For this reason, humans need to establish a sense of direction so that they will know which way to orientate themselves. It is perhaps to this end that bad examples are also given – the worst of which is Iblis, the personification of evil in Islam. According to most Islamic scholars, Iblis was initially among the believing jinn, yet when God created humankind and asked Iblis to prostrate before Adam, he refused. From arrogance and sheer envy he turned away from God and attempted to drag humankind with him towards damnation. Since God had initially created Iblis and was therefore the master of his actions, it was also God's decision to allow Iblis's betrayal and his ever-proceeding attempts to drag believers away from the truth. In the cosmology of Islam, this primordial event marks the beginning of the divine testing of humankind.

A broad continuum extends between the perfect example of goodness at one end and the ultimate example of evil at the other, as embodied by the Prophet and Iblis, respectively. Along this continuum, we find a range of examples that can be said to be neither absolutely good nor absolutely evil. Rather these examples offer a mixture of good and evil, and it is often not possible to discern whether good or evil has the upper hand. It is in this territory of the in-between that we find the failed or incomplete examples – the examples that embody a degree of either evil or goodness, but which simultaneously drag along a part of the opposite as a half-hidden shadow side. These examples are failed in the sense that it is not quite clear what they exemplify. The struggle of neo-orthodox Muslims to emulate the good example of the Prophet, to become a good example for others to follow, and to turn away from the bad example of Iblis is carried out in this unknowable middle ground of the always failed or incomplete example. It is in this intermediate region of imperfection, half-appearances, and distorted images between the visible and the invisible that most of these Muslims' lives are played out (see also Pandolfo 1997).

On this particular evening in Gellerup, the screening of the YouTube exorcism appears to ignite an unintended discussion. The video was meant to provide visual evidence of the existence of both invisible jinn and angels. As such, it was intended not so much as an example for proper Islamic conduct, but rather – as in the correspondence model in much Western social science – as a model and illustration of reality as it actually is. Instead, however, it has provoked a debate about the extent to which it is possible, necessary, or even desirable to believe in such almost grotesque visual displays, or whether they could in fact be make-believe on the part of either jinn, patient, shaykh, or filmmaker. Just as much doubt as certainty flows from these images, and, as we shall see, the scepticism aroused does not confine itself to the space of the image, but spills over to other instances of possession that the young men have witnessed or heard about.

Invisible visibility?

Just as the possessed body and the image of the possessed body seem to evoke both doubt and certainty as to what they purport to exemplify, so the exemplifying power of images and film has been the object of considerable criticism and anxiety within the academic discipline of anthropology. Hastrup's failed ram photography is a prime example. For Hastrup (1992: 11), her disappointing photographic experience leads to a subordination of photographic imagery as necessarily being inferior to the written word in its capacity for producing anthropological knowledge. Both Hastrup and the shaykh in our YouTube video struggle to squeeze an essentially invisible phenomenon into the visible façade of an image. Somehow their words appear better at containing the kind of invisibility that they argue persists beneath the visual façade.

For many visual anthropologists, the issue has been not how to contain the invisible within the image, but rather how to counteract anthropology's tendency to over-amplify intangible cultural differences through excessive textual abstraction. David MacDougall points out how the visible features of human life have 'largely disappeared as signifiers of culture' (1998: 255) and how anthropology has detached itself from observable reality to such a degree that it is often impossible to discern any resemblance between lived life and the cultural formations being described. For MacDougall, the ethical potential of ethnographic film and photography lies in its way of returning us to the concrete and detailed features of persons and their environments. Visual media have, as Lucian Taylor also argues, a capacity for exceeding theory and for 'showing anthropologists' purchase on the lived experience of their subjects to be rather more precarious than they would like to believe' (1996: 88).

Journal of the Royal Anthropological Institute (N.S.), 96-112
© Royal Anthropological Institute 2015

At the basis of Taylor's and MacDougall's critique of the abstractions of written anthropology is a particular understanding of how the medium of film allows us to explore the role played by ordinary lived time and space in the constitution of social life. As MacDougall points out, photographic images and film have a way of counterbalancing the strangeness of even the most exotic people with 'a sense of familiarity' (1998: 245) – that is, a sense of how, despite cultural differences, we are ultimately all subject to the same plane of embodied spatial and temporal existence.

Both MacDougall and Taylor are pivotal figures within the formation of observational cinema – a distinctive style of realist filmmaking that applies the mimetic powers of the camera not simply to mirror everyday reality, but also to facilitate a process of merging the object of perception with the body of the perceiver. Through long uninterrupted shots, the camera is used as 'a physical extension' of the cameraperson's perceptual organs, thus allowing viewers intimate access to the filmmaker's engagement with the social life portrayed (Grimshaw & Ravetz 2009: 548; Henley 2004: 114; L. Taylor 1996: 75). In this way, ethnographic filmmakers of the observational tradition seek to apply a holistic approach that avoids the fixation on verbal meaning, theoretical abstractions, and 'invisible' cultural differences in much written analysis (Grimshaw & Ravetz 2009: 539; Suhr & Willerslev 2012). Against Hastrup's critique of the incapacity of visual media to show the invisible, MacDougall (1998: 252) asks us to appreciate the image for its way of showing the visible commonalities of being human, which, in his view, have disappeared from much contemporary anthropology. How do these claims for and against the image and its capacity for showing invisible realities or pan-human commonalities make sense in relation to the video of young Muslims in Gellerup watching exorcism on YouTube?

Salt and pepper

'Say: It has been revealed to me that a group of jinn listened to the Qur'an'.

The shaykh in the YouTube video has started exorcizing the aged Congolese jinn from the possessed man through the recitation of Surat al-Jinn (Qur'an 71:1). This verse is often quoted as evidence of the existence of jinn as real beings who, like humans, have been endowed with the will and freedom to accept the divine message. When used in exorcisms, the verse may remind the intruding jinn of how it has betrayed the law of God, but how it still has the possibility of escaping eternal torment by surrendering to the absolute deity. In this case it seems to have an effect. The possessed body is coughing loudly. The shaykh continues to recite:

'They [the jinn] said: Verily, we have listened to a wonderful recital. It guides to the right path and we have believed therein and we shall never join anything with our Lord'.

Imad points out to us that the jinn has finally been persuaded to take the Islamic creed – *al-shahāda*:

'He testifies that there is no other god than God. He testifies that Muhammad is the messenger of God'.

Once more the jinn starts to cough. Mubarak concludes: 'Now it's leaving the body. Something is coming out of his mouth'.

The shaykh is talking in Kurdish again. Chya translates:

'He says that he has been possessed, this is evidence for those who don't believe in jinn. He's happy that he got rid of it'.

Khalil has grown increasingly sceptical during the viewing of the video: 'I don't know how many stories I have heard like this. Who knows whether they are true?'

Journal of the Royal Anthropological Institute (N.S.), 96-112
© Royal Anthropological Institute 2015

Imad looks at him with dismay: 'You could start to believe . . .'.

Khalil: 'Seriously, we know jinn are real – but I have heard so many stories that are totally . . .'.

Adrees attempts to stop an argument from developing again: 'Some people tend to exaggerate. Some people like to add salt and pepper to any story that they hear'.

Khalil interrupts: 'Why believe it, you don't know if it's real?'

Imad: 'If there are witnesses'.

Khalil: 'It could be true but it could also be false'.

Chya: 'Don't you believe your brother?' Chya refers to the previous discussion about two cases of possession that some of the members of the group have personally witnessed.

Khalil: 'He has experienced something. I'm not saying it's untrue. But many of the examples we have talked about . . .'.

Imad interrupts: 'If, for example, I tell you that I have seen all this with our Bosnian brother, would you trust me? Yes, because I have experienced it myself'.

Khalil replies: 'Yes, you have seen it, but when I hear a story that someone has heard from another – I can't use it for anything. Why should I care?'

Adrees tries again to end the argument: 'I do understand you. You can never use such a story as evidence. Evidence of what is allowed and what is forbidden. But such stories can awaken you – awaken your seriousness. They teach us that we have to protect ourselves – from evil spirits and magic – by reading those verses that the Prophet, peace be upon him, has taught us. It's good if we read them'.

Khalil, still not satisfied: 'Just before, I heard this story. He said that the trees could move during the night and that they could enter into the rectum of some animal . . . I don't have this from the Qur'an or the *Sunnah*. Why should I accept it?'

Again Adrees makes an effort to settle the discussion:

'But in any case – the conclusion of this is – that such stories are not obligatory for you to believe in. It's not demanded of you to believe in them. But what you and all Muslims have to believe is what the Prophet, peace be upon him, has said. For example, the Prophet said that the jinn can fly. Then we believe it. Okay, this is possible for jinn. But if we hear some other story – then you can question it. Okay, maybe I believe this story or I don't believe it – because the storyteller is a liar or something else. But I believe that a jinn can fly. That this is possible. I just don't know if this particular story is true. Like with any other story – who tells it? Who has witnessed the story? Does the story seem realistic?'

Confusion

Somehow the reality depicted by the YouTube video appears to fall apart as we watch it. The group of young Muslims hoped to show each other and the viewers of my film a visual example that proved the existence of jinn and the efficacy of the Qur'an in getting rid of these malicious creatures. The video showed precisely how to get rid of jinn by reading the Qur'an, how a dark magical substance was thrown up at the climax of the exorcism, and how finally the human subject repossessed his body. Nevertheless, the video shows so much that the whole event almost takes on the appearance of a parody. Somehow, the overly explicit and robotic display makes it difficult to appreciate the video as clear evidence of the miracle of the Qur'an. Some of the young men might have been inclined to believe or to react sceptically from the outset of the discussion, but as the discussion continues it is clear that no one gets their presuppositions fully affirmed.

At the moment of filming, I attempted – in the style of observational cinema – to let the camera blend in and not unnecessarily intrude in the unfolding of the discussion. Obviously, however, the presence of the camera does impact significantly on the discussion. The declared aim of the young Muslims is as best they can 'to be the face of the Prophet of God in Denmark'. However, in this case the camera, as witness to their embodiment of divinely ordained conduct, frames the discussion so that what should have resulted in an exemplification of the truth of God ends up as a rather muddled conversation about falsity and mischief.

The most basic demand on the neo-orthodox Muslim is to bear witness to the existence of the invisible domain of God, paradise, hell, angels, and jinn (Qur'an 2:2–5). The religious duty, however, is not simply to take at face value any visual illustration of the invisible. In fact, many of the Muslims I worked with stated that any attempt at visualizing the invisible was not only impossible but also forbidden (see also Wahhab 1996: 174). As a shaykh once explained to me, there would be no meaning to faith, testimony, or God's test of humankind if people could already see the invisible (al-ghayb).

The invisible, as understood in the context of neo-orthodox Salafi Islam, is precisely that which cannot be reached through the senses. Hence it is not a job for human beings to attempt to do this. But when the invisible appears to intrude into the visible world, it is difficult to know how one should react. In this case, the visual display of the invisible divides the participants in the discussion. While some, like the shaykh in the YouTube video, strive to claim the image as an evidential example of the existence of jinn, and therefore a platform upon which they can testify to divine truth, others in the discussion feel obliged to react with scepticism at the visualization of the invisible.

Several of the young men find themselves incapable of not bursting out laughing as they witness the scene. For them, perhaps in a similar way as for filmmakers and visual anthropologists of the observational tradition, the visual display points towards a more 'ordinary' reality, standing in marked contrast to the extraordinary verbal claims of the shaykh. In MacDougall's (1998: 250) view the 'ordinary' signifies human commonalities that radically transcend the cultural difference invoked in much written anthropology. For the young Muslims, however, the ordinary is also the realm of pretend and make-believe, which, in their view, has become increasingly dominant in modern society.

When I watch these film examples of young pious Muslims watching exorcisms, I am not at all sure whether it leads me to a recognition of radical impermeable difference or more ordinary human commonalities. Rather, I think what it leaves me with is confusion. By no means does it display the kind of fullness and homogeneity of space and time favoured by observational filmmakers. Instead, the observational scene seems to shuffle indistinctly between the actual and virtual, past, present, and future. This heterogeneous meshwork issues from the cohabitation and juxtaposition of multiple realities, temporalities, objects, appearances, and voices that completely exceed the limited space and temporality of the film-image. I simply do not know where to situate the 'normal human participant' (Henley 2004: 114) who allegedly has the capacity of a pan-human perception in this setting. Could this be me as the camera operator? Is it the shaykh? Is it the possessed? The jinn? Is it those young men who cannot see or believe in the evidential proof presented to us? Or is it those who do see it and believe in it? If there is an element of pan-human perception that we share in this conglomerate of vision, then it can only be located in the failure of perception and in the situatedness and obvious limitation of human perception.

In a recent article, Charles Hirschkind points out how Muslim YouTube surfing of this kind can best be described as an 'adventure, that one sets off across a quixotic, unpredictable landscape whose every twist and turn presents not the threads of an unfolding discourse or the development of a deeper understanding but the sudden surprise of an affect, the pleasure or shock of an unexpected discovery' (2012: 5).

Hirschkind is exploring primarily the practice of watching sermons (khuṭub) on YouTube. Based on the comments left by Muslim viewers, he concludes that the prime attraction of such videos is their capacity to move the viewer towards experiences of pious tranquillity (iṭmiʾnān), stillness of the soul (sakīna), and humility (khushūʿ). Videos that arouse the heart towards such ethical and devotional dispositions are frequently described as muʾaththir – a term indicating that something is effective, moving, exciting, and so on (Hirschkind 2012: 6). Muslim YouTube viewers often leave comments in the form of small supplications (duʿāʾ) – a kind of visual and ethical testament to repeated acts of drawing close to God. However, according to Hirschkind, the moral space that is created by these commentaries is highly vulnerable. If YouTube viewers leave derogatory comments, the effectiveness of the videos in arousing the correct emotional response seems to decrease dramatically.

Hirschkind (2012: 13) looks at khuṭbas as well as videos of beautiful Swedish babies and awe-inspiring natural phenomena, all of which could be said to embody good examples in the sense of constituting 'modest images'. By contrast, I draw attention here to videos that are very difficult to think of as good examples, yet still produce a kind of shock that attracts pious Muslim youth. When watching these exorcisms, the shock of the image provokes amazement and wonder, but also a kind of rib-tickling entertainment verging on the inappropriate. The comical and the potentially inappropriate appear not, however, to distract Muslim viewers from the videos. Despite highly disparaging comments about 'barbaric Arabs' or the 'backwardness' of Islam, large numbers of viewers continue to watch, comment, and copy '7000 year old jinn inside man'. Somehow, the capacity of these rather immodest, failed images to arouse a devotional response is not as easily polluted as the YouTube sermons analysed by Hirschkind. In fact, it seems that accusations of falsity as well as anti-Islamic comments left by non-Muslims stimulate the popularity of and debate around these videos. How can we make sense of this?

The notion of an audio-visual 'shock' used by Hirschkind to describe the experience offered to pious Muslims by YouTube brings to mind a style of filmmaking very different from the realist schools discussed so far in this paper. Most ethnographic filmmakers in the observational tradition have been preoccupied with the 'cinema of duration' as advocated by André Bazin (2005 [1967]: 39; Grimshaw & Ravetz 2009: 539) – that is, the ability of the camera to capture events and actions in human life in the order and pace in which they actually occur. Rather than shocking the viewer, the aim is to allow the viewer to become immersed in the observation of a single moment in a particular place. In contrast, the early Soviet cinema of filmmakers such as Sergei Eisenstein and Dziga Vertov was aimed precisely at producing cinematic shocks. In Eisenstein's (1949) conception, 'intellectual montage' as opposed to 'mundane montage' referred to a juxtaposition of dissimilar objects which, when put in confrontation with each other, would shock the viewer into recognizing a reality far larger than could possibly be seen from a single subjective viewpoint. Rather than aligning viewers with a certain reality,

Journal of the Royal Anthropological Institute (N.S.), 96-112
© Royal Anthropological Institute 2015

Eisenstein saw in cinema the essential tools for people to stand up to oppressive ideas of what counts as the real. In his words: 'The representation of objects in the actual (absolute) proportions proper to them is, of course, merely a tribute to orthodox formal logic ... [d]isplacing the expressiveness of archaic disproportion for regulated "stone tables" of officially decreed harmony' (Eisenstein 1949: 34–5).

For Eisenstein, realism was by no means the correct form of perception. Rather, realism was to be seen as a function of a certain form of social structure. By contrast, the cinema of montage implied an aesthetics where each juxtaposition of film shots constituted a qualitative leap out of the perceptual regimes that dominate human action and thought (see also Deleuze 2005a [1986]: 38). Instead of the correspondence model of observational cinema, the filmmaking pursued by early Soviet filmmakers aimed at the transgression of the observable. Here validity was to be measured not by the resemblance of a film to the 'pro-filmic', but rather by its power to force the viewer out of the pro-filmic and into empathy and passionate engagement in the joint production of an industrial communist utopia (see, e.g., Vertov 1929).

Contemporary neo-orthodox Muslim YouTube viewing can be understood as a consumption of images akin to that imagined by Eisenstein and Vertov. In exposing themselves to videos such as '7000 year old jinn inside man', these young Muslim men are not uniting their perception with that of a camera. Rather, the juxtaposition of elements internal to this video, to other videos, and to the experiences and comments of other viewers creates fissures that force the pro-filmic display outside of itself. The grotesque character of the display, the bird's-eye view camera, the bold postulates of the shaykh, the strange discontinuous YouTube subtitling, and the harsh debate left by hundreds of viewers all work to forge cracks in the visible façade. For Eisenstein, the perceptual disruptions facilitated by cinema were necessary for the emergence of the communist paradise. Perhaps Muslim YouTube viewers are using these videos in a similar way, as a vehicle to enhance the ethical conduct and sensitivity required for entering the Gardens of Everlasting Bliss (Qur'an 19:72).

Surely part of the attraction for the group of young Muslims in viewing exorcisms of jinn is entertainment. Yet it is not only entertainment. The excitement and horror of viewing these videos stems from the small gaps of ontological insecurity that are produced. For pious Muslims, these cracks into the unknown may be useful because they produce a degree of doubt. Doubt (*shakk*) is often described as one of the most dangerous forms of illness. Yet doubt is an unavoidable condition and perhaps, in fact, a necessity. Without doubt, there would be complete certainty and therefore no possibility of faith as an active submission of consciousness to the divine. The emphasis on such paradoxical movements of faith is present in a number of religious traditions within and beyond Islam. The Danish philosopher Søren Kierkegaard, whose translated work is being used by a number of Islamic scholars, argued, for example, that doubt is indeed the very engine of faith (Kierkegaard 2005 [1843]; see Bektovic 1999; Kassim 1971; Suhr 2013a; Tomlinson 2014).

By being exposed to '7000 year old jinn inside man', the consciousness and analytical capacity of the Muslim viewer is stretched to accommodate degrees of both belief and unbelief. Combining belief with unbelief is dangerous within neo-orthodox Salafi Islam. How can one know whether one is laughing at the individual case example or at the more general use of the Qur'an to exorcize spirits as it was practised and advocated by the Prophet? The latter is, in the understanding of these Muslims, tantamount to expelling oneself from the people of paradise (*ahl al-janna*). As a shaykh explained to some of the young men during their weekly lecture in basic Islamic doctrines ('aqīda), laughing at or in any way ridiculing the practices of the Prophet is one of the greatest sins. The enforced stretching of consciousness between belief and unbelief is not so far from the most dangerous illness of all – namely, the illness of nifāq: hypocrisy or double dealing. Al-munāfiq, the hypocrite, is, it is said, the person who gets the lowest position in hell. Indeed, ordinary heathens will have the debatable pleasure of standing with their feet on the heads of al-munāfiqūn. Entering the territory between belief and unbelief is consequently also to enter a limbo between prospects for eternal life in paradise and an eternity at the very bottom of hell.

The intention with the YouTube video discussed here is that it should work as an example in the Geertzian sense – as a model *of* and a model *for*. For some it may work in this way. Yet because of its grotesque visual façade, it also provokes a different form of religiosity, perhaps more akin to the form of humility that may arise when encountering phenomena such as a storm or a weird dream (Schilbrack 2005: 430), and hence the kind of devotion, submission, asking for help, or thankfulness that arises when standing in front of the totally invisible. It is dangerous to laugh at practices that could be of prophetic origin, or to claim to be able to identify the visible form of something invisible, but reactions like this are almost unavoidable when viewing such videos as '7000 year old jinn inside man'. In this way, the obscurity of the video pushes moral imagination and perception to their limits. While a genuinely 'good example' that is both a model *of* and a model *for* may create a path and direction for human agency, these failed images give no clear direction. Rather, they seem to dismantle the capacity for human action. Instead of devices for producing clarity or evidence, these failed images work as amplifiers of invisibility.

'It gives us a way to remember to read our daily prayers', Adrees concludes, after deciding that '7000 year old jinn inside man' cannot, after all, be taken as proper indisputable evidence of the divine truth. While some of the young men initially appeared convinced and argued for the truth value of the YouTube exorcism and others fiercely argued against it, this synthesis proposed by Adrees is what they all finally agree on. If the proposed visual evidence only testifies to the fact that ultimately there is no tangible evidence, then what it provides is instead a test of one's trust in God – al-tawakkul 'alā Allāh – and a test of one's willingness to surrender all scepticism to the fact that the invisible is invisible and therefore cannot be seen. By collapsing any possibility of coherent signification, the failed image flows with ambiguity – speaking to its recipient from no single identifiable position, about nothing and everything at once. This is the curse of the failed image, but also its attraction and marvel, since the failure creates an ideal condition for leaps of faith, submission, and surrendering of the self to the unknown. I suggest that in this way, these odd videos become productive as a means of establishing the attitude of humility (khushū') that Hirschkind points out is so pivotal in the practice of Muslim YouTube consumption.

The image in anthropology
What may YouTube videos such as '7000 year old jinn inside man' teach us with regard to the use of photographic imagery for exemplification in anthropology? Apparently images do not work well in visually exemplifying for us the kinds of textual invisibility of which Hastrup writes. Nor do they in any clear-cut way show us the pan-human commonalities proposed by ethnographic filmmakers of the observational tradition. My argument so far can be summarized by the statement that, for all their failure and

incompleteness, images as examples may, however, still be productive in establishing the possibility of a stance of humility and an appreciation of the invisible as invisible: that is, as something that cannot be seen from the perspective of a human. In a roundabout and perhaps accidental way, the failed image comes to share a similarity with the kind of 'ethical writing' that philosophers such as Emmanuel Levinas and Maurice Blanchot associate with forms of poetry that bespeak the unknown. In Blanchot's words:

> To speak the unknown, to receive it through speech while leaving it unknown, is precisely not to take hold of it, not to comprehend it; it is rather to refuse to identify it even by sight ... To live with the unknown before one ... is to enter into the responsibility of a speech that speaks without exercising any form of power (1993 [1969]: 302).

For Levinas and Blanchot, to encounter the failed image is the potentially traumatic exposure of oneself to the unknown other. It is a confrontation of the self with an alterity that cannot be grasped in any definite form (Bankovsky 2004). The image, in this sense, becomes not a looking-glass to or representation of another world; rather, in the words of Gerald A. Bruns it becomes 'the materialization of being, the way a cadaver is the image of the deceased, a remainder or material excess of being ... not a reproduction of a thing but ... a withdrawal of it' (2006: 215). By blocking consciousness, the failed image disables the possibility of meaning, of turning the world into a symbol. As Levinas points out, the failed image does not 'extend between us and a reality to be captured'. Instead, as a 'symbol in reverse', it pushes us to an ontological dimension outside the order of the visible (Levinas 1987: 5–7).

If we cannot fully appreciate the image for what it succeeds in depicting, then I propose, following Levinas and Blanchot, that we appreciate it for what it fails to depict. What is interesting about the video image discussed in this article is not primarily its actual visible content. Just as interesting is what it fails to show: that is, the invisible parts of reality that it brings to our attention. In some way, all images evoke the invisible simply by their framing, their carving out of a certain space, their limited range of contrast, colour reproduction, and delimitation of a certain period of time. Chained as it is to the messy and disturbing particularities of life, the image captured by a camcorder or a camera is, almost by default, exemplary in the negative – always capturing a little too little and a little too much. For Roland Barthes (2010 [1980]), this photographic viewing experience of a lack and a surplus is captured by the notion of 'punctum' – often described as the visual detail that somehow constantly drags the eye outside the frame towards an invisible excess of untamed, unanalysed, perplexing life. This is also what Lucian Taylor points to when arguing how, rather than reducing people's lives to abstract analytical categories, the shots of a camera drag us into the 'ambiguity of meaning that is at the heart of human experience itself' (1996: 76).

Here I have speculated upon a particular video image depicting an instance of spirit possession. Visually extreme manifestations of spirit possession have long captured the minds of ethnographic and documentary filmmakers (see, e.g., Aaltonen 2001; Connor, Asch & Asch 1980; Deren 1985; Rouch 1955). Perhaps a part of the uncanny attraction of these phenomena lies in the way in which their visual display evokes a broader experience of possession: namely, the way in which human vision itself almost indispensably is possessed by the visible.

In Levinas's formulation, '[S]ight is ... an openness and a consciousness, [and] even in its subordination to cognition, sight maintains contact and proximity. The visible caresses the eye. One sees and one hears like one touches' (1987: 118). In this notion of sight as the visible's caress of the eye, a certain passivity on the part of the beholder is also emphasized (see also Deleuze 2005b [1989]: 124). Yet, perhaps vision in Levinas's sense – as the effect of the visible's caress – is too weak a concept. At least we may note how, at times, we feel exposed to a form of unwanted caress – a violence of sorts – from which we may attempt to find shelter by closing our eyes. This defence is only frail, however. Having first intruded into the retina, the visible continues to work in our imagination regardless of whether we want it to or not. As our life is given to us at birth by a still-unknown donor, vision is forced into us from outside our perspective as a wanted or unwanted gift which, regardless of our views on the matter, transforms us in ways we cannot possibly master or repay. The primordial indebtedness of vision is impressed on us by the visual display of spirit possession and the photographic image, which always and necessarily is possessed by what it depicts.

Sometimes our ability to move around with our gaze – to select that which we wish to look at or to close our eyes to it – results in a commonsensical understanding of vision as centred upon the perceiver. The wide array of cinematic manipulations available to the film editor also conjures this illusion of optical mastery. It is exactly this that is brought into question by the tension and limited visual display of the possessed image. Just as the body in the image is allegedly possessed by a jinn, so the image itself is possessed by the figure of two men, someone outside the frame to whom they are speaking, a physical space, and an observing camera – all of which extends beyond what can possibly be contained within the image, yet determines how we can see the image and our options with it. The failed image serves here as a warning against the clarity and security we may feel through the use of seemingly 'good' examples that too easily confirm preconceived understandings of the immediately visible. The power of visual exemplification lies not only in what an image shows, but just as much in the incompleteness and failure of the image, its manner of 'punctum', the way in which it does not quite signify that which it appears to record: the way it leads us outside the frame.

NOTES

This paper is based on conversations with young Muslims in Aarhus, Denmark, during eighteen months of ethnographic fieldwork conducted between 2010 and 2012 with a prime focus on Islamic conceptions of healing and illness. I wish to thank the editors of this volume as well as three anonymous reviewers who all gave in-depth critique of and suggestions for the analysis presented. The study was made possible by the generous support of the Aarhus University research programmes 'Camera as Cultural Critique' and 'EpiCenter', the Moesgaard Museum, and the Danish Council for Independent Research (DFF-1321–00169).

[1] The video entitled '7000 year old jinn inside man', with English subtitles, was originally accessed on YouTube on 14 May 2012 at *http://www.YouTube.com/watch?v=mo1WfroDCVc*. Since 2012 the video has been reposted and debated on several different channels with different titles, including 'Real jin 7000 years old': *https://www.youtube.com/watch?v=p42lyC5ZCls* and 'Shoking [*sic*] 7000 year old jinn inside man': *https://www.youtube.com/watch?v=wowGQ6DR7jQ*.

REFERENCES

BANKOVSKY, M. 2004. A thread of knots: Jacques Derrida's homage to Emmanuel Levinas' ethical reminder. *Invisible Culture* 8, 1-19.

BARTHES, R. 2010 [1980]. *Camera lucida: reflections on photography* (trans. R. Howard). New York: Farrar, Straus and Giroux.

BAZIN, A. 2005 [1967]. *What is cinema?* vol. 1 (trans. H. Gray). Berkeley: University of California Press.

BEKTOVIC, S. 1999. The doubled movement of infinity in Kierkegaard and in Sūfism. *Islam and Christian-Muslim Relations* 10, 325-37.

BLANCHOT, M. 1993 [1969]. *The infinite conversation* (trans. S. Hanson). Minneapolis: University of Minnesota Press.

BODDY, J. 1989. *Wombs and alien spirits: women, men, and the zār cult in northern Sudan.* Madison: University of Wisconsin Press.

BRUNS, G.A. 2006. The concepts of art and poetry in Emmanuel Levinas's writings. In *The Cambridge companion to Levinas* (eds) S. Critchley & R. Bernasconi, 206-33. Cambridge: University Press.

DELEUZE, G. 2005a [1986]. *Cinema 1: the movement-image* (trans. H. Tomlinson & B. Habberjam). London: Continuum.

——— 2005b [1989]. *Cinema 2: the time-image* (trans. H. Tomlinson & R. Galeta). London: Continuum.

DRIESKENS, B. 2008. *Living with djinns: understanding and dealing with the invisible in Cairo.* London: Saqi Books.

EISENSTEIN, S. 1949. *Film form: essays in film theory* (ed. & trans. J. Leyda). New York: Harcourt Brace.

GRIMSHAW, A. & A. RAVETZ 2009. Rethinking observational cinema. *Journal of the Royal Anthropological Institute* (N.S.) **15**, 538-56.

HASTRUP, K. 1992. Anthropological visions: some notes on visual and textual authority. In *Film as ethnography* (eds) P.I. Crawford & D. Turton, 8-25. Manchester: University Press.

HENLEY, P. 2004. Putting film to work: observational cinema as practical ethnography. In *Working images: visual research and representation in ethnography* (eds) S. Pink, L. Kürti & A.I. Afonso, 109-30. London: Routledge.

——— 2006. Spirit possession, power, and the absent presence of Islam: re-viewing *Les maîtres fous. Journal of the Royal Anthropological Institute* (N.S.) **12**, 731-61.

HIRSCHKIND, C. 2012. Experiments in devotion online: the YouTube *khuṭba. International Journal of Middle East Studies* **44**, 5-21.

KASSIM, H. 1971. Existentialist tendencies in Ghazālī and Kierkegaard. *Islamic Studies* **10**, 103-28.

KIENER, W. 2008. The absent and the cut. *Visual Anthropology* **21**, 393-409.

KIERKEGAARD, S. 2005 [1843]. *Fear and trembling* (trans. A. Hannay). London: Penguin.

LEVINAS, E. 1987. *Collected philosophical papers* (trans. A. Lingis). Dordrecht: Martinus Nijhoff.

MACDOUGALL, D. 1998. *Transcultural cinema.* Princeton: University Press.

MARCUS, G.E. 1994. The modernist sensibility in recent ethnographic writing and the cinematic metaphor of montage. In *Visualizing theory: selected essays from V.A.R. 1990–1994* (ed.) L. Taylor, 37-53. New York: Routledge.

PANDOLFO, S. 1997. *Impasse of the angels.* Chicago: University Press.

PHILIPS, A.A.B. 2007. *The exorcist tradition in Islam.* Birmingham: Al-Hidaayah.

SCHILBRACK, K. 2005. Religion, models of, and reality: are we through with Geertz? *Journal of the American Academy of Religion* **73**, 429-52.

SEDGWICK, M. 2010. Contextualizing Salafism. *Tidskrift for Islamforskning* **1**, 75-81.

SUHR, C. 2013a. *Descending with angels: the invisible in Danish psychiatry and Islamic exorcism.* Ph.D. thesis, Aarhus University.

——— & R. WILLERSLEV 2012. Can film show the invisible? The work of montage in ethnographic filmmaking. *Current Anthropology* **53**, 282-301.

——— & ——— (eds) 2013. *Transcultural montage.* New York: Berghahn.

TAYLOR, C. 1990. *Philosophy and the human sciences: philosophical papers 2.* Cambridge: University Press.

TAYLOR, L. 1996. Iconophobia. *Transition* **69**, 64-88.

TAYMIYAH, S.I.I. 2007 [1409]. *Essay on the jinn* (ed. & trans. A.A.B. Philips). Riyadh: International Islamic Publishing House.

TOMLINSON, M. 2014. Bringing Kierkegaard into anthropology: repetition, absurdity, and curses in Fiji. *American Ethnologist* **41**, 163-75.

WAHHAB, S.I.M.A. 1996. *The book of monotheism.* Riyadh: Darussalam.

WEINER, J. 1997. Televisualist anthropology: representation, aesthetics, politics. *Current Anthropology* **38**, 197-235.

WILLERSLEV, R. 2011. Frazer strikes back from the armchair: a new search for the animist soul. *Journal of the Royal Anthropological Institute* (N.S.) **17**, 504-26.

Films

AALTONEN, J. 2001. *Kusum.* 69 min. Helsinki: ILLUME.

CONNOR, L., P. ASCH & T. ASCH 1980. *Jero on Jero: a Balinese trance seance observed.* Watertown, Mass.: Documentary Educational Resources.

DEREN, M. 1985. *Divine horsemen: the living gods of Haiti.* New York: Mystic Fire Video.

ROUCH, J. 1955. *Les maîtres fous.* 24 min. Paris: Films de la Pléiade.

SUHR, C. 2013*b. Descending with angels.* 75 min. Aarhus: Persona Film & Watertown, Mass.: Documentary Educational Resources.

VERTOV, D. 1929. *The man with the movie camera.* 68 min. Kiev: VUFKU.

Défaillance de l'image et possession : exemples d'invisibilité dans l'anthropologie visuelle et dans l'islam

Résumé

L'exploration des réponses aux média visuels dans l'islam néo-orthodoxe peut-elle apporter de nouvelles réponses aux interrogations récurrentes sur la valeur des images en anthropologie visuelle ? Le présent article avance que l'image photographique partage une étrange ressemblance avec le corps des personnes possédées par les esprits invisibles appelés djinns. En tant qu'exemple ou modèle défaillant de la réalité, l'image fonctionne, comme le corps possédé, en tant qu'amplificateur de l'invisibilité, pointant vers ce qui ne peut être vu, dépeint visuellement ou représenté par écrit. Cela suggère une épistémologie négative, dans laquelle la valeur des images proviendrait non pas de l'adéquation de leur correspondance avec la réalité perçue, mais plutôt de la manière dont elles échouent à donner en exemple ce qu'elles semblent représenter.

7

Paradoxical paradigms: moral reasoning, inspiration, and problems of knowing among Orthodox Christian monastics

ALICE FORBESS *London School of Economics and Political Science*

Whilst anthropological discussions of morality tend to be rooted in Aristotelian ethical theory, this paper highlights an alternative Christian moral reasoning rooted in Neoplatonist/Christian hybrids and visible in contemporary Eastern Orthodox monastic practice. The analytical move proposed here is to focus on the disjunctures between different ethical traditions within Christianity in order to show how they produce diverse forms of moral reasoning that rely on particular uses of exemplarity and exemplification. It is argued that the Aristotelian lens, with its stress on compliance, piety, obedience, and the daily practice of self-perfection, can produce impoverished accounts of ascetic life by excluding the more anarchic and idiosyncratic forms of spiritual training. Christianity has a long tradition of deploying paradox and perplexity to explode facile certainties, thereby carving out a space, at the limits of human knowing, where a divinity conceived as radically alter to the created world can be directly engaged with.

When I first met Abbot Serafim[1] at his remote island monastery on Montenegro's lake Skadar, he was dozing alone before a table laden with the remains of a Homeric feast of meats and alcohol. The friend who had brought me by boat over vast wild marshes to meet this exceptional holy father (*duhovnik*) hastened to explain that the abbot had release to eat meat only on this particular day of the year – although the next day, at his monastery's patron saint feast (*slava*), he led the revels late into the night. Serafim was well on his way to becoming a popular *duhovnik*, as attested by the guests to this feast, who included the Serbian minority presidential candidate, numerous local businessmen, professionals, artists, and media figures, as well as Montenegrin, Serbian, and Russian monastics and religious tourists. *Duhovnici* – senior monks ordained as confessors – occupy a special place in the Orthodox imagination thanks to charismatic reputations propagated through stories of uncanny knowledge and efficacy in prayer. They are seen as repositories of 'direct', unmediated knowledge of God, which is considered superior to texts, motivating people to travel thousands of kilometres for their blessings or advice.

When I discussed Serafim with the nuns from a neighbouring convent, it emerged that they too thought he was eccentric. Yet far from trying to conceal potentially embarrassing idiosyncracies, they laughingly pointed them out, saying he sometimes failed to show up to say mass or bored them with endless talk of football. They showed me an interview with Russian *GQ Magazine* – which had profiled him as an up-and-coming holy man – where, asked if whilst fighting in the Bosnian war in his teens, prior to becoming a monk, he had killed many people, he laconically replied 'Many'. When I inquired how he was regarded within the church, Sanja, a novice from Belgrade, came straight to the point:

> He stretches the rules too much and some [in the church] don't like him. But he has the gift to move in different worlds. People think God loves him. There are many ways to have that authentic relationship with the truth, no 'one size fits all' ideal, no single type of the *duhovnik*. As with the saints, there is great variation in personalities and paths to God. Some hierarchs act holy and refined, others love to be flamboyant. Saints are completely mad, but they're mad for Christ, not themselves.

Various Orthodox believers offered slightly different, yet mutually consistent, interpretations of Serafim's persona. The embarrassment of the friend who introduced me to him stemmed from the assumption that I would misinterpret Serafim's behaviour, seeing him as a negative example. The nuns were aware he was a bit controversial but accepted the archbishop's judgement of Serafim's basic inner soundness, expressed in the decision to make him an abbot. Their confidence was reinforced by the fact that the archbishop was their confessor as well as Serafim's. The businessmen who funded Serafim's projects clearly related to his heroic charisma and no-nonsense personality, which fitted well with the ideas of masculinity of Montenegrin highland clans, and also appealed to Russian religious tourists. Finally, staff at the archdiocese seemed slightly wary, but valued his contacts and ability to get things done, demonstrated by his restoration work on ruined ecclesiastical buildings.

Unsurprisingly, whenever I tried to explain Serafim to Western interlocutors, they tended to assume he was a negative example. This led me to wonder what ethical presuppositions one should make to be able to view him as a saintly exemplar, as many sincere Orthodox believers clearly did – rather than as an embarrassing exception, as Western interlocutors would. The comments of Orthodox informants suggested they were responding particularly to the paradoxical, contradictory nature of this colourful figure. Sanja explained Serafim's unconventionality by assimilating him to the Christian exemplar of the mad, wild desert prophet. She said that his confessor, the archbishop, had instructed Serafim as follows: 'Son, you are given the call of the desert. The work is hard but the rewards are great'. This was interpreted as an act of divinely inspired insight that had matched the man with his correct place in God's unfolding plan of creation. She and other informants 'read' Serafim as an extension of other paradoxical Christian exemplars, such as (in Orthodoxy) the holy fool or divine madman (*jurodiv*) (see Ivanov 2010). I suggest that such 'wild' exemplars capture something important regarding the way in which Orthodox monastics and laypeople think about spiritual achievement. It encapsulates, on the one hand, a keen awareness of and concern with the limits of human knowledge and the elusiveness of true insight, and, on the other hand, the tantalizing possibility that this elusive knowledge might occur in anyone, however unlikely, as a result of charismatic revelation.

Journal of the Royal Anthropological Institute (N.S.), 113-128
© Royal Anthropological Institute 2015

The fieldwork and its context

Before proceeding with the argument, a few observations are needed regarding my fieldwork and Orthodox monasticism more generally. I undertook research among Serbian Orthodox monastics in Montenegro and Kosovo (which belong to the same Serbian Orthodox Church archdiocese) between 2007 and 2009. This involved living inside two convents and in the archdiocesan town Cetinje, and travelling with monastics to visit other monasteries and convents. Prior to this, I had undertaken two years' fieldwork in a Romanian Orthodox convent. Although national Orthodox churches have parallel institutional structures, all Orthodox faithful are in communion with each other, meaning the two fieldworks were mutually relevant from my informants' point of view. Whilst my argument here might apply both to my Romanian and Serbian data, I draw only on Serbian examples for the sake of simplicity.

In discussing 'Orthodox theology', I am keenly aware of the dangers of essentialization. However, it is valid to speak of this theological tradition in the singular because these churches form a federation of equal, parallel national institutions, united by a common dogma which is safeguarded by a joint central council (Synod). Differences between the churches do arise, but the themes discussed here are central enough to Orthodox monastic training to be widely agreed upon within the two churches I studied.[2] During my fieldwork in the Serbian and Romanian Orthodox churches, I found dogmatic uniformity to also stem from the sharing of theological texts and writings by *duhovnici* across church/national borders. For instance, when I asked a priest who taught theology in Kosovo for a good text on Serbian saints, he referred me to a treatise on mysticism by a Romanian author. When I pointed out the author's nationality, he said this was irrelevant – what mattered was that it was a good text.

I chose to work with monastics because in the Orthodox context they are a powerful institutional elite. Each national church has a single monastic order which forms its institutional backbone. Priests are required to marry before ordination, and this bars them from entering the higher clergy, who are all monastics. Although nuns are barred from priesthood, they can wield considerable power as abbesses of important convents or assistants to the clergy. Unlike the Catholic case, where a plurality of monastic orders compete against each other and the territorial church to attract the faithful and generate revenues (see, e.g., Bax 1985; 1995), Orthodox monastics do not normally perform life-cycle rituals, leaving these to priests. Monasteries obtain most of their revenues through the church's territorial organization, within which they are integrated. This integration and separation of priestly and monastic tasks results in far less competition than exists within Catholic institutional contexts. Orthodox monastics tend to be less focused on charity work than their Catholic counterparts. They are religious experts whose visible aloofness from society and geographical isolation makes them attractive to ordinary folk in need of inspiration and an infusion of divine charisma. In later life some become hermits, emplaced sources of charisma tapped by worldly individuals, and resembling Tambiah's (1984) Thai Buddhist forest saints.

In making Orthodox theology one of the central themes of this paper, I am not implying that this faith is rooted in its theological wellsprings rather than the product of socially and historically situated actors and forces. However, it is important to consider how theological ideas relate to practice, or fail to (Turner & Turner 1978). Although different degrees of direct theological awareness existed among both monastics and the faithful, theological thought infiltrated mundane activities and everyday religiosity in substantive ways, partly owing to a sustained engagement between monastics and

Journal of the Royal Anthropological Institute (N.S.), 113-128
© Royal Anthropological Institute 2015

laity in Orthodox contexts. Many monastics had formal studies, yet their engagement with theology was not primarily theoretical, but, rather, intrinsic to everyday life within the 'living tradition' of the church, envisioned by them as a continuous intersubjective community extending back to the Apostles (Stewart 1994). Through their extensive daily liturgical practice, they engaged in a form of theological contemplation which, like that of the early church fathers, was not a kind of objectified, academic knowledge, but rather an inter-subjective form of address, communion, and contemplation. This manner of engagement pervaded their relations with saintly exemplars and divine beings, and was also central to their interactions with seniors and confessors (*duhovnici*), on the one hand, and with ordinary folk, on the other.

Joel Robbins (2006) offers three answers to the question of how anthropology and theology can interact. First, anthropology should examine the role of theological ideas in its own formation. Secondly, it can approach theology as data, analysing how it informs lived practice. Finally, the two disciplines can initiate a dialogue grounded in their common interest in alterity. This paper seeks to engage in all three ways. On the first front, it draws attention to the need critically to explore the limitations of the Aristotelian ethical assumptions which have helped frame anthropological debates on morality. Secondly, approaching theology as data, I analyse how the prolix writings of Neoplatonist church father Pseudo-Dionysius the Areopagite inform mainstream Orthodox monastic training and the uses of exemplarity and exemplification thereof. Finally, Robbins argues that whilst anthropologists are very good at discovering and describing difference, theologians are better at relating alterity back to one's own self and culture. Anthropologists, he says, should 'take on the challenge to find real otherness at the fundamental level of social ontology' (Robbins 2006: 292). Accordingly, I seek to describe uses of the exemplary in this particular Neoplatonist Orthodox ontology, but also to highlight its connections to wider themes and tensions within Christianity and asceticism more generally, and to the very human dilemma of attempting to cope with, and transcend, the limits of knowing.

The exemplary as an index of moral living

The 'exemplary' – as in striving to live an exemplary life – has tended to do heavy conceptual work in anthropological discussions of morality and asceticism. Owing to its close relationship to the ascetic Ideal, it is made to stand simultaneously for the method of ascetic life – continual self-perfection – and the end-goal, fashioning an exemplary self and life (Foucault 1997). Through Foucault's influence, an Aristotelian-based ethics that foregrounds virtuous practice, understood as daily positive action aimed at self-perfection, came to shape anthropological assumptions and debates regarding morality (Schielke 2009: S35). Particularly within the anthropology of Islam (Asad 1986; 2003; Hirschkind 2006a; 2006b; Mahmood 2003), but also in influential classic studies of Christian monastic and ascetic discipline (Asad 1993; Dumont 1985; Foucault 1997), the focus of discussions of morality has been on piety and self-perfection. In line with a mainstream reading of Aristotelian ethics,[3] this conceptualization of moral reasoning assumes the goal of ascetic life to be a 'fixed end' (Dewey 1967) which is known and can be reached by striving to follow the rules and/or the commands of one's master, to the point of obliterating one's own individuality (Foucault 1997: 246). These a priori assumptions may be useful as an analytical starting-point (Lambek 2000), but they should be used critically. To take it for granted that informants share them is to ignore the fact that the exemplary can do different kinds of conceptual work in different ethical systems.

Journal of the Royal Anthropological Institute (N.S.), 113-128
© Royal Anthropological Institute 2015

Hence, the philosophical assumptions of any 'living' system of ascetic training, and the ways in which they compare with the (mostly Aristotelian) assumptions of a Western scholarly audience, should be problematized. How is the exemplary understood by informants: what is it, and how does one come to know or learn it? How does grasping the exemplary relate to the project of trying to be exemplary? How do informants frame the relationship between exemplarity and other concepts that may have a bearing upon their ethical reasoning: knowing and doing, mimesis and creativity, reason and perplexity?

The use of paradox as a means of pursuing an ever-deepening understanding of truth has, historically, been a key Christian (and biblical) theme, manifested in various ways across different versions of the faith. However, this area of Christian thought has rarely received the analytical attention it deserves. The stress on compliance and zealous self-perfection has, I argue, led to impoverished accounts of morality that exclude the more anarchic and idiosyncratic forms of spiritual training. Over the past decade, several authors have begun engaging with the topic of how the paradoxes thrown up by religious commitments are experienced (Bandak 2012; Cannell 2006; Engelke 2005; 2007; Robbins 2004; and, in an Islamic case, Schielke 2009). This paper resonates with this body of work.

I argue that the Aristotelian lens, when applied to the analysis of morality, can obscure the productive and creative valences of the subversive, uncertain, and baffling, and indeed the power of certain types of negation in ascetic life. In the case of Christian asceticism, an unquestioned reliance on Aristotelian ethics obscures the presence of a quite different ethical system inspired by Neoplatonist and early Christian philosophical hybrids, which is very visible within contemporary Orthodox theology and practice. When Western interlocutors are asked to consider Serafim's example, they apply to his case the premises of Aristotelian ethical reasoning, seeing him as glaringly imperfect. Meanwhile, Orthodox monastics are more inclined to use the lens of Neoplatonist ethics, viewing their own faculties for knowing God's ways as glaringly imperfect. Whilst the former ethics centres on *doing*, on right living through virtuous practice, the latter hinges on *knowing* by questioning the possibility of understanding the true meaning of virtues, and yet predicating moral achievement upon gaining this elusive insight.

Before going further, let me briefly elaborate the contrast I draw between Platonist and Aristotelian ethics. Both Plato and his pupil Aristotle produced eudaimonistic ethics, taking human well-being, the result of the cultivation of virtue, to be the highest aim of moral thought and conduct (see Ackrill 2001; Irwin 1995; 2007). The difference between them lies in their understandings of well-being and the good life. For Plato, in light of the Socratic project, the definitions of virtues are far from self-evident, meaning that right living involves a continual, austere struggle to discard selfish aims which disguise themselves as virtuous motivations. This striving is to be carried out using theoretical means which are aimed at recovering an unmediated knowledge of the truth. Plato wished to ground his ethics in such a knowledge, modelling it on mathematics, placing at its centre a search for unitary principles, equally applicable to the microcosm of human life and to the order of the entire universe. His moral project thus centres on knowing, understood as 'anamnesis' – the recall of a set of paradigmatic entities, the Forms (see Irwin 2007; Kraut 1992).

Aristotle follows Plato in regarding ethical virtues as complex rational, emotional, and social skills, but rejects his idea that a training in the sciences and metaphysics is a necessary prerequisite for a full understanding of the good. For him, well-being is not a theoretical project, but, rather, a practical one, carried out through the inhabituation of virtues resulting from daily right living (Irwin 2007). Living well consists in those lifelong activities that actualize the virtues of the rational part of the soul, creating a self-sufficient state for the active individual (Kraut 1989). Yet by moving away from Plato's preoccupation with the elusiveness of true understanding, Aristotle arguably loses some useful complexity. The Socratic dialogues themselves are powered by bafflement, which was viewed by Plato (1984), in *Meno*, as a wholesome intermediary stage on the way to knowledge. Plato thus assigns a positive role to negation and perplexity, but this is lost in Aristotelian ethics.

The analytical move I propose is not a return to Plato's ethics, discounting Aristotle. Rather, I aim to highlight a Neoplatonist version of Christian ethics which, despite already being a part of the Christian repertoire and conceptual vocabulary as applied to questions of morality, knowledge, and normativity, has failed, so far, to inform anthropological thought on these topics. My aim is to expose the discontinuities within Christianity between different ethical projects, by pointing out a Neoplatonist ethical project which was successfully adopted into the faith around the fifth century AD and continues to inform the practices of many Christians. This project does not centre on Plato's Forms, but rather on the Neoplatonist idea of the Good (see Corrigan 2004; Siorvanes 1996), which developed the notion of the Good in Plato's late work – described by Plato in the *Republic* (Plato 2000) as the absolute measure of justice, the Form that gives meaning to all other universals and transcends Being itself. Neoplatonist church fathers later used this concept to reflect philosophically on the nature of the Christian God. Neoplatonist ethics, I argue, encapsulates a set of questions that are more relevant than the Aristotelian equivalent to Serbian or Romanian Orthodox monastics' understanding of their vocation, imagined by them as the quest for a deeper, hidden truth through an ongoing engagement with radical alterity.

Paradigm and paradox in Orthodox monastic training

Thomas Kuhn (1970) has pointed out that in the scientific education learning involves mastering a series of paradigmatic examples. The training of Orthodox monastic novices also involves pondering exemplars of saints and great *duhovnici*. Such figures are paradigmatic because they illustrate a variety of right ways to live out different vocations (scholar, warrior, hermit, king/queen, martyr, cleric, monastic) as pathways to God. Despite vast differences between them, saints are said to share a radical motivation to serve God's plan; as Sanja expressed it, they are 'mad for God, not themselves'. Owing to their inscription into the liturgical calendar, such lives are celebrated periodically. On the day assigned to each saint, his/her story is read and prayers are offered from matins to vespers, prompting meditation throughout the day on the challenges and victories of the saint's life which use a heroic rhetoric. Year after year, as these calendrical occasions recur, one comes to feel one is revisiting an old friend, especially since saints are thought of as being synchronous, alive and active in the present. Monastics are encouraged to draw parallels with their own lives, and derive great comfort from the saints' difficulties. Anything can recall a saint's story. Whilst driving us along the craggy Montenegrin coast, Sister Tatjana, a Bosnian novice, was moved by the evocative arid landscape to tell us about Saint Anthony's life in the desert. Seemingly ignoring the wheel as the car drifted towards the edge of the craggy road, she turned to us describing the saint's trials and key life encounters, and the command he gave to his body when feeling restless: Legs go,

Journal of the Royal Anthropological Institute (N.S.), 113-128
© Royal Anthropological Institute 2015

I am staying! As we grew silent, puzzling this out, it occurred to me that great examples are as baffling as they are revealing.

Bafflement, I argue, is a pedagogical tool self-consciously used within Orthodox monastic training to motivate people towards an ever more profound engagement with the subject of their meditations. Such deployment is not unique to Orthodoxy, as attested by the 'anthropological conundrum', the puzzling ethnographic anecdote that opens many an essay. However, I would argue that, because of Neoplatonist influences, bafflement plays a particular role in Orthodox thinking about truth and the knowability of God. This is illustrated by a technique of meditation developed by Neoplatonist church father Pseudo-Dionysius the Areopagite (henceforth Ps-Dionysius), which relies on the use of example as a subversive tool used to probe, and attempt to transcend, the limits of what can be known and said about God. In the context of this exercise, bafflement is taken as a sign of being in touch with divinity, on the right spiritual path.

Assumed to be a disciple of the fifth-century Athenian philosopher Proclus, Ps-Dionysius[4] was the first to elaborate theologically the connections between Christianity and Neoplatonism. The rest of this section describes his elaboration of the role of example in Christian meditation. His works (Pseudo-Dionysius 1987) attempt a theoretical examination of knowing through a philosophical mediation on the names of God and the nature of divine hierarchy. He was influential in Western Christianity up to the Middle Ages and is a key Orthodox theological and philosophical voice (see, e.g., Corrigan 1996; Hathaway 1969; Rorem 1993). His opus was known to my monastic informants in Montenegro mainly through the popularizing efforts of Maximus the Confessor (580–662 AD), a widely read and emulated saint who defended it from charges of heresy, pressing for its inclusion into the Christian canon.

My monastic informants at Montenegro's archdiocesan see were highly educated and intellectually inquisitive people, many with postgraduate studies abroad, nurtured by an archbishop schooled in Bern, Rome, and Athens. The abbess of the convent where I continued fieldwork had a degree in psychology and a substantial library endowed with social science and theological texts. Though others are less well schooled, I argue that Ps-Dionysius' use of bafflement and paradox, his ideas regarding the subversive use of example, and his elaboration of the idea of mystical, unmediated knowledge of God have filtered into the mainstream, becoming part of the Orthodox common sense. Indeed, his use of subversive examples is a key part of the living instruction received by monastics and the faithful from their spiritual fathers (*duhovnici*), informing the inter-subjective understandings fuelled by such relationships.

Ps-Dionysius' work focuses on the question of how a God who is by definition utterly unknowable, unrestricted being, transcending even goodness, can become manifest in and through the whole of creation in order to bring back all things to the hidden obscurity of their source. How can you exemplify the unexemplifiable? Meditation on the names and attributes of God leads Ps-Dionysius to develop a mystical (a term he took to mean simply 'hidden') theology concerned with getting beyond the limitations of language: affirming our affirmations, then negating them, and then negating the negations in order to ensure that we do not make an idol out of a God about whom we, ultimately, know nothing (Corrigan 1996).

Ps-Dionysius starts from the observation that most people can only understand the attributes of God if they are incarnated into visible and sensible things. Life and wisdom are not seen in themselves, but rather through the medium of a being who is living and wise. Other names of God, termed symbols by Ps-Dionysius, refer to visible things that have no inherent relation to the godhead. Their literal signification is restricted to the realm of the sensuous (the created), and they must be turned into metaphors if they are to be useful to theology. Ps-Dionysius chooses an example from David's Psalms: the Lord awoke like a strong man, powerful and reeling with wine. Applied to God, drunkenness and sleep become what Ps-Dionysius calls dissimilar similarities: examples that compel the reader to make an imaginative leap, from the easily comprehended literal meaning to a more difficult, abstract terrain, where sleep becomes withdrawal from the world, and drunkenness an excess of attributes within God, who is also their source (Corrigan & Harrington 2011). Dissimilar similarities strike one as exceptionally unworthy of God – they are counter-intuitive. Yet they reveal a truth that can lead up to Him. Ps-Dionysius prefers these to the more appropriate divine names, such as 'luminous' or 'wise', arguing that the latter create the illusion that, by using the name, we have adequately comprehended the godhead.

For my monastic friends, Serafim's example works as a dissimilar similarity: he renders obvious God's impenetrability and omnipotence, as well as the human failure to come even close to predicting or understanding His mysterious movements. The choice of such an unlikely instrument to fulfil divine purposes (such as rebuilding ruined monasteries) highlights for them the fact that God is not circumscribed by human logic. It also points to the fragility of people's judgements of others – Serafim, despite appearances, might be a very holy man. These reversals are disempowering, eroding certainties and creating an urge continually to peel away layers of illusory knowledge. Dissimiliar similarities, through their obvious inadequacy for the task of describing God, thus force one to search for a deeper truth.

Ps-Dionysius goes further: dissimilar similarities are better than more appropriate examples because they are negations. All names and representations of God, after being affirmed, must be denied in order, finally, to arrive at a real understanding of the godhead, only possible when both affirmations and negations have been transcended. As Sanja put it, making a similar point, 'Maximus Confessor said that God is none of the things you think he is'. Used in this way, exemplification becomes a subversive practice, a way of exploding presuppositions and false claims to knowledge. Around this deconstruction, Ps-Dionysius builds a contemplative method, the result of which will be accentuated mystery rather than revelation: after all the speaking, reading, and comprehending of the names ceases, there follows a divine silence, darkness, and unknowing (Corrigan 2006). Ps-Dionysius' theology is complex because it explores what can be said about God, what such statements can mean, and takes this line of thought to its extremity, 'discovering the necessity to talk too much about God, and to push language forms to their breaking points, and then to see what we cannot say about God' (Corrigan & Harrington 2011).

Used as a subversive practice, example can point to increasing complexity, and becomes the engine that drives a perpetual, ever-deepening meditation. Dissimilar similarities, counter-intuitive or paradoxical examples are thus vehicles for understanding, not because they elucidate, but because their prolixity is productive, triggering a type of contemplation that is perpetual and necessarily open-ended. This contemplation is a form of prayer, a reverential philosophical thought and receptivity, stretching ourselves out, as Gregory of Nyssa put it, so as to be lifted up (Corrigan 1996). In liturgical practice, the sensory symbols deployed in rites (sounds, smells, sights) are also supposed to trigger and stimulate this contemplative process, and for this reason are valued above the mere reading of texts. An example would be the scent of myrrh incense burned during religious services, a concrete reminder of the omnipresence of divine energies and their ability to envelop one invisibly. At the same time, this particular scent is said to be exuded naturally by the dead bodies of saints, which have been so infused with divine charisma as to become incorruptible: it is thus literally the smell of charisma (Serbian: *blagodat*).

In order to be effective, contemplation must remain radically open-ended, and paradoxical examples or negations are instrumental in producing this effect. According to Ps-Dionysius, if we say that God is good, we have the illusion of knowing entirely what we mean, and thus close off the thought. If, however, we say God is a worm, we subvert our own comfortable tendencies by being shocked into filling the image with inquiry. The Psalmist who uses the worm image hides the sacred from those who do not understand and yet points to it in a new way (Corrigan & Harrington 2011). In other words, Ps-Dionysius sees scripture as providing the basis for a deeper understanding of attribution or predication that will lead us beyond our own merely human capacities (Rorem 1993). The constant tension of hiddenness and openness pervades his meditative practice of theology. As a result,

> his practice of writing is a complex and necessarily deceptive or subversive process of reading the encoded insight (or contemplation) in created things in such a way that neither the perceptual beauty of the material thing nor the deeper hidden beauty of the sign becomes a trap, an idol, or a vanishing point but, instead, an activity that opens up an irresistibly beautiful world in and to God (Corrigan & Harrington 2011).

In subsequent Orthodox thought, this complex theory of signification became known as 'negative' or *apophatic* theology: the attempt to define God by negation only, which underlies a mystical approach to divine truth. This is opposed to the cataphatic theology which applies to created entities (Lossky 1997). The distinction between the two reflects a radical ontological break between created and uncreated objects of knowledge. Orthodox *duhovnici* often say that whilst human language and reason are sufficient for understanding the created world, uncreated divinity is not an object that can be grasped or described using these faculties. The kind of knowing appropriate to the latter is faith, a form of affect that 'reaches out', inviting charisma to lift one to the divine plane where truth can be experienced directly, free of all mediation (Savin 1996).

Performing the presence of the alter

How, then, does grasping the exemplary relate to the project of trying to be exemplary in Orthodox monastic life? How does the concern with retaining the possibility of experiencing the ineffable, of engaging with the radically alter, translate into day-to-day behaviour in the monastery or convent? Sanja's openness and humour about Serafim were far from unusual. Rather than trying to represent themselves as perfect or conceal instances of 'unexemplary' behaviour, monastics seemed to relish exploding pretensions from within with disarming candour and humour. Over time, I came to see this as a performance of intellectual honesty and humility, a form of authenticity intended both to signal and generate a sense of closeness to God.

For instance, during my first interview with Sava, abbot of the archdiocesan monastery, a highly respected *duhovnik*, he reached within his ample robes to reveal a tiny Sony camera on which he had filmed a spoof video of his monks. Dressed up as Obama bin Laden and his entourage, the bushy-bearded monks uttered Arabic words (a prayer learned by the abbot in Jerusalem) and nudged the newest novice, in civvies, to play the part of the suicide bomber. The abbot added that he had entered the best Osama impersonator in his phone memory under Bin Laden, and used this to prank American tourists by pretending to put them in touch with the terrorist. When I discussed these pranks with Abbot Serafim (whose relationship with Sava was rather competitive), he commented seemingly without any self-irony: 'Sava has the mind of a 16 year old'.

Serafim's eccentricity was thus only a more extreme example of a certain playfulness cultivated by many monastics, who, in daily life, often enjoyed being humorous, rude, outrageous or provocative. For instance, whilst travelling with some nuns in a car, we heard a clap of thunder, prompting one nun to burst out singing 'Thunder' by AC/DC. (She explained that she had been a 'rocker' in her lay existence.) When one describes such occasions, singling them out, it seems that monastics behave thus deliberately in order to shock. In some cases, such as Sava's video, there is an undeniable element of this. However, this is also a normal way of acting in the monastery and, as part of their training, monastics are encouraged to act playfully or spontaneously, to cultivate instinctively child-like behaviour. This may play against foreign visitors' preconceptions of what constitutes exemplary behaviour for a monk or nun, and in that sense there is an engagement with preconceptions of the exemplary. However, by bursting out into 'Thunder' by AC/DC, the nun was not trying to teach us anything. It would be more accurate to say that monastics are simply encouraged to express themselves in this way, that it is considered good and desirable. This interpretation is supported by the fact that monks and nuns were not surprised by others' crazy behaviour and often did not even bother discussing it. For the most part, playfulness was quite instinctive, seamlessly integrated into the way they were trained. It did involve a form of imitative action, though not a slavish, uncreative mimesis but rather an imitation of not imitating too much. Used in the right way, spontaneous and childlike behaviour could subvert facile assumptions, creating a tension that might lead to God.

Unconventional behaviour, particularly in *duhovnici*, was explored for signs of charisma. For instance, when I once returned to the convent after a long absence, Sanja described her impressions of a visiting *duhovnik* (and former bishop) who was famous for his rudeness and unpredictability. During an all-night prayer vigil, just as everyone was about to fall asleep, the *duhovnik* entered the church, muttering angrily to those who tried to kiss his hand: 'Don't touch me, don't touch me', and thrusting a flower at someone, ordering them to put it in water. The commotion had awakened everyone in an instant.

Not all *duhovnici* or monastics acted in striking, charismatic ways, and those who were charismatic often had a polarizing effect on other people. For instance, the archbishop, an imposing prophet-like figure, was universally considered to be very charismatic, but his detractors argued that, owing to his involvement in politics, he had 'fallen' and become evil. The underlying assumption here, common in monastic circles, was that the more spiritually advanced one was, the more one would be tested. It was expected that monastics would sometimes 'fall', but it was not always possible to distinguish clearly between someone whose incomprehensible actions were motivated by divine charisma and someone who had yielded to temptation. The only way to make such a determination was through the fruits of their actions – in light of an assumption that cause and effect are essentially alike, a now mainstream idea elaborated by Ps-Dionysius (Hathaway 1969). Thus, a period of time had to pass before the sources of inspiration, divine or demonic, could be determined with greater certainty.

Journal of the Royal Anthropological Institute (N.S.), 113-128
© Royal Anthropological Institute 2015

My monastic informants expected the operations of divine charisma to appear arbitrary from their vantage-point, assuming they are part of God's plan, the complexity of which cannot be grasped by the human mind. In this semiotic ideology (Keane 2007), it is impossible to know the Ideal one is trying to reach when one sets out to reach it. In the early stages of monastic life, which are the most traumatic, monastics know they do not understand the 'true', deeper meaning of their vocation because human contents of the mind obscure clarity of vision with respect to divine realities. Instead, the Ideal is expected to reveal itself along the way, as one is mentally and physically transformed through infusions of divine charisma, understood to be an impersonal 'energy' which, by attaching itself to people, things, or contexts, lifts them to a different ontological level. I have argued elsewhere that the ambiguity at the heart of this notion of charisma creates a space where ontological transformations can occur (Forbess 2005; 2010).

This schema of divinity places God and His charisma outside any human paradigm of power. If it is truly alter, immanent divinity cannot be encompassed by human intellect and has a propensity to rupture any man-made order. In such a context, jocularity and transgression are far from anti-religious, and indeed they help articulate a link between self and divinity. Conversely, the attempt to eliminate the unknown, ambiguous, and unexpected would render impossible the manifestation of God *qua* real alterity, preventing true closeness to the divine. Thus, in Orthodox monastic life as I observed it, subversiveness is an important part of the semiotic ideology, the grit in the oyster which helps to banish facile stereotypes and pushes novices out of their comfort zone, stimulating them to seek an ever-deepening engagement with their vocation. To the cynical observer these monastics may seem engaged in a battle to keep routinization at bay, and in a sense they are, but real intellectual and emotional fulfilment is derived from this way of engaging with the world and oneself.

When I met her, Sanja was one of three novices in a newly re-established historical monastic foundation populated by five nuns. She was given tasks by the abbess, in rotation with the other nuns, and spent her days meditating and wrestling with her vocation whilst fishing out in boats, preparing the church for services, or reading out and singing prayers. When she felt confused or troubled, she sought advice from the abbess, her monastic sponsor, or, more rarely (every few months), her confessor, the archbishop. These seniors acted as conduits of charismatic inspiration, having to intuit what she needed and helping, through often cryptic answers, to redirect her thoughts in a creative direction, staving off frustration. Sanja told me that meetings with her *duhovnik* were particularly inspiring. On one occasion she walked in to find him talking with someone and, seeing a dark form kneeling before him, assumed he was hearing someone else's confession. However, when she looked again, they were alone, the implication being that Christ had been in the room. Such incidents reinforced her conviction.

In the kind of exemplification involved in this training, one was not expected to imitate one's superiors exactly, or to eliminate one's own individuality, but rather to grasp the essence of the advice given in light of its timing and one's own deepest thoughts and questions. Divine charisma could work through the *duhovnik*, the sponsor, or even a complete stranger without his or her even being aware of it, conveying to the novice the message s/he needed to hear. This unknown quantity could thus suddenly engender a leap between the mundane and divine immanence. Expecting this, monastics tried to act as if they were open to an authentic connection with God, inviting charisma in by looking for ways to reframe ambiguous situations.

Journal of the Royal Anthropological Institute (N.S.), 113-128
© Royal Anthropological Institute 2015

Concluding remarks: paradigm, paradox alterity, perplexity

How, then, does this idea of charisma, and its often chaos-inducing interventions, relate to exemplarity? Caroline Humphrey (1997) has contrasted two styles of morality: the rule-centred, which she associates with Western forms of Christianity, and which aims to be clear, consistent, consequential, and universally applicable; and the morality of exemplars, detected by her in Mongolia, which thrives on multivocality and pliability, allowing people to choose from a range of possible ethical models and ponder their relevance for themselves. At first glance one is tempted to argue that Serbian Orthodox monastics also tend towards a morality of exemplars instead of rules. This is supported by the centrality of the *duhovnici* and saints in novices' training, and by a certain distrust of excessive zeal, which is read as an index of pride, the chief sin that caused Satan's fall from paradise. To assume that closeness to God can be earned through personal merit would, in this reasoning, instantly cancel out one's genuine spiritual achievement. Consequently, an excessive literalism in following rules is seen as potentially harmful because it can foster self-righteousness and cut one off from divine inspiration. Rather than ticking all the right boxes, Neoplatonist exemplary behaviour is played out as a creative interaction with one's *duhovnik* or sponsor, aimed at capturing an essence he embodies and learning how to perform and invite inspiration.

At the same time, however, Orthodox theology has its own engagement with normativity. Ps-Dionysius, for example, develops the Neoplatonist idea of justice into the underlying principle of the divine hierarchy (Hathaway 1969). There are two kinds of law, he argues: human 'custom', which is less important, and the *nomos*, or divine natural law, which is inscribed in the very essence of things, meaning that, when they are true to their essence, they are following this law. In other words, although Orthodox monastics may not seem especially concerned with rule following, they are in fact very much preoccupied with trying to follow this 'hidden' and less easily grasped divine rationale for their existence. Each form of Christianity has its own ways of using both exemplars and rules.

Exemplarity and exemplification, I have tried to show, can have very different meanings or purposes in different ethical schemas. Educational philosopher Bryan Warnick (2008) shows that whilst classical philosophers believed imitation to be compatible with creativity, Enlightenment thinkers like Kant came to contrast it to the development of independent reason: genius was opposed to the spirit of imitation. Humphrey seems to view rule-centred forms of morality as less creative than the morality of exemplars, which allows improvisation and choice regarding which exemplars to emulate and which to ignore. For Orthodox monastics, both exemplars and rule-centred moral forms are creative because enacting them is predicated on being attuned to, and creatively deciphering, the mysterious workings of divine charisma. Rule following involves reflecting on the hidden aspects of the *nomos*, whilst exemplar following requires one to 'read' the example in relation to one's unique individual circumstances.

To become a fully fledged monastic, one has to learn to discover and cultivate sources of charismatic knowledge and power in one's own life, as well as competently handle disruptive forces within oneself and others. The routine of monastic life is often upsetting because it seems to lack the charismatic, extra-ordinary quality described in the lives of saints or experienced during visits to other monasteries. However, it would be a mistake to conclude that charismatic knowledge is just a myth. This idea of knowledge has real effects precisely because it causes monastics to expect and *actively search* for

Journal of the Royal Anthropological Institute (N.S.), 113-128
© Royal Anthropological Institute 2015

profound experiences. Performances of charismatic insight create a social space for deliberation about morality and the monastic Ideal. The repertoire of charisma, with its ambiguity, creates space for personal issues to emerge and be creatively resolved. Temptations can thus be handled without blind obedience, withdrawing into oneself, or repressing desires, aspirations, and individual quirks. Instead, these are socialized so as to no longer be 'of the world', but rather 'of the world of Orthodoxy'. Notions of charisma act as the lubricant in this process, allowing novices to discover new potentials within themselves and play an assertive, creative role in their own training. This is reminiscent of the pedagogical techniques used by Bernard de Clairvaux with worldly-wise monastic recruits: '[T]he overall aim of this monastic project was not to *repress* secular experiences of freedom but *to form religious desires out of them*' (Asad 1993: 143, emphasis added). The monks 'stayed in the cloister because they creatively exercised virtue not because they were beaten into submission' (Asad 1993: 161-2).

In some ways, the Orthodox use of paradigmatic saintly exemplars is akin to scientific training – but in other, important, ways it is not. Specifically, whilst scientific exemplification and the resulting paradigms are intended to pinpoint the specific in order to accurately 'cut' that which is being examined from other similar things and thereby create as firm a closure as possible, reigning in the inherent slipperiness of example, Ps-Dionysius' practice of exemplification is intended to achieve exactly the opposite: a perpetual open-endedness and mutability – as with the unruliness of examples mentioned in the introduction. God is the ultimate unstable example. For the monastics trying to live in the spirit of this instruction, the paths to God not only can, but *must* boggle the mind. Being baffled is a sign of communion with God, reassuring one that one hasn't lost one's way spiritually. To lose the element of surprise could be read as having lost one's way. Serafim and others like him go to great lengths to keep this element of surprise alive.

I have tried to draw attention to such diverse uses of exemplification also as a way of exploring how informants' usages intersect with social science analysis. Martin Holbraad (2009) observes that in light of anthropology's profound preoccupation with alterity, the data which most resist collection and explanation are most 'anthropological'. Yet, paradoxically, what counts as truth in anthropology, and the available explanatory concepts, can distort such data, making them seem misguided or absurd. The problem then is how to find concepts that distort the data as little as possible. What sorts of assumptions would an anthropologist have to make about the truth in order to avoid this? In this paper the alter data were Serafim's seemingly inappropriate actions. His paradigmatic character as a revered *duhovnik* was hard to reconcile with the paradox of his seemingly unexemplary behaviour. If one views Serafim as a holy fool, one may be tempted to argue, with Sergey Ivanov that his indecorous behaviour 'can be edifying only if he abandons his disguise – for otherwise how would one tell him apart from a real, non-pretend fool or delinquent? . . . Yet, if he does reveal himself, he subverts his own vocation' (2010: 1, 6). However, I do not think Serafim was confronted with this dilemma of constant slippage towards being either an ordinary fool or a fraud. Ivanov's social science conception of truth pushes him to attempt to secure closure, to 'cut' the holy fool from either one or the other possibilities, or to express the impossibility of his slippery position, forced to straddle the two. For Serafim, his Neoplatonist open-ended form of exemplification raises no such dilemma. He is neither trying to be a fool, nor trying to disguise his true righteous nature. This is not an elaborate performance, but merely a reaching out towards radical alterity and hoping it will honour the invitation.

Journal of the Royal Anthropological Institute (N.S.), 113-128
© Royal Anthropological Institute 2015

The paradoxes and bafflement it instigates are highly useful in a broader context where they mark off a divine borderland.

NOTES

I thank the British Academy of Arts and Sciences for its generous support in granting me the Postdoctoral Fellowship that made possible the research for this paper. I am also grateful for their valuable comments to the editors of this issue, to Oliver Weeks, and to the participants to the workshop 'The Power of Example: Anthropological Explorations in Persuasion, Evocation, and Elucidation', held at the Department of Cross-Cultural and Regional Studies, University of Copenhagen, 8-9 September 2011.

[1] The names of informants are pseudonyms.

[2] Differences between parallel churches arise both in terms of the emphasis placed on different elements of the faith and through unique local traditions. An example of the latter would be the cult of saints in the Serbian church, which has a distinctive flavour owing to unique divine kinship practices (see Forbess 2013), including the widespread canonization, since the Middle Ages, of national heroes.

[3] Aristotle himself, despite writing intensively about ethics (Aristotle 1998), never developed this work into a coherent system, and the thrust of his ethical theory remains to an extent open to debate (Walsh & Shapiro 1967). However, his work does re-focus moral reasoning on practice, eliminating Plato's essentialist preoccupation with finding a transcendental basis for ethics, and this fact is sufficient for the purposes of the current argument.

[4] He wrote anonymously under the name of a legendary member of the Athenian Areopagus, who was instantly converted by Saint Paul. This was a common literary device at the time. (For a discussion of his possible identity, see Hathaway 1969: 3-30.)

REFERENCES

ACKRILL, J.L. 2001. *Essays on Plato and Aristotle.* Oxford: Clarendon Press.

ARISTOTLE 1998. *Nicomachean ethics* (trans. D.P. Chase). Mineola, N.Y.: Dover.

ASAD, T. 1986. *The idea of an anthropology of Islam* (Occasional Papers Series). Washington, D.C.: Center for Contemporary Arab Studies, Georgetown University.

——— 1993. *Genealogies of religion: discipline and reasons of power in Christianity and Islam.* Baltimore, Md: Johns Hopkins University Press.

——— 2003. *Formations of the secular: Christianity, Islam, modernity.* Stanford: University Press.

BANDAK, A. 2012. Problems of belief: tonalities of immediacy among Christians of Damascus. *Ethnos: Journal of Anthropology* Special Issue: Foregrounds and backgrounds: ventures in the anthropology of Christianity (eds) A. Bandak & J.A. Jørgensen, **77**, 535-55.

BAX, M. 1985. Popular devotions, power, and religious regimes in Catholic Dutch Brabant. *Ethnology* **24**, 215-27.

——— 1995. *Medjugorje: religion, politics and violence in rural Bosnia.* Amsterdam: VU Uitgerverij.

CANNELL, F. (ed.) 2006. *The anthropology of Christianity.* Durham, N.C.: Duke University Press.

CORRIGAN, K. 1996. 'Solitary' mysticism in Plotinus, Proclus, Gregory of Nyssa, and Pseudo-Dionysius. *Journal of Religion* **76**, 28-42.

——— 2004. *Reading Plotinus: a practical introduction to Neoplatonism.* West Lafayette, Ind.: Purdue University Press.

——— & M.L. HARRINGTON 2011. Pseudo-Dionysius the Areopagite. In *The Stanford encyclopedia of philosophy* (Fall edition) (ed.) E.N. Zalta (available on-line: *http://plato.stanford. edu/archives/fall2011/entries/pseudo-dionysius-areopagite/*, accessed 15 January 2015).

DEWEY, J. 1967. The nature of aims. In *Aristotle's ethics: issues and interpretations* (eds) J. Walsh & H. Shapiro, 47-56. Belmont, Calif.: Wadsworth.

DUMONT, L. 1985. A modified view of our origins: the Christian beginnings of modern individualism. In *The category of the person: anthropology, philosophy, history* (eds) M. Carrithers, S. Collins & S. Lukes, 93-122. Cambridge: University Press.

ENGELKE, M. 2005. The early days of Johane Masowe: self-doubt, uncertainty and religious transformation. *Comparative Studies in Society and History* **47**, 781-808.

——— 2007. *A problem of presence: beyond scripture in an African church.* Berkeley: University of California Press.

FORBESS, A. 2005. Democracy and miracles: political and religious agency in an Orthodox convent and village of South Central Romania. Ph.D. thesis, University of London.

————— 2010. The spirit and the letter: monastic education in a Romanian Orthodox convent. In *Eastern Christians in anthropological perspective* (eds) C. Hann & H. Golz, 131-57. Berkeley: University of California Press.

————— 2013. Montenegro versus Crna Gora: the rival hagiographic genealogies of the new Montenegrin polity. *Focaal: Journal of Global and Historical Anthropology* **67**, 47-60.

FOUCAULT, M. 1997. *Ethics: subjectivity and truth* (trans. R.E.A. Hurley). New York: New Press.

HATHAWAY, R.F. 1969. *Hierarchy and the definition of order in the letters of Pseudo-Dionysius: a study in the form and meaning of the Pseudo-Dionysian writings.* The Hague: Martinus Nijhoff.

HIRSCHKIND, C. 2006a. Cassette ethics: public piety and popular media in Egypt. In *Religion, media, and the public sphere* (eds) B. Meyer & A. Moors, 29-52. Bloomington: Indiana University Press.

————— 2006b. *The ethical soundscape: cassette sermons and Islamic counter-publics.* New York: Columbia University Press.

HOLBRAAD, M. 2009. Ontography and alterity: devining anthropological truth. *Social Analysis* **43**: 2, 80-93.

HUMPHREY, C. 1997. Exemplars and rules: aspects of the discourse of moralities in Mongolia. In *The ethnography of moralities* (ed.) S. Howell, 25-47. London: Routledge.

IRWIN, T. 1995. *Plato's ethics.* Oxford: University Press.

————— 2007. *The development of ethics from Socrates to the Reformation*, Vol. **1**. Oxford: Clarendon Press.

IVANOV, S.A. 2010. *Holy fools in Byzantium and beyond.* Oxford: University Press.

KEANE, W. 2007. *Christian moderns: freedom and fetish in the mission encounter.* Berkeley: University of California Press.

KRAUT, R. 1989. *Aristotle on the human good.* Princeton: University Press.

————— (ed.) 1992. *The Cambridge companion to Plato.* Cambridge: University Press.

KUHN, T. 1970. *The structure of scientific revolutions* (Second edition). Chicago: University Press.

LAMBEK, M. 2000. The anthropology of religion and the quarrel between poetry and philosophy. *Current Anthropology* **41**, 309-20.

LOSSKY, V. 1997. *The mystical theology of the Eastern church.* Yonkers, N.Y.: St Vladimir's Seminary Press.

MAHMOOD, S. 2003. Ethical formation and politics of individual autonomy in contemporary Egypt. *Social Research* **70**, 837-66.

PLATO 1984. The Meno. In *The dialogues of Plato*, vol. 1 (trans. R.E. Allen), 151-86. New Haven: Yale University Press.

————— 2000. *The Republic* (trans. B. Jowett). Mineola, N.Y.: Dover.

PSEUDO-DIONYSIUS 1987. *The complete works* (trans. C. Luibheid & P. Rorem). London: Society for the Promotion of Christian Knowledge.

ROBBINS, J. 2004. *Becoming sinners: Christianity and moral torment in a Papua New Guinea society.* Berkeley: University of California Press.

————— 2006. Anthropology and theology: an awkward relationship? *Anthropological Quarterly* **79**, 285-94.

ROREM, P. 1993. *Pseudo-Dionysius: a commentary on the texts and an introduction to their influence.* Oxford: University Press.

SAVIN, I.G. 1996. *Mistica si ascetica ortodoxa.* Sibiu: Tipografia Eparhiala.

SCHIELKE, S. 2009. Being good in Ramadan: ambivalence, fragmentation, and the moral self in the lives of young Egyptians. *Journal of the Royal Anthropological Institute* Special Issue: Islam, politics, anthropology (eds) F. Osella & B. Soares, S24-40.

SIORVANES, L. 1996. *Proclus: Neoplatonic philosophy and science.* Edinburgh: University Press.

STEWART, C. 1994. *Demons and the Devil: moral imagination in modern Greek culture.* Princeton: University Press.

TAMBIAH, S.J. 1984. *The Buddhist saints of the forest and the cult of amulets: a study of charisma, hagiography, sectarianism and millennial Buddhism.* Cambridge: University Press.

TURNER, V.W. & E. TURNER 1978. *Image and pilgrimage in Christian culture: anthropological perspectives.* New York: Columbia University Press.

WALSH, J. & H. SHAPIRO (eds) 1967. *Aristotle's ethics: issues and interpretations.* Belmont, Calif.: Wadsworth.

WARNICK, B. 2008. *Imitation and education: a philosophical inquiry into learning by example.* Albany: State University of New York Press.

Paradigmes paradoxaux : raisonnement moral, inspiration et problèmes de la connaissance parmi les moines chrétiens orthodoxes

Résumé

Alors que les débats anthropologiques sur la moralité sont souvent enracinés dans la théorie éthique aristotélicienne, le présent article met en lumière un autre mode de raisonnement moral chrétien, au carrefour du néoplatonisme et du christianisme, qui se manifeste dans la pratique monastique contemporaine des chrétiens orthodoxes d'Orient. Le changement d'angle d'analyse proposé ici se concentre sur les disjonctions entre différentes traditions éthiques au sein du monde chrétien, afin de montrer comment celles-ci produisent des formes diverses de raisonnement moral, basées sur des usages particuliers de l'exemplarité et de l'exemple. L'auteure avance que la grille de lecture aristotélicienne, mettant l'accent sur l'observance, la piété, l'obéissance et la pratique quotidienne du perfectionnement de soi, peut susciter des récits appauvris de la vie ascétique en excluant des formes plus anarchiques et idiosyncrasiques de discipline spirituelle. Depuis longtemps, le christianisme a recours au paradoxe et à la perplexité pour battre en brèche les certitudes faciles, et s'est ainsi taillé un espace aux limites du savoir humain, dans lequel il peut directement s'adresser à une divinité conçue comme radicalement différente du monde créé.

8

How to do things with examples: Sufis, dreams, and anthropology

Amira Mittermaier *University of Toronto*

In this paper I explore how members of a Sufi community in Egypt use dream-stories as examples to evoke an otherwise invisible realm, and how I, in turn, use their stories ethnographically. My Sufi interlocutors use examples to invite others into the realm of the imagination, to draw listeners into the shaykh's spiritual aura, and to offer a model for emulation that sometimes triggers similar experiences in others. Their approach to examples poses a challenge to the logic of representation, in which a particular stands in for a larger whole. Instead it points to an evocative logic in which examples do not merely represent; they also *do* things. Whereas ethnographic examples tend to oscillate between representation and evocation, referential language ideologies largely obscure the example's evocative power. I suggest that my interlocutors' use of, and approach to, examples can help us think about the example as evocative and performative, including the ways in which examples act upon and through anthropologists.

I begin with an example. One of the moments in which my interlocutors' modes of exemplification stopped me in my ethnographic tracks.

It was long past midnight. I was sitting in the courtyard of an Egyptian mosque where the weeklong celebration (*mawlid*) in honour of Sayyida Nafisa, one of the Prophet Muhammad's saintly descendants, was slowly coming to an end. I was tired and just about to head home when 'Umar came over to tell me that Shaykh Qusi had given me permission to take a look at the Book of Visions. I couldn't believe my luck. The Book of Visions is a handwritten book in which the shaykh's followers for many years have been recording their dream and waking visions.[1] I had been doing fieldwork with Shaykh Qusi's community for months, and ever since I had learned of the book's existence I had been asking whether I could make a copy, or at least take a look. In response, I had been told numerous times that the book is full of secrets (*asrār*) and that I wouldn't be allowed to see it. Now, unexpectedly, the shaykh had changed his mind. Later I was to learn that an order (*amr*) had come to him in a dream, instructing him to make public his community's extraordinary spiritual experiences. And so, that night in the Sayyida Nafisa mosque, 'Umar brought me the Book of Visions, led me to a quiet corner in the courtyard, and told me I was allowed to select some dreams for my dissertation. He gave me a piece of paper and instructed me to write down which of the carefully numbered dream-stories I wanted.

And so I chose. I chose what I took to be a representative sample: some dreams of the shaykh, some of the Prophet, the saints, the dead; waking visions, visions that occurred during the *hadra* (the group's spiritual gatherings), during *mawlids* (saints' day festivals), and at home; some short dream-accounts, some long ones; some told by women, some by men. Different styles, a bit of each kind, covering a broad spectrum of dreamers, dream-types, and dream content.

About half an hour later 'Umar came to check on me. He looked at the examples I had chosen, decided I had chosen badly, and said he would select dream-stories for me instead. He ended up choosing fifty-eight narratives, Xeroxed copies of which he gave me in a purple plastic folder the next time I saw him. I viscerally remember the sense of disappointment I felt as soon as I leafed through the copies. Unlike me, trying to get a bit of each, 'Umar had chosen recurrent dream-visions almost all of which affirm the shaykh's high spiritual state. The stories he had selected were all very similar. The goal for him was not to come up with a representative sample that covers a broad spectrum; it was to find *effective* examples that make a particular point.

I repeatedly tried to reproduce the other dream-stories I had read – those I had chosen but 'Umar had not. I wanted to preserve these invaluable examples but struggled to remember the details. Only slowly did I come to accept that, in this instance, I would have to submit to my interlocutors' choice of examples and, with it, their logic of exemplification. The copies 'Umar had made for me became a material reminder of the fact that, just as I render Shaykh Qusi and his followers into my 'informants' or 'interlocutors', I am caught in their modes of signification, story-telling, and exemplification – modes which can pose a challenge to (and open up new possibilities for) doing ethnographic research, writing ethnography, and thinking anthropologically.

Using this example of divergent exemplifications as my starting-point, I suggest in this paper that my interlocutors' attention to the evocative power of examples sheds light on blind spots inherent in referential or representational logics of exemplification. 'Umar did not seek to come up with a neutral sample; he was committed to a particular story and he was highly conscious of the addressee to whom his examples were directed: me, my future readers, and an amorphous yet powerful notion of the 'West'. He wanted the examples to do something: to direct us to, make us curious about, and draw us into the shaykh's spiritual aura. Anthropologists, too, use examples to convince and seduce their readers. They, too, do things with examples. And, 'Umar, too, wanted to represent something, albeit something evasive: a spiritual reality. Accordingly, my goal in this paper is not to construct a dichotomy between anthropological and Sufi modes of exemplification. Rather, I use my interlocutors' exemplifications to draw into view what a representational language ideology tends to obscure: the evocative power of examples.

Besides thinking about what examples do, we need to ask who is doing what with examples. In the example above, I chose examples, and so did 'Umar. Examples are selected and crafted. As Alexander Gelley puts it: 'Examples do not fall into speech like leaves to the ground' (1995: 1). And yet, examples, once embedded in a text or narrative, are not contained by the author's intention; nor do they evoke a stable referent. Examples are inherently unstable. In ethnographic texts, examples point downwards into the messiness of life from which anthropologists pick their examples (like leaves off the

Journal of the Royal Anthropological Institute (N.S.), 129-143
© Royal Anthropological Institute 2015

ground), and they point upwards toward abstract terms that enable comparisons and allow for theoretical claims to be made. In Clifford Geertz's classical essay on 'Thick description', anthropologists move from miniatures to 'wall-sized culturescapes of the nation, the epoch, the continent, or the civilization'; they move from the microscopic to Power, Faith, Work, and Oppression (1973: 21). They move from the particular to the general, to grand schemes. For Geertz, '[S]mall facts speak to large issues, winks to epistemology, or sheep raids to revolution, because they *are made to*' (1973: 23, emphasis added). Matthew Engelke links the perceived oddity of anthropology to the 'penchant we have for using a vignette or anecdote about what we observed one Tuesday morning in an open-air market outside Timbuktu eighteen years ago to explain the workings of political power in Mali, or African economies, or globalization' (2009: 12). Undoubtedly, writing about large-scale national or global developments, or even just about one particular community, based on seemingly serendipitous encounters, involves large leaps of faith and almost magical acts of translation and generalization. At the same time, the microscopic, the miniature, the wink, and the vignette have a special status in anthropology, a discipline that thrives on details, particularities, characters, and moments, one that often stays close to the ground or even aims to make 'common cause with [its] objects' (Gordon 2008: 21).

To unravel different meanings of exemplarity, I begin by contrasting evocative and representational logics of exemplification. I then offer some background on Shaykh Qusi and the importance of dreams within his community, and introduce some of the meanings of *mathal* ('example' in Arabic). Having laid the ground for a more polyvalent understanding of the example, I present three ways in which Shaykh Qusi's followers engage with, and use, exemplary dream-stories in everyday conversations: as invitations that evoke the invisible; as embedded within a divine order; and as a mode of orientation and guidance. Together these three forms of engagement point to an appreciation for what examples *do* – and as such, they have something to contribute to this collective endeavour of rethinking the power of example in anthropology. If, as Lars Højer and Andreas Bandak suggest in the introduction to this volume, 'exemplification [is] a distinct anthropological way of theorizing' (p. 3), then we might do well in exploring the example's performative potentials, not only by rereading anthropological literatures with an eye to what examples do in them, but also by cultivating an openness towards learning from how our interlocutors put examples to work.

Representational and evocative logics

One could say 'Umar was not choosing examples, and neither was I. Each of us, rather, was selecting a sample with which I was to work when writing my dissertation. Yet our understanding of what constitutes a good sample was intimately tied to our assumptions about what kinds of examples I should have at hand later. I wanted to represent a sociological spectrum of inspired dreamers (men and women, young and old, etc.) and a variety of dreams and dream categories. I wanted to capture a whole through and in its variety. 'Umar wanted to present a particular spiritual state. He wanted to make a point. Whereas I was interested in the dreamers' backgrounds, to 'Umar their age and gender were irrelevant because divinely inspired dreams come to and through the dreamer; they do not index her or his personal circumstances or life-histories. I wanted the narratives to point back to a source, to represent a community. 'Umar was more interested in a 'vector forward' (Gelley 1995: 2) – potential addressees and future effects.

Journal of the Royal Anthropological Institute (N.S.), 129-143
© Royal Anthropological Institute 2015

As such, 'Umar and I brought different logics of exemplification to the same text. Whereas I tried to work systematically towards a vague goal of representativeness, 'Umar whole-heartedly embraced the evocative power of the example. He did not use the stories as seemingly neutral windows into a broader whole, but he wanted them to have a particular effect: to draw us into the shaykh's aura, to instill a sense of awe, and to confirm the shaykh's authority. Far from trying to capture a social spectrum, 'Umar's examples all point in the same direction: towards something that, ultimately, is intangible and evasive.

Arguably, I was choosing examples under the spell of a still quite powerful logic of representation. The 'representative', according to the *Oxford English dictionary*, 'stands in the place of', 'serves as a sign or substitute for', and 'speaks or acts on behalf of a wider body or group of people'. A representative example is one that can stand in for a larger whole. The use in which an example serves this function dates from the nineteenth century (Freadman 2005: 306). We can understand the representative example also within the context of the rule of the norm, which Foucault (1977) takes to be closely related to the disciplinary order of modernity, and which Ian Hacking (1990) relates to the rise of statistics. The modern subject is to aspire not to being exceptional, but to being as close to the norm as possible. Similarly, within this order, the example can be measured with regard to its representativeness, to how typical it is. The example here is by definition substitutable.

I wanted the stories that I chose from the Book of Visions to be as representative as possible. I wanted them to be typical instances of dreams within the shaykh's community, or Sufism more broadly, or Islam at large. The logic of representation offers a way of stabilizing examples, of ordering them. When faced with the evasive world of dreams or other invisible phenomena, this temptation, arguably, is even stronger. As Stephan Palmié (2002: 3) has noted, nothing brings out positivism more quickly than ghosts. Similarly, I think, the temptation to ground and order dream-stories through sociological categories might be enhanced by their ultimate refusal of the sociological.

More broadly, the anthropologists' search for representative examples mirrors representational or referential understandings of language which are dominant in Euro-American contexts (e.g. Crapanzano 1992; Holbraad 2012; Irvine 1989; Keane 2007). A referential language ideology tends to obscure the pragmatic or evocative dimensions of language. Looking for fixed meanings, it 'ignore[s] the complex interlocution – the arguments, assertions, accommodations, seductions, and surrenders, perhaps the echoes of text-silenced voices still sounding somewhere' (Crapanzano 2000: 5). Similarly, a representational logic of exemplification tends to ignore the ways in which examples can take on a life of their own – the example's unruliness, its seductiveness. Michael Taussig suggests that such are the demands of academic talk and writing: 'the demands for an explanation, the demands for coherence, the denial of rhetoric, the denial of performance' (1992: 7). In brief, referential language ideologies tend to overlook the ways in which language does not merely mirror a reality out there but also *makes* realities.

The title of this paper is inspired by J.L. Austin's *How to do things with words* (1962), which ruptures a purely referential language ideology. Austin points out that at least some words do not represent; they *do* things. In particular, Austin was interested in speech-acts – statements that have no truth-value but perform a certain kind of action (such as, 'I hereby pronounce you husband and wife'). A number of thinkers have extended this argument beyond speech-acts, arguing that *all* words (and examples) do things (e.g. Butler 1997). Anthropologists furthermore have noted that language functions differently in different places and that 'the ways of thinking about language and about human agency and personhood are intimately linked' (Rosaldo 1982: 203).[2] The same holds true for examples, which, too, are linked to ideas about agency, personhood, and relationality. In some places, the evocative role of examples is less obscured.

According to the *Oxford English dictionary*, the evocative is that which 'calls [and] draws forth'. An evocative example, then, does not merely *re*-present. It does not render present again something that is given and stable. It rather creates worlds. It makes visible what otherwise could not be seen. Significantly, what is drawn forth in 'Umar's examples is literally the unobservable, invisible, intangible.

Ethnographic examples, too, do not merely represent. They also evoke. As Højer and Bandak note in the introduction, the example, including the ethnographic one, 'excels in exploring the tension between, and the instability of, the specific and the general, the concrete and the abstract . . . , and it does so by never fully becoming one or the other' (p. 6). The example's unstable place between specific and general is related to a different tension and instability: that between representing and evoking. Anthropologists frequently list a handful of key fieldsites or key interlocutors, implying that they could have chosen many others: that these sites and interlocutors are substitutable; that they are representative of larger trends, communities, or 'cultures'. But they simultaneously tend to imply that these sites or people are particularly good examples: that they stand out. Anthropologists use anecdotes and examples to persuade and to create particular lines of force. A good ethnographic example is and isn't substitutable. It is generalizable and unique, both at once.

Thus, while we sometimes use the language of 'sample' and generally try to make a case for representativeness, the examples we end up including in our ethnographies are often not the most typical but the most striking, charismatic, extraordinary. They are chosen because they help make a particular point. A profound ambiguity surrounds the ethnographic example, and ultimately it might be precisely the oscillation between representation and evocation that constitutes its power.

My goal is not to undo this oscillation. I do believe, however, that it would be helpful to dwell more on the evocative and to consider how examples – be they dreams, stories, interlocutors, places, or particular moments – work upon and through us. It might mean being a little less apprehensive about the power of examples. As such, it might also call for rethinking ethnographic representation in ways less opposed to the evocative. Michael Taussig, for instance, advocates 'an understanding of the representation as contiguous with that being represented and not as suspended above and distant from the represented' (1992: 10). This is a representation that refuses being translated fully into 'large issues', one that never erases the particularity of the example.

As Højer and Bandak point out, examples are so interesting to think with because they belong to no one in particular. Unlike the language of 'cases' or 'data', that of 'examples' brings our interlocutors right into the conversation. They offer themselves up as examples, present stories as examples, might be dissatisfied with being degraded to being 'just another example', and have views on what constitutes a good or bad example, and on what examples can and should do. By bringing my interlocutors into the conversation not just as examples of examples but also as theorists of examples, I contrast three takes on exemplification: (1) a social-scientific model in which examples are taken to represent something predefined (gender, age, etc.); (2) the evocative power of examples, exemplified here by my Sufi interlocutors; and (3) ethnographic examples that oscillate between representation and evocation. That is, I turn to Shaykh Qusi's community not because our own examples *don't* do things but because my interlocutors are more attuned to, and less apprehensively put to work, the power of examples.

Shaykh Qusi, dreams, and the meanings of *mathal*

Originally from a small town in Upper Egypt, Shaykh Qusi held a graduate degree in chemistry from a Czech university. He lived and worked in Egypt, Germany, Spain, Turkey, and Saudi Arabia. In addition to his scientific and cosmopolitan background, he studied key texts of the Islamic tradition from an early age and said he was particularly influenced by al-Ghazālī (d. 1111) and Ibn al-'Arabī (d. 1240), two medieval Sufi thinkers.[3] In the early 1990s, Shaykh Qusi was subjected to a spiritual calling. Disciples gathered around him, mostly in Egypt but also elsewhere, forming a spiritual community called Al-Ashrāf al-Mahdiyya (The Guided Honorables). Most of the shaykh's followers are highly educated, and many hold influential positions in the Egyptian military, banks, and large companies. The group organizes biweekly *hadras*, gatherings during which a spiritual text is collectively recited, and they participate in saint's day celebrations and organize a large Ramadan table (*mā'idat al-rahmān*) every year where they serve food to thousands of people on a daily basis throughout the month of fasting. Although in many ways the group resembles a Sufi community, the shaykh rejected this label. He pointed out that, whereas Sufis concern themselves with developing the self (*al-nafs*), he worked directly on the spirit (*al-rūh*). This rejection of the Sufi label is likely also related to the fact that Sufism is widely associated with the 'lower classes' and ignorance in Egypt. Despite their unease with the label, I tend to frame the group as a 'Sufi community' in much of my work, and the shaykh often serves as my 'Sufi example'. Sufism offers a slightly misleading but readily accessible *general* through which to locate the *particular* of Shaykh Qusi's community.

Since the shaykh's death in 2008, his followers have continued along his spiritual path, and they speak of his continuous spiritual presence. They still often see him in their dreams and waking visions, which have long been central tools of communication within the community. Drawing on Islamic traditions of dream interpretation, Shaykh Qusi's followers distinguish between three kinds of dreams: those that reflect the dreamer's wishes and worries; those sent by the Devil or evil spirits; and those that are divinely inspired.[4] Divinely inspired dreams can be invited through spiritual practices but ultimately are understood to come from an Elsewhere. They constitute a channel of communication with the Prophet Muhammad, his saintly descendants (*ahl al-bayt*), and the dead. They can point to the future and more broadly offer glimpses of *al-ghayb*, the world of the Unknown. According to a number of prophetic sayings, they constitute a part of prophecy. Divinely inspired dream-visions, called *ru'a* (sing. *ru'yā*) in Arabic, are central to many spiritual communities and individual believers in Egypt but are eyed with suspicion by reformist, rationalist Muslim scholars, who tend to argue that the gates of prophecy are closed, that the dead are truly dead and cannot be communicated with anymore, and that we should rely on our minds and not our dreams.[5] Prophetic dreams, as such, are profoundly valued and heavily contested, both at once. My fieldwork consisted of tracing how such dreams are understood, invited, interpreted, and dismissed and how they move dreamers in their waking lives. When I first met Shaykh Qusi and told him about my research, he smiled and said I had come to the right place; his followers were all 'experts in dreaming'.

Journal of the Royal Anthropological Institute (N.S.), 129-143
© Royal Anthropological Institute 2015

The shaykh's followers often tell and retell dream-stories, and they record them in the Book of Visions. Because of the dream-vision's high epistemological value, referring to dreams can be just as valid as (or even more convincing than) telling stories about waking life. As such, in everyday conversations dreams can be tokens, rhetorical devices, and even pieces of evidence. When recounting particular dreams, the shaykh's followers sometimes frame them with the word *mathalan* ('for example') to mark a shift in the flow of conversation. 'For example, last week Mahmoud saw how the Prophet Muhammad came to Shaykh Qusi and said . . .'.

The Arabic word *mathal* brings with it a range of associations (see also Andreas Bandak's contribution to this volume). It can be translated as example, instance, analogy, or proverb. The related preposition *mithla* means 'like': 'A is like B'. Closely associated with likeness, in the Qur'an examples mostly function as allegories. Generally, translators of the Qur'an render the term *mathal* as 'similitude', 'likeness', or 'parable'. For instance, the effects of charity in the Qur'an are compared to (they are *mithla*) 'a grain of corn [which] grows seven ears, and each ear has a hundred grains' (Qur'an 2:261; Muhammad Asad's translation). Interpreters explain that in the Qur'an examples from the natural world serve to make the abstract benefits of charity more graspable. Something known (a grain of corn) is brought together by way of comparison (*tashbīh*) with something unknown (a divine truth or abstract principle). The comparison grounds the abstract in the everyday while simultaneously framing the natural world as concrete and accessible. The Qur'an explains, 'And [all] such parables (*amthāl*, sing. *mathal*) we propound unto men, so that they might [learn to] think' (59:21; Muhammad Asad's translation). As such, Qur'anic examples function, in Alexander Gelley's terms, 'as illustration, as an aid in understanding, in visualizing' (1995: 2).

In the hadith, the record of the Prophet Muhammad's deeds and sayings, we find a slightly different meaning of example.[6] The Prophet's life as recorded in the hadith is not *an* example but *the* example *par excellence*. I return to this meaning shortly.

In a third textual source relevant to Shaykh Qusi's community, writings by medieval Sufi thinkers, *mathal* evokes the realm of the imagination, *'ālam al-mithāl*. Sometimes translated as world of images, *'ālam al-mithāl* refers to a realm between the spiritual and the material; it is a space and a mode of perception. In Sufi writings the imagination offers access to knowledge that circumvents the limitations of rational thought. Al-Ghazālī, a medieval Sufi thinker whose works have influenced Shaykh Qusi, highlighted the limits of reason and argued that we should take dreams seriously as a source of knowledge. As Ebrahim Moosa (2005) notes, al-Ghazālī gave primacy to the logic of the imaginary that embraces 'both/and' while disowning the limiting embrace of the 'either/or' of rational logic. Similarly, in his work on Ibn al-'Arabī, another influential medieval Sufi thinker, William Chittick explains, '[O]ne of the reasons for Ibn al-'Arabī's extraordinary stress on the importance of imagination [was] his attempt to make people aware of the disservice to understanding done by rational extraction and abstraction'. In Ibn al-'Arabī's view, '[T]he more that rational thinkers reflect upon God, the further away they push Him' (Chittick 1998: xi, xxxvi). In contrast to reason, the imagination embodies. It creates closeness. It is inherently rooted in *tashbīh* (immanence), which sees the cosmos as a locus of God's continual self-disclosure, a realm of likeness.[7] Reason differentiates between symbol and symbolized; between Creator and creation. The imagination, by contrast, perceives how the symbol partakes in what it symbolizes. As such, dreams of the Prophet do not offer a symbolic representation; the Prophet appearing in the dream *is* the Prophet. William Chittick, who has translated a number of Ibn al-'Arabī's works into English, notes that a problem of translation is posed by the prevalence of abstraction in the English language (1998: xxxv). Abstraction pushes towards *tanzīh* (transcendence), which is the opposite of *tashbīh* (immanence). The former foregrounds difference, the latter similarity. We might say that Michael Taussig's approach to ethnography, too, calls for a form of *tashbīh*, a mode of imagination and writing that stays close to, or is even contiguous with, the represented and is not suspended above and distant from it. In line with this understanding of the imagination, those stories or examples that work best are not the most representative or typical but those that move the listeners or readers, that draw them in, creating closeness rather than abstraction.

These three meanings of *mathal* – Qur'anic allegory, the Prophet's exemplary life, and the world of images and likeness – open up a field of associations that diverge from a quasi-scientific language of samples which is concerned with how and whether examples adequately represent a larger whole. Instead, the meanings of *mathal* draw our attention to the kinds of things examples *do*.

Examples as invitations

Many conversations in Shaykh Qusi's community revolve around divinely inspired dreams and waking visions: who has seen what, where, and at what time. Followers often tell and retell dream-stories – at the group's spiritual gatherings, at *mawlids*, during car rides, and over tea. Because it is usually assumed that the dreamers themselves might not be able to understand or interpret their dreams, dreams are first reported to those spiritually close to the shaykh (during his lifetime they would have been recounted to the shaykh himself). Once approved as meaningful, dream-stories enter into wider circulation within the community.

Some dreams are dreamed collectively (e.g. by two people in different cities who have identical, overlapping, or complementary dreams). Dreams can also inspire other similar dreams. Listening to dream-stories can hone one's receptiveness. As such, dream-stories refer to past spiritual experiences, but they also invite the listener into a realm of in-between-ness: between invisible and visible, spiritual and material, divine and human. Examples draw things into view, and in Shaykh Qusi's community they draw into view what otherwise would remain invisible. As such, dream-stories differ from anthropologists' fieldwork stories in that they do not claim to re-present an observable reality. Fieldwork anecdotes promise, as Stephen Greenblatt (1997) would put it, a 'touch of the real' or, in Clifford Geertz's (1989) words, they prove the anthropologist's 'having been there'. By pointing to a particular place at a particular time, they are more stubbornly tied to a representational, referential logic. By contrast, it is impossible to prove or disprove what someone else claims to have dreamed.[8] Dream-stories offer evidence too, but they point to a realm that is accessible not through the body's senses or the mind but through the imagination.[9] In Shaykh Qusi's community, having access to this realm, even through other people's dreams and stories, means being connected to the Prophet and his saintly descendants, and to the world of hidden, inner truths (*al-bātin*). As such, the most relevant question here is not which stories are most *representative* but which are most *evocative*. Thus, often after having been told a dream-story, I was asked not simply what I thought about the story but also what I *felt* about it. Dream-stories were presented to me not simply as evidence but also because they are expected to offer a taste of an otherwise inaccessible, invisible realm, *al-ghayb*.

Journal of the Royal Anthropological Institute (N.S.), 129-143
© Royal Anthropological Institute 2015

In an article on remembering as moral practice, Michael Lambek (1996) distinguishes between two conceptualizations of memory. Echoing the distinction between representational and evocative, one conceptualization frames memory as a more or less accurate representation of the past; the other understands it as moral practice, a set of claims, and a function of (and constitutive of) social relationships. Lambek holds that memory is never morally or pragmatically neutral: '[T]o remember is never solely to report on the past so much as to establish one's relationship toward it' (1996: 240). He turns to practices of spirit possession in Madagascar to highlight this often-obscured aspect of memory, arguing that this understanding is not absent from 'Western' epistemologies but is largely obscured by hegemonic understandings. I similarly dwell on my interlocutors' attunement to the ways in which examples can invite us to see differently, not because I want to reinscribe a West-Islam dichotomy, but because my interlocutors' insights are themselves invitations. They invite us to see what is obscured by a representational logic and to think beyond concerns with representativeness.

Like memory among Lambek's interlocutors in Madagascar, dream-stories in Shaykh Qusi's community are never pragmatically neutral. They are expected to move the listeners, to draw them into an otherwise invisible realm, to confirm the shaykh's spiritual state, and sometimes to invite more dreams of the same kind. Yet, unlike memory in Lambek's account, dreaming (and telling dreams) in Shaykh Qusi's community is not only a moral but also a spiritual practice. The dream embeds the visible social world within a web of invisible relations – to the dead, the Prophet, the saints, and ultimately God. Seeing, telling, and inviting dreams are all modes of cultivating relationships that exceed the visible world.[10] The dream as a mode of relationality and as a message from an Elsewhere resonates with how my interlocutors understand their place in my ethnography: not as a randomly chosen example but as something that always already exceeds my choice and intentions. Just as dream-visions undo the myth of the self-contained subject, my interlocutors' understanding of their place in my ethnography undoes the assumption that anthropologists are fully in control of their fieldwork and writing.

Beyond randomness

Many people, in Egypt and elsewhere, have asked me how I met Shaykh Qusi. The story I usually tell in response is one of serendipity. One day, during my fieldwork, I was visiting a small saint's shrine in Islamic Cairo. There I met Mona, a woman in her late forties who had known Shaykh Qusi for a number of years. (She later told me that she rarely visits this particular shrine but for some reason had ended up there that day.) We chatted a little, and Mona invited me to come along to a nearby mosque where Shaykh Qusi was gathered with his followers. I had no other plans, spontaneously decided to join her, and met the shaykh. He was welcoming and had lots to say about dreams. I continued seeing him and his followers.

A few months later, I sat in a coffee shop in downtown Cairo with a middle-class friend from a town in Upper Egypt. I happened to have a book of Shaykh Qusi's poetry with me. My friend skimmed through the book and frowned: 'Who is this guy? Why are you talking to him? Isn't he just one of those charlatans?' I encountered similar scepticism later on when giving talks to academic audiences in North America. So who is this Shaykh Qusi? How does he fit into the larger landscape? Why did I choose him? How does he compare to other shaykhs? Is he really representative of Egyptian Sufism?

Journal of the Royal Anthropological Institute (N.S.), 129-143
© Royal Anthropological Institute 2015

And isn't Sufism itself marginal in Egypt? In my own moments of doubt I scolded myself for not having worked more systematically, from above, so to speak. If I wanted to include a 'Sufi example' in my study, I should have started by contacting the Egyptian Higher Council of Sufi Affairs, asked for a list of all current Sufi orders in Cairo, scheduled meetings with the shaykhs of the leading orders, conducted preliminary interviews, and from there chosen a representative example.

And yet, if I had taken that route, I would have never met Shaykh Qusi. His group is not one of the registered Sufi orders that a systematic search for a representative example could have ever led me to. At the same time it is only through them that I came to appreciate more fully a different understanding of the imagination and the profound ways in which the visible world can be disrupted by, or enfolded in, the invisible.

Concerns with randomness rarely arose when I was *with* Shaykh Qusi and his followers. In their view, I had met them for a reason. Still today they tell the story of how I met Mona and how she directed me to them. But for them it is not a story of serendipity. In their version, my encounter with the shaykh was meant to happen. It would have occurred with or without Mona. The underlying understanding of fate and temporality does not preclude choice but acknowledges the limits of human agency. This understanding also finds expression in the kinds of dream-stories I was collecting. Divinely inspired dreams connect different moments in time: they draw together the moment when the dream is seen and the moment when it comes true. Many Sufis furthermore explained to me that divinely inspired dreams are always already written on the Eternal Tablet (*al-lawh al-mahfūz*), a tablet in heaven on which all fate is inscribed. Present, future, and eternity merge here, disrupting linear temporalities and causalities by embedding each moment – whether dream or waking life – within a larger order. Similarly, my encounter with Shaykh Qusi took place at a particular moment in time but, in the eyes of his followers, it was always already written (and might well have already been dreamed). It was far from random or serendipitous.

This understanding does not preclude that, in the eyes of Shaykh Qusi and his followers, many other encounters during my fieldwork were random or even pointless. Which encounters are deemed relevant (and which dreams are considered divinely inspired) is always a matter of interpretation. Nevertheless, the underlying understanding of fate lifts my meeting with Shaykh Qusi out of the realm of randomness and pushes back against the question of whether he really is a representative example. It challenges the assumed directionality and temporality of the example. The shaykh is not an example chosen by me – carefully or not carefully enough. He had a place in my ethnography before I ever met him.

In the prologue to his book on Afro-Cuban religions, Stephan Palmié contrasts his own rationalizations of his fieldwork with the explanations offered by a professional diviner and a priest. They insist that he was driven to their doorsteps by the spirit of a dead slave – 'a solution straightforwardly plausible within the world of Afro-Cuban religion but … utterly fantastic within the universe of meaning that I inhabit' (Palmié 2002: 1). Palmié uses this example to challenge habituated understandings of history and, in particular, the pastness of the past. Similarly, in an article drawing on her research on Sufism in Pakistan, Katherine Ewing reflects on what it means for the anthropologist to become 'the recipient of a dream sent by a saint' (1994: 574). In one of her examples, a Sufi saint (*pir*) tells her that he will come to her while she is sleeping. He says he can reach her even in America. That same night she dreams of the saint, feels touched in the dream, and wakes up startled. Others whom she tells about the dream take it as proof of the saint's spiritual power; she remains doubtful, however. Later, towards the end of her fieldwork, she meets another Sufi saint in Peshawar, and the following night again has a vivid dream. She returns to the saint, tells him about the dream, and he says she will know her teacher or spiritual leader in the years to come. Through these examples, Ewing reflects on what she calls an 'anthropological atheism', or the 'refusal to acknowledge that the subjects of one's research might actually know something about the human condition that is personally valid for the anthropologist: it is a refusal to believe' (1994: 571). To get beyond such a refusal, one does not need to 'go native'. But one needs to be open to considering how different understandings of fate, agency, and history push back against habituated assumptions. By drawing attention to how dreams, inspiration, and examples act upon and *through* us, Shaykh Qusi's followers and their stories help decentre the anthropologist's role in selecting and crafting examples.

Maybe anthropologists do not always choose their examples but sometimes are also chosen by them. Maybe, similarly, examples are not simply 'made to' speak to larger issues, as Geertz suggests, but also have their own story to tell.

The best of examples

Once it is freed from a purely representational logic, the example is allowed – even expected – to take on a life of its own. Shaykh Qusi's followers tell their dream-stories not simply to point to what is possible when one has reached a high spiritual state, but also as examples in the sense of model. In German we would say such stories are not simply *Beispiele*; they are *beispielhaft*. They are not only an example *of* but also an example *for*.

The example-as-model diverges from the logic of sample and data – the idea that a particular can stand in for a larger whole. Here, rather, the example is not just *any* particular but a very *particular* particular. It is not the ordinary and substitutable but the most extraordinary. In the context of Shaykh Qusi's community, the best of all examples is the Prophet Muhammad. He is literally referred to as the best or highest example (*al-mathal al-aʿlā*), the ideal. The Qurʾan (33:21) also calls him a 'beautiful example' (*uswa hasana*; see also Christian Suhr's contribution to this volume). It is for this reason that many people in Egypt, instead of telling me about their own lives, referred to the Prophet Muhammad's life by way of citing hadiths, written accounts of the Prophet's deeds (see also Hoffman-Ladd 1992). As Saba Mahmood (2009) points out, understanding this profound identification with the Prophet – the constant aspiration to embody his life as best as possible, the degree to which one's sense of self is bound up with him – is crucial for understanding the sense of injury caused in 2005 by the publication of the controversial Danish cartoons depicting him.

What makes the Prophet the best example is not the fact that he is most representative or typical but rather that he is an ideal. He is an exemplar. The same holds true for the Prophet's saintly descendants (*ahl al-bayt*), whose lives offer models for emulation. In Shaykh Qusi's community, the shaykh, too, offers a model of orientation and emulation.

Referring to a different context, Ian Hacking offers the helpful image of a 'radial order'. He distinguishes the best example from other, ordinary examples, ones which radiate away:

> Thus, many people, asked to give an example of a bird, apparently say, 'robin'. People seldom offer 'ostrich' or 'pelican' straight off. The robin is a best example ... We cannot arrange all birds in a

Journal of the Royal Anthropological Institute (N.S.), 129-143
© Royal Anthropological Institute 2015

single linear order of birdiness, saying that pelicans are more birdy than ostriches but less birdy than robins. If we must draw a diagram, it should be a circle or sphere (Hacking 1995: 23-4).

In this radial order, different birds are related by chains of family resemblance, and in the middle of these chains lies a prototype. Similarly, in Sufi contexts, good examples – such as the Prophet's saintly descendants and Sufi shaykhs – radiate out from the Prophet Muhammad, the best of all examples.

In ethnographies, too, the notion of the best example often lurks behind the example as substitutable instance. More broadly, Alexander Gelley (1995) argues, examples in the Western philosophical tradition have long hovered between these two sets of meaning: an example is a standard, model, or paradigm; but it is also an instance. Some uncertainty always remains: 'Is the example merely *one* – a singular, a fruit of circumstance – or *the One* – a paradigm, a paragon?' (Gelley 1995: 2, original emphasis). By calling Shaykh Qusi a key interlocutor in my book (Mittermaier 2011: 23), I, too, imply something slightly different than if I called him merely an example or informant. It means he is an example and exemplary, both at once. As anthropological modes of story-telling fluctuate between representational and evocative aspirations, they can overlap with Sufi modes of story-telling but can also diverge from them. Ethnographic examples are caught between being suggestive and descriptive.

Thus far I have argued for a shift in focus from the representational towards a more nuanced appreciation of the evocative. I have relied on Shaykh Qusi's followers to illuminate what is obscured in a representational logic. So far in my account these different logics have coexisted rather peacefully. Sometimes, however, different styles of exemplification can also enter into conflict. Let me illustrate this final point through yet another example.

In 2011 I returned to Egypt with my published book in hand. I gave a copy to Shaykh Qusi's followers. They flipped through its pages and were pleased to find the shaykh's picture along with a chapter dedicated entirely to their community. At the same time, they questioned my choice of having devoted only one chapter to the shaykh. Why not write about all the other topics in which I was interested through the shaykh? In his followers' eyes, Shaykh Qusi offers an all-encompassing perspective on life, the imagination, and Islam; there was no need to include other shaykhs and dreamers in my ethnography. Besides having to confront questions about my decision to *reduce* Shaykh Qusi to being merely an example, I have on occasion been called upon to help organize a speaking tour for the shaykh's followers, who hope to spread his message in North America. The shaykh, even beyond his death, confronts me with expectations I cannot always meet. At times, it seems that there is a misunderstanding, a disconnect, between my approach to the shaykh – as *an* example – and his followers' understanding of how I should use the shaykh in my work – as *the* example.

The space between these two modes of exemplification is not always one of creativity and dialogical engagement. It can also be a space of discomfort and unease.

Conclusion

I have reflected in this paper on strategies of exemplification in Shaykh Qusi's community alongside my own use of examples. The shaykh and his followers tell particular dream- and vision-stories not to offer representative data but to *move* listeners – to invite them into the shaykh's aura and community, to draw them into a world of the hidden (*al-bātin*) and invisible (*al-ghayb*) and into their own dream-worlds. Examples here are not neutral, substitutable instances but rather are appreciated for their evocative power, for their ability to draw listeners into an otherwise inaccessible realm. I suggest that anthropologists, too, often use examples evocatively but that a representational language ideology tends to obscure these evocative dimensions. In anthropology, examples oscillate between a representational and an evocative logic. And while it is this very oscillation that lies at the heart of the example's ethnographic power, I hope to have shown that an ethnographic engagement with our interlocutors' approaches to, and use of, examples can help illuminate the example's evocative dimensions.

Readers might find that there is something infinitely regressive about my use of examples to address other modes of exemplification. I begin with 'Umar yet quickly reduce him to representing Shaykh Qusi's community. The community, in turn, is framed as a 'Sufi community' and is linked to the Islamic tradition through references to the Qur'an, hadith, and medieval Sufi thinkers. Despite beginning with a concrete example of other modes of exemplification, I arguably fall back into the generalizations that follow a familiar pattern from particular to general. Maybe, by the very act of framing and representing, I push the ability to apprehend other modes of understanding and story-telling just out of reach. And yet, representing other modes of exemplification might be the only way to engage with them – to let them undo the logic of representation from within. Recall here that Shaykh Qusi's community would challenge the very idea that I am fully in charge of choosing my examples. It is ironic that I have to rely on examples to make a point about examples. But it is equally ironic that Shaykh Qusi has once again claimed a space for himself as the key example in this paper.

Ultimately, not only our interlocutors are moved by analogies and examples but so too are we as ethnographers, readers, and writers.[11] The examples that we end up using in our ethnographies might be meaningful in ways that exceed our intentions and chosen modes of argumentation. We might then need to consider how – at the same time as we craft, select, and manipulate examples – we are also *acted upon* by examples. My interlocutors' insights into the seductive, performative, and evocative power of example can open up a space for thinking about different approaches to story-telling, strategies of exemplification, practices of imagining, and modes of evidence – ones that might enrich our vocabulary and appreciation for the things examples do.

Importantly, the difference between evocative and referential does not map onto an Islam/West dichotomy. Setting up such a dichotomy would be highly problematic – particularly in light of the long history of Orientalist discourses that portray Arabs, Muslims, or more generally the Other as incapable of thinking abstractly or logically. An example of this kind of Orientalist discourse can be found in the book *The Arab mind*, originally published in 1973 and reprinted after 9/11, in which anthropologist Raphael Patai (1983 [1973]) argues that the very nature of the Arabic language renders its speakers incapable of abstract thought. In Patai's account, Arabs are imprisoned in a world of analogies: they cannot but think in examples. My interlocutors are keenly aware of such Orientalist stereotypes and often worried about their examples being taken out of context and having unwanted effects.

Rather than contrast Islam and the West, I want to close by suggesting that the dichotomy between 'typical instances' and 'invitations' is itself highly unstable. Invitations hold the potential for being or becoming typical instances, just as 'scientific representations', especially in anthropology, may be – and be thought of as – invitations to think and imagine. Maybe, in letting other modes of story-telling speak back to our modes of listening and writing, we might be able to embrace the power of example

Journal of the Royal Anthropological Institute (N.S.), 129-143
© Royal Anthropological Institute 2015

with a little less hesitation – the power of examples that we choose *and* those that write themselves through us.

NOTES

For comments on earlier drafts of this paper I would like to thank Andreas Bandak, Lars Højer, the participants in the workshop 'The Power of Example', *JRAI*'s anonymous reviewers, as well as Katie Kilroy-Marac and Alejandra Gonzalez Jimenez.

[1] For a discussion of the relationship between poetry and prophecy in the Book of Visions, see Mittermaier (2007). On Shaykh Qusi's community, see also chapter 4 in *Dreams that matter* (Mittermaier 2011).

[2] For anthropological accounts that foreground the performative dimensions of language, see also Keane (1997) and Tambiah (1979).

[3] All dates in this paper are CE.

[4] In classical dream manuals, a dream that reflects the self's wishes is called *ḥadīth nafsī*; one that is sent by the Devil or evil spirits is called *ḥulm*; and one that is divinely inspired is called *ru'yā*. Widely used dreams manuals include those by Ibn Sīrīn (d. 733) and al-Nābulusī (d. 1731). For a comprehensive history of dream interpretation in the Islamic tradition, see Lamoreaux (2002).

[5] I use the term 'dream-vision' to translate *ru'yā* because the latter can refer to a divinely inspired dream or waking vision. Shaykh Qusi's followers often do not differentiate whether they were awake or asleep when seeing a particular vision. On Egypt's rich but contested dream landscapes, see Mittermaier (2011).

[6] The hadith literature also contains many analogies. For example, the Prophet said: *mathalu aṣḥābī ka-mathal al-milhi fī al-ta'am* ('The likeness of my Companions (among people) is like salt in the food'). Cited in Suyuti's *al-Jami' al-Saghīr*, 8160.

[7] *Tashbīh* comes from the verb *shabbaha*, which means making something similar, comparing, highlighting commonalities.

[8] However, according to prophetic sayings, lying about one's dreams will be severely punished in the hereafter.

[9] The kind of imagination that figures in Shaykh Qusi's community is not the same as fantasy but refers to a prophetic mode of perception and to the space between the divine and the human. In Sufi epistemologies more broadly, the visible world (*zāhir*) can be misleading, whereas dream-visions and other forms of inspiration can offer glimpses of hidden, inner truths (*bātin*).

[10] Divinely inspired dreams can be invited but are not produced by the dreamer. Elsewhere I discuss the dreamer's being acted upon to highlight limits of 'self-cultivation' – a trope used widely in the anthropology of Islam (Mittermaier 2012).

[11] Thinkers such as William Connolly (1999) highlight how visceral and affective dimensions shape our political and analytical stands. Acknowledging the visceral underpinnings of our academic work implies paying more attention to the ways in which things have a hold on us, move us, repel us, or compel us forward – in our research design, fieldwork, and writing.

REFERENCES

Austin, J.L. 1962. *How to do things with words*. Oxford: Clarendon Press.

Butler, J. 1997. *Excitable speech: a politics of the performative*. New York: Routledge.

Chittick, W. 1998. *The self-disclosure of God: principles of Ibn al-Arabi's cosmology*. Albany: State University of New York Press.

Connolly, W.E. 1999. *Why I am not a secularist*. Minneapolis: University of Minnesota Press.

Crapanzano, V. 1992. *Hermes' dilemma and Hamlet's desire: on the epistemology of interpretation*. Cambridge, Mass.: Harvard University Press.

——— 2000. *Serving the word: literalism in America from the pulpit to the bench*. New York: New Press.

Engelke, M. 2009. The objects of evidence. In *The objects of evidence: anthropological approaches to the production of knowledge* (ed.) M. Engelke, 1-20. Malden, Mass.: Wiley-Blackwell.

Ewing, K. 1994. Dreams from a saint: anthropological atheism and the temptation to believe. *American Anthropologist* **96**, 571-83.

Foucault, M. 1977. *Discipline and punish: the birth of the prison* (trans. A. Sheridan). New York: Pantheon.

Freadman, A. 2005. Representation. In *New keywords: a revised vocabulary of culture and society* (eds) T. Bennett, L. Grossberg & M. Morris, 306-9. Oxford: Blackwell.

Geertz, C. 1973. Thick description: toward an interpretive theory of culture. In *The interpretation of cultures*, 3-30. New York: Basic Books.

Journal of the Royal Anthropological Institute (N.S.), 129-143
© Royal Anthropological Institute 2015

———— 1989. Being there: anthropology and the scene of writing. In *Works and lives: the anthropologist as author*, 1-14. Stanford: University Press.

GELLEY, A. 1995. Introduction. In *Unruly examples: on the rhetoric of exemplarity* (ed.) A. Gelley, 1-24. Stanford: University Press.

GORDON, A. 2008. *Ghostly matters: haunting and the sociological imagination*. Minneapolis: University of Minnesota Press.

GREENBLATT, S. 1997. The touch of the real. *Representations* **59**, 14-29.

HACKING, I. 1990. *The taming of chance*. Cambridge: University Press.

———— 1995. *Rewriting the soul: multiple personality and the sciences of memory*. Princeton: University Press.

HOFFMAN-LADD, V. 1992. Devotion to the Prophet and his family in Egyptian Sufism. *International Journal of Middle East Studies* **24**, 615-37.

HOLBRAAD, M. 2012. *Truth in motion: the recursive anthropology of Cuban divination*. Chicago: University Press.

IRVINE, J. 1989. When talk isn't cheap: language and political economy. *American Ethnologist* **16**, 248-67.

KEANE, W. 1997. Religious language. *Annual Review of Anthropology* **26**, 47-71.

———— 2007. *Christian moderns: freedom and fetish in the mission encounter*. Berkeley: University of California Press.

LAMBEK, M. 1996. The past imperfect: remembering as moral practice. In *Tense past: cultural essays in trauma and memory* (eds) M. Lambek & P. Antze, 235-54. London: Routledge.

LAMOREAUX, J. 2002. *The early Muslim tradition of dream interpretation*. Albany: State University of New York Press.

MAHMOOD, S. 2009. Religious reason and secular affect: an incommensurable divide? In *Is critique secular? Blasphemy, injury, and free speech* (eds) J. Butler, T. Asad, S. Mahmood & W. Brown, 64-100. Berkeley: University of California Press.

MITTERMAIER, A. 2007. The book of visions: dreams, poetry, and prophecy in contemporary Egypt. *International Journal of Middle East Studies* **39**, 229-47.

———— 2011. *Dreams that matter: Egyptian landscapes of the imagination*. Berkeley: University of California Press.

———— 2012. Dreams from Elsewhere: Muslim subjectivities beyond the trope of self-cultivation. *Journal of the Royal Anthropological Institute* (N.S.) **18**, 247-65.

MOOSA, E. 2005. *Ghazālī and the poetics of imagination*. Chapel Hill: University of North Carolina Press.

PALMIÉ, S. 2002. *Wizards and scientists: explorations in Afro-Cuban modernity and tradition*. Durham, N.C.: Duke University Press.

PATAI, R. 1983 [1973]. *The Arab mind*. New York: Charles Scribner's Sons.

ROSALDO, M.Z. 1982. The things we do with words: Ilongot speech acts and speech act theory in philosophy. *Language in Society* **11**, 203-35.

TAMBIAH, S.J. 1979. *A performance approach to ritual*. Oxford: University Press.

TAUSSIG, M. 1992. *The nervous system*. New York: Routledge.

Comment faire les choses avec des exemples : soufis, rêves et anthropologie

Résumé

Le présent article explore la manière dont les membres d'une communauté soufie égyptienne utilisent les récits de rêves comme exemples pour évoquer un royaume invisible par ailleurs, et comment l'auteure, à son tour, utilise ces récits à des fins ethnographiques. Ses interlocuteurs soufis utilisent des exemples pour inviter les autres dans le royaume de l'imagination, pour attirer les auditeurs dans l'aura spirituelle du sheikh et pour offrir un modèle à imiter qui déclenche parfois des expériences similaires chez les autres. Leur approche des exemples est un défi à la logique de la représentation selon laquelle un élément particulier représente un tout plus grand. Au lieu de cela, elle suggère une logique de l'évocation, dans laquelle les exemples non seulement représentent, mais aussi *font* les choses. Alors que les exemples ethnographiques oscillent souvent entre représentation et évocation, les idéologies du langage référentiel occultent largement le pouvoir évocateur de l'exemple. L'auteure suggère que l'utilisation des exemples par ses interlocuteurs et leur approche de ceux-ci peuvent nous aider à envisager l'exemple comme évocateur et performatif, notamment dans la manière dont il agit sur et à travers les anthropologues.

9

Anthropological tropes and historical tricksters: pilgrimage as an 'example' of persuasion

SIMON COLEMAN *University of Toronto*

I explore the implications of example-making for both informants and ethnographers through an analysis of the history of the refoundation of the Anglican shrine at Walsingham during the twentieth century. I argue for an appreciation of distinctions between examples as 'models' and 'instances', but also for a focus on relations between the inchoate and the specific in processes of exemplification. The paper shows how an examination of the making of examples by actors in the field can speak to the creation of examples in writing and analysis, and may introduce elements of 'serendipity' more normally associated with encounters in the field.

Introduction: anthropology, Anglicanism, and exemplification

Some time ago, when I was briefly left to my own devices in the library of the Anglican pilgrimage shrine at Walsingham, I had a quick scan of the bookshelves. Amid the works of theology, history, and so on, I found one by an anthropologist: an edition of Frazer's *Golden Bough* (1890), which had developed a satisfying patina of age, in keeping with my medieval – and medievalized – surroundings. No doubt some of the more cynical commentators on Walsingham, particularly those from the kind of nonconformist background that Frazer experienced as a child, would have seen his textual presence in the library as all too appropriate: the work of a partly forgotten author located in an anachronistic site of Christian worship whose only links with the past seem to consist of dubious relics and a curious collection of stones taken from scattered sites of religious ruination: fragments from a flourishing culture of pilgrimage that crumbled in the wake of the Reformation and the Dissolution of the Monasteries.

But perhaps Frazer's book evokes other, more fertile resonances in relation to the shrine in Norfolk. For at the time that the Walsingham pilgrimage was being roused from its post-Reformation slumber, the Anglo-Catholicism that it came to champion was undergoing a literary as well as a liturgical renaissance (Waller 2011: 170), 'exemplified' by the fiction of Charles Williams, a writing associate of J.R.R. Tolkien, as well as the poetry of T.S. Eliot. Eliot's *The Waste Land* acknowledges the influence of Frazer in its footnotes, and his poem deployed a trope of restless wandering, almost pilgrimage, in its search for spiritual meaning and coherence – a coherence that Eliot would subsequently find and express in writing that would become saturated with the kind of Marian imagery that was also beginning to re-permeate Walsingham in the 1920s.

Despite their religious differences, what Eliot had in common with Frazer, and what both shared with the re-emergence of Anglican Walsingham, was a powerful if tendentious method of tracing scholarly and imaginative threads through fragments of history and culture. Rane Willerslev (2011: 504) has suggested, in a lecture ostensibly devoted to Frazer's pupil and nemesis Bronislaw Malinowski, that *The Golden Bough*'s bundling together of disparate cultural materials did not try to reflect ethnographic reality, but rather attempted to overcome it in order to further an overall project of constructing imaginative speculations as to the interconnections between the shrine at Nemi[1] and other hugely dispersed religious phenomena.

It was Malinowski's rather different method of making connections, of seeking a more explicitly holistic coherence through the integrating eye of the fieldworker, that would triumph in the anthropological world, and it is difficult to know what would have happened if Eliot had tried to use *Argonauts of the Western Pacific*, published like *The Waste Land* in 1922, as his inspiration rather than Frazer's monumental work. The modest dinghy that sets Malinowski down at the beginning of *Argonauts*, the part-industrial, part-Elizabethan barge that takes Eliot along the Thames as it threads through his poem, and the antique 'bark' that drops Frazer back at Nemi after his long textual journey all drew on fluid imagery in depicting the respective authors' quests for varieties of enlightenment, but Malinowski's process of discovery *begins* when he is 'set down', while Frazer's *ends* with him finally coming ashore and to rest back at Nemi; meanwhile, Eliot shifts between different authorial voices and metaphorical vessels, neither fully at rest nor constantly in motion, reflecting somewhat gloomily on 'These fragments I have shored against my ruins'.

But still, the American poet and the Polish anthropologist, both *émigrés* to England, did share some common ground in their use of tropes of part and whole. Marc Manganaro has suggested that Malinowski's depiction of the *kula* 'serves as a striking analogue to Eliot's conception of the objective correlative' (2002: 73). So both Malinowski's *kula* and Eliot's correlative encouraged the reader to perceive, and be persuaded to believe in, the existence and unity of something greater, which each pointed to and partially embodied. In Manganaro's terms, 'Every article attached to the correlative that is the Kula is, by virtue of being interpreted according to it, filled with meaning that orients and makes sense of the whole' (2002: 73; see also Jarvie 1964: 83). And for a time within Anglo-Saxon anthropology, the *kula* probably became *the* ethnographic exemplum that helped to spawn other exempla, involving as it did an in-gathering not of pre-Reformation stones or poetic shards, but rather of dispersed islands into a supposed unity that led the scholar towards a particular conceptualization of cultural coherence.

Almost a century later, examples are still used to conjure up larger ensembles. Synecdoche remains a vital aspect of our disciplinary aesthetics and identity, a prime tool to think with and engage in the act of description. Despite everything, anthropology still engages, albeit gingerly, with a Malinowskian inheritance that provides both historical genealogy and transhistorical paradigm for much of our work. At the same time, we have lost much of our faith in the idea of easily definable or functioning sociological wholes, and we are less confident about locating stable contexts of interpretation (Dilley 1999). A further problem relates to *how* an example is perceived to be exemplary. As ethnographers, we run the risk of conflating distinctions between 'being an example of' and 'being exemplary', in other words between providing a generic or 'typical' embodiment of some phenomenon, and instead highlighting the best and therefore in a sense most *exceptional* manifestation of it. In this vein, Alexander Gelley (1995) refers to the inherent unruliness of examples, the ways in which they can move between *setting* an example and *giving* an example, the model and the instance.[2] And it may be in the very conflation of these two, in the often strategic presentation of model as 'mere' instance, thus concealing the exceptionality of the former in the banality of the latter, that we can see both the workings of ideology and some of the besetting problems of ethnographic description. In his analysis of early modern rhetoric, John Lyons makes a parallel point when he notes how 'example is a way of taking our beliefs about reality and reframing them into something that suits the direction of a text', so that the example may therefore qualify as the most ideological of figures, in the sense of being a figure intimately bound to a representation of the world and yet one 'that most serves as a veil for the mechanics of that representation' (1989: ix). In their introduction to this volume, Lars Højer and Andreas Bandak refer to the power of the exemplar to extend itself in concrete examples and thus to mould the world in its own image. Gelley (e.g. 1995: 3–4) further recommends us to look closely at *how* a part is made to stand for a whole, whether through analogy or some other means, and to ask whether the 'whole' pointed to is perceived as having been lost or as maintaining an existence that is best viewed through the part. In other words, when examining the claims of either ethnographers or informants, do we observe the part being presented as a fragment of something that has been destroyed but that can be reconstructed, or rather as the means through which to gain a more concrete understanding of an existing but abstract entity that is difficult to grasp in conceptual or imaginative terms?

None of these ruminations should prompt us to abandon the use of examples or to stop asserting the importance of context in our ethnography. But it seems reasonable to focus more than we have done on the very making of examples, both as anthropologists constructing texts and as ethnographers observing informants engaged in practices or strategies of exemplification. This paper will reflect on anthropological understandings of examples through looking at specific cases of self-conscious construction of examples (as well as the exemplary) from my field, that of the revived Anglican pilgrimage to Walsingham over the past century or so. The cases I shall focus on represent key – and therefore in some respects exceptional – points in the ongoing revival of the shrine, but also two very different ways of asserting connections between parts and wholes, and constructing such wholes, separated by some sixty years in the life of the shrine as it moved from its refoundation in the 1920s and 1930s to the consolidation of its position in the religious landscape of Britain in the 1990s. While conceding the fact of their historical exceptionality and attempting to avoid either cultural or historical determinism, I argue that both ways can also be regarded as being very much of their time, and therefore revealing of shifts in how the wider cultural significance of Walsingham could be asserted by those wishing to persuade others of its importance.

I explore how presenting and comparing these forms of example-making, itself a strategic choice on my part, can speak to me as an ethnographer, providing disruptive but highly suggestive ways in which to reformulate my own ideas as to what Anglican Walsingham might be exemplary *of*. Serendipity, so often asserted as a hallmark of the field, can surely also occur in the analytical process of attempting to isolate and examine 'emic' forms of exemplification. And in this sense I am exploring a further potentially

Journal of the Royal Anthropological Institute (N.S.), 144-161
© Royal Anthropological Institute 2015

unruly dimension of exemplification, not merely the interplay between instance and model but also how a focus on example-making from the field can suggest connections that I would not originally have considered salient to my understanding of the site.

Of course, the crossing of supposed divides between ethnographic and analytical worlds has long been at the heart of anthropology, but I want to show that it is not merely the content of any given example, but *how* it is constructed, as well as shifts over time of methods of construction, that can be unruly in ways that are analytically productive. Caroline Humphrey (1997: 25) indicates something of this approach in her fertile tracing of the ways in which the ethical discourse of exemplars in Mongolia provides 'social space' for deliberation about ways of life that have been successfully achieved. This space emerges through the ways in which a local, exemplar-focused way of thinking about morality counteracts Western models of learning right conduct through performing ritual and etiquette, or the holding up of general ethical precepts as emanations of God or society. In Mongolian forms of exemplification (Humphrey 1997: 33–4), precepts tend to be 'authored' and emerge in relationships as tied to the personalities of both mentor and follower. At the same time, the subject is required to do some work, to ponder the meaning of the exemplar for him- or herself, so that exemplars as forms of moral discourse are open-ended and unfinished. One conclusion Humphrey draws from this analysis (1997: 43) is that in their flexibility, diversity, and embeddedness in relationships, Mongolian exemplars seem very unlike the 'cultural schemas' of Sherry Ortner (1989), which place emphasis on the structural and implicitly constraining nature of cultural models.[3]

The examples I shall explore in this paper have been created in social and cultural spaces far away from those described by Humphrey. But it may be that much learning in Euro-American contexts also occurs through exemplars, and in fact what interests me is her depiction of relatively unpredictable social spaces of exemplification that require or assume effort from the subject, the sense that examples may therefore provoke and not merely fix ways of thinking about exemplification. Walsingham is a pilgrimage site ostensibly rooted in a text-based, dogma-driven, world religion. And yet my comparison of examples of exemplification will reveal ambiguities, battles, shifts over the relationship between precept-orientated and more open-ended ways of proceeding, centred not only on the social space, but also on the literal, material space of the site.

My approach will therefore focus on the early to mid-twentieth-century Anglican revival of the shrine at Walsingham as involving a complex and controversial process of exemplification. Those who contributed to the revival of the shrine justified its reconstruction through presenting it as piecing together fragments of the past to provide models for the present and future, but also as exemplary in the very way it *made* connections. In tracing such reconstruction and association claims to making connections, I shall point to chains of exemplification and calibration between the biblical, the medieval, and the modern in relation to place and text but also in relation to particular persons, including the key figure in the modern, Anglo-Catholic revival of Walsingham, Father Alfred Hope Patten. Patten it was who in that productive year of 1922 publicly announced the re-establishment of devotion to Our Lady of Walsingham at the tiny Norfolk village to which he had come as vicar just a year earlier (Yelton 2006). And it was Patten who not only gathered stones from assorted monasteries and other sacred buildings destroyed in the Dissolution, but then also had them attached to the walls of an entirely new shrine that was built in the 1930s. In such an act of accumulation

Journal of the Royal Anthropological Institute (N.S.), 144-161
© Royal Anthropological Institute 2015

and display there could hardly have been a more potent and suggestive juxtaposition of part and whole – temporally, materially, geographically, theologically.

At the same time, numerous questions remain (for the ethnographer as well as the visiting pilgrim) about the character of the conjunctions that Patten asserted. Did they refer to a wider whole (the pre-Reformation church) that, in Gelley's terms, had been destroyed but could somehow be restored? Was Patten faithfully reviving Walsingham as an example of the medieval church or creating a new, composite whole in ancient guise, where the medieval was now being evoked through modernist lenses? And was he asserting conjunctions with the past through mere analogy or rather through forms of materiality that advocated and embodied a fundamentally sacramental, ontologically much more charged, view of history?

In turn, I want to extend my examination of such potential chains of exemplification and calibration beyond Patten himself, by historicizing his own praxis of remaking history. Stretching our perspective over time, we see how Patten and his works remain exemplary in contemporary Walsingham, a half-century after his death, but certainly not in the way that he intended.[4] I want to argue that the direction and force of the synecdochal and potentially sacramental orientation of such works have changed in the hands of Patten's successors, so that they point to and construct a very different kind of whole, using the same site to produce a different set of assemblages, and indeed deploying different methods of assemblage.[5] Key to understanding this shift is another dimension of exemplification that must be acknowledged: not merely the relation of part to whole, but also how the specific relates to the inchoate. This latter issue forces us to acknowledge that exemplification may work not merely through seeming to concretize thought and association, but also through keeping aspects of the example vague and at least initially underdetermined, full of potentiality. So before we take a closer look at the shrine and its continued revival, I want briefly to invoke a theoretical approach that will allow us to consider the importance of the inchoate in the analysis but also the creation of the exemplary.

Exemplification: between intimation and intimacy

In a 2008 paper, Michael Carrithers presents what he calls a 'theory fragment' that points to a wider body of theoretical analysis, that pertaining to so-called 'rhetoric culture'. Here, I only have space to present a tiny piece of Carrithers' fragment. I am particularly interested in his characterization of the fluid workings and constructions of culture through shifts between opacity and clarity. His assumption (2008: 183) is that human life plays out against a background comprised at least in part of inexpressibility, and he sees Kant as perhaps the most obvious patron of this perspective, given the latter's positing of the existence of the 'thing-in-itself', the reality which stands beyond the devices of human understanding, but towards which human understanding orientates itself. For Carrithers, employing a perspective more rooted in the micro-interactions and rhetorics of human social life, a key relationship is between events and interpretation, between a happening and the subsequent ways in which it is converted into a more generally comprehensible and perhaps persuasive and exemplary narrative. But the schemas of thought that we use to comprehend the sheer historicity of life are plastic and mutable, the material of constant symbolic play, 'so that we cannot read off the ways in which people respond to events, or in which they seek to shape events, simply from a schedule of their ideologies, or their cultural schemas, or their social organization' (2008: 161).[6] Carrithers (2008: 164) draws on the work of James Fernandez (1986) in reflecting on the importance of the inchoate – that which is *un*formed, undeveloped, the material on which the culturally *in*formed imagination is going to work – in exploring understandings of how a situation may move from the relatively formless through successive stages of particularity, from a bare intimation of something to an apparently intimate relationship with it.

The inchoate and the intimate may also coexist in striking ways. An example provided by Carrithers is taken from Gertrude Stein's extraordinary *Wars I have seen*, first published in 1945. Stein's life spanned numerous wars, and her problem in the book concerns how to write about and indeed how to 'see' war. One of her techniques is to give us a perspective on such general world events from a particular, local, domestic perspective. We perceive the large through the small, the whole through the part, but in a way that also complicates their distinction. Thus Carrithers (2008: 173) points to Stein's striking use of indefiniteness and the inchoate in her writing about her domestic life, the way she avoids vivid details while making reference to the idea of family – generically expressed as 'wife', 'husband', 'mother'. Stein evokes intimacy but not conventional specificity, bringing the reader into the domestic circle even as she uses it to help us to 'see' the larger frame of 'war'.

What do all these points have to do with the work of exemplification? I think Carrithers is pointing to the possibility of seeing examples 'in the making' through shifting processes of particularization that are also inevitably processes of editing and framing, as certain *kinds* of connections are asserted above others in attempts to stabilize interpretation. We see how fragile the relationship between part and whole may be, how unclear or shifting the links, and how this fragility may emerge from the inchoate character of 'events' that come gradually to be domesticated and 'seen' as exemplary – at least for a time. And while the example, understood as a form of rhetoric culture, invites others to come closer in order to examine its potential meanings and implications, it may also establish certain forms of distance from its intended recipients. Furthermore, note that, as in Humphrey's discussion of Mongolia, we see a shift away from fixed cultural schemas and towards the labour that is performed to tease out social and moral implications of events or examples. Indeed, it is precisely the need to do such work that might make examples engaging.[7]

In the case of Walsingham, the two cases of exemplification that I shall discuss demonstrate attempts to negotiate relationships between the inchoate and the particular. These negotiations are themselves forms of persuasion, meant to engage recipients (pilgrims and other visitors) in certain ways. Both involve what one might call 'performative exemplification', using the example to assert the existence of wider wholes whose existence is arguably in doubt. Part of the work to be done by the pilgrim/visitor is deciding whether and/or how to assent to becoming a co-creator of that whole. And yet of course part of my point will be that, despite the commonality of the site, the gap of sixty years between the two cases is instructive precisely because it reveals different wholes being performatively constructed, different connections being made, different understandings of the appropriate relationship between the inchoate and the particular being displayed, and different understandings of how 'instances' can also be 'models'.

Alfred Hope Patten: entrepreneur of the exemplary

If you enter the main door of the Anglican shrine at Walsingham, you are presented with an impressive panoply of material culture. Directly in front of you is a large relief

Journal of the Royal Anthropological Institute (N.S.), 144-161
© Royal Anthropological Institute 2015

depicting the Annunciation, a central biblical image for the shrine in its focus on Mary's relationship to Jesus, visual revelation, and sacred landscape. According to the legend surrounding the shrine's foundation, the Virgin Mary appeared to a local aristocratic woman, Richeldis, in 1061, and transported her in a vision to the Holy Land so that she could record the measurements of Jesus' childhood house in Nazareth and build an exact replica of it in Norfolk. The relief is fixed to the back of the western wall of what appears to be a church within a church, but is in fact part of the copy of the Holy House that Patten had built (using private donations) in the 1930s. On the same and adjoining walls are placed Patten's gathering of stones from ruined buildings. Effigies of two figures flank the wall, on either side of the Annunciation scene: one is of Richeldis, eyes turned upwards, holding a model of the Holy House; the other is of Patten's grave, constructed to look like a medieval stone effigy, his feet resting on yet another copy of the Holy House.

The relations between these forms of material culture provide only the briefest of introductions to the vast numbers of symbols, relics, and images contained by the shrine, but I want to dwell on them briefly as I see them as providing an instructive part of a wider whole – not only in telling us something of the story of the shrine, but also in indicating the workings of such exemplification as a form of Anglican praxis. Note that on entering we are greeted with a vision of a vision: we gaze at the Annunciation, and at Mary as she gazes at Gabriel; but we may also look at Richeldis, herself a visionary of Mary, and at Patten, who did not claim to have been granted Marian apparitions but who did talk of seeing ghosts and having visions of the Middle Ages. So there are chains and translations of forms of sacred seeing evident here, forms which lead us repeatedly and reflexively towards the Holy House itself. The entrance is depicting four or five versions of the House all at once: there is the domestic scene of the Annunciation, then the mini-houses attached to the effigies of Richeldis and Patten, then the back wall of Patten's House, and then – more implicitly and contentiously – the fact that the ground we are standing on was claimed by Patten, erroneously, to be the archaeological site of the medieval Holy House constructed by Richeldis.

Of course I am presenting here a one-dimensional reading of the material culture of the shrine church. None the less, I hope that we are gaining an inkling of the symbolic resources Patten had at his disposal. From the standpoint of the 1920s and 1930s, he was able to draw on all of the main historical periods in which Walsingham had previously been a significant presence in English religious and cultural discourse (Janes & Waller 2010: 3): medieval, post-Reformation, and Victorian. Contained in such history were not one but two periods of flourishing just before disaster. The date of 1061 refers to a time just before the Norman invasion, while the period between the mid-twelfth century and 1538 (Janes & Waller 2010: 5) saw Walsingham become the most important centre for the cult of the Virgin in England before it was destroyed on the orders of Henry VIII.

Patten's revival came at another key period in post-war English history. The parish of Walsingham was already a supporter of the Anglo-Catholic revival in the country, of the sort that Patten had absorbed during his upbringing in Brighton and which had been represented most clearly by the High Church orientation of the Victorian Oxford Movement. The last two decades of the nineteenth century had seen a dramatic increase in 'ritualist' practices (Yates 2010: 132), and in 1904 the British Parliament, no less, had tried to resolve disputes over ritual by setting up a largely ineffectual Royal Commission on Ecclesiastical Discipline. So-called 'Ultra-Catholics' were even subject

Journal of the Royal Anthropological Institute (N.S.), 144-161
© Royal Anthropological Institute 2015

to physical attacks (Yates 2010: 139), including those by 'Protestant raiders' who replayed the Reformation by smashing up some of the material sites of Anglo-Catholic revival.[8] Patten was also reconstructing his shrine in parallel with the Roman Catholic rediscovery of Walsingham, which was to result by the end of the 1930s in the village hosting two competing Catholic shrines, each with its own growing pilgrimage tradition, lending a further complexity to themes of translation, transformation, and exemplification.

Patten was reviving Walsingham at a time when it clearly mattered, when the themes that it raised had considerable resonance with wider ecclesiastical, social, cultural, and political debates in English culture. He apparently knew little of contemporary political and cultural trends, but he was both a keen actor and what one might call a master tropologist, playing skilfully on themes of restoration and replication so that Walsingham could represent an example of two original types simultaneously: both medieval England and the biblical landscape, with the result that a visit to the shrine could represent a 'pilgrimage to Englishness' (Janes 2010: 160) as well as to what had long been called 'England's Nazareth'. He was certainly not above using archaeology in the service of liturgy, as when he suggested (Patten 1934) that excavations sponsored by him revealed that he was rebuilding on the original site of the shrine (Coleman 2012). Thus Walsingham could be made to materially embody a part physically dramatizing a whole that was believed to have been lost. What was being restored might be interpreted as both a single shrine and the whole of medieval Christianity. Furthermore, it was both a unique place and meant to be a contemporary example for other Anglo-Catholics of how to re-create the pre-Reformation (but not 'Roman') church. Thus a revived Walsingham was an example of what could be done in the future, and much of its potential lay in its ability to inspire acts of restoration elsewhere (see also Lyons 1989: 8), so that the multiplication and accumulation of such examples might actually go on to *create* and not merely invoke a wider class of restored Catholic places of worship. Patten also conflated model with instance by claiming that what was actually the most exceptional and successful example of such restoration in England was simply following a standard, middling liturgical path between two extremes. In defending himself to his hostile bishop (who had refused to attend the translation of the statue of Our Lady of Walsingham to the new shrine), Patten wrote:

> [W]e ... affirm that we are not members of a separate body, cut off from the rest of Christendom ... We Catholics are wearied at the perpetual jibes of English Romans and their taunt that we are no ministers of the church, just as in the same way our patience is almost exhausted by the agitation and blasphemy of the militant protestant section (quoted in Yelton 2006: 97).

Such words implied that 'we Catholics' represented the true Church of England, legitimated by both historical precedent and biblical precept. If Christian theologians have more frequently talked of the value of prefiguration in the Bible, Patten was providing a *post*-figurative connection to a wider historical whole, in the process transforming the scale of his exemplification of the past. In his resurrection of the shrine, he was bringing together stones not merely from Walsingham but also from other parts of England and even beyond, just as he gathered relics from trips around continental Europe.[9] Each stone provided a physical commemoration of both an original building and the event of destruction of that building; each lent legitimacy to the newly built shrine but also gained new significance precisely through being juxtaposed with other stones that had suffered a similar fate but pointed to a similar potential future. Thus the material and liturgical stakes were high, since exemplification of the right sort of

Catholic Christian practice could increase the scope of its ambitions in the present.[10] From 1931, the shrine of England's Nazareth was located no longer in a diocesan, 'parochial' space, but rather one that was 'sectarian' in its location within the landscape of the Church of England yet all-encompassing in its ambitions for its vision of the true church.

Many decades later, our appreciation of how Patten's actions were interpreted by others, and particularly pilgrims, is limited. However, some clues exist, even if they present interestingly contradictory evidence. We know that the local bishop was not the only Anglican to be deeply wary of what was going on at Walsingham: even other Anglo-Catholics of the time felt the shrine to be extreme in its material expression of a world where the Reformation might never have happened, so that it was perceived to be 'on the outer fringes of the Movement' (Yelton 2006: 98).[11] We also know that, in its early years, the shrine attracted a tiny number of visitors, not even a hundred a week. However, Patten was largely popular with local villagers and parishioners, and he relied on their co-operation for his transformation of the shrine. Numbers began to grow, so that by the mid-1930s perhaps up to 30,000 were coming to the shrine in a given year. Gradually, Patten's aim of bringing together scattered fragments in one place in order to constitute a model for others also began to bear fruit, as shrines of Our Lady of Walsingham in churches across the country and abroad started to appear (Yelton 2006: 99). And, perhaps most intriguingly, while Walsingham may still have seemed extreme in Anglican circles, it resonated with secular, cultural trends in ways far beyond Patten's control or probable comprehension. Yates (2010: 146) argues that, for all his medieval pretensions, Patten's initiative reflected the flamboyant cultural aspects of the interwar years, the shrine's liturgical smells and bells providing a religious counterpart to transformations in the secular imagination, not least those of the cinema.

As a 'tropologist' as well as a revivalist, Patten seems to have made his mark through providing an excess of materiality that was assumed to give privileged access to the past, combining archaeology, liturgy, and dramaturgy in ways that demonstrated the power of the shrine through the sheer accumulated detail of its references to other sacred figures, places, and times.[12] The highly suggestive, expressively powerful exemplification that he orchestrated collapsed what in Frazerian terms would have been interpreted as similarity and contagion, resemblance to the past (the shrine as a model of the biblical original) and actual contact with it (the stones and relics taken from medieval sites); but it also tells us something about the exemplifier, the figure who in life dwelt not just *on* but also *in* the past and who after his death became materially conjoined with it. Patten emerged as a kind of trickster figure, evoking and conflating High Anglican versions of the two forms of exemplification that I mentioned at the beginning of the paper, apparent typicality and a kind of transgression through excess.

This quality of a certain elusiveness prompts me to compare Patten, no doubt incongruously, with Gertrude Stein, as mediated through Carrithers' discussion of rhetoric culture. For Patten resembles Stein in the way his tricksterism was expressed through a combination of the inchoate and the intimately known. Whether he liked it or not, the pilgrimage landscape he bequeathed to Walsingham juxtaposed the materially involuted shrine church, stuffed like a Victorian parlour with sacred objects in every nook and cranny, with the centre of the village where the actual ruins of the former site remained a largely blank space, a permanent reminder of dissolution and a sense that the actual presence of the past would remain irredeemably inchoate, an ideal to which one might constantly stretch but never quite reach. For the centre of the village

Journal of the Royal Anthropological Institute (N.S.), 144-161
© Royal Anthropological Institute 2015

and most likely original site of the pilgrimage remained in the possession of a family with Quaker roots and inclinations, who would not allow their grounds materially to be converted to Anglo-Catholic purposes. Restoration was fated to co-exist permanently with fragmentation, to create wholes in spite of absences that would always be present, no matter how many relics Patten gathered, or how frequently processions were led through the village from his restored shrine. Patten was forced to juxtapose the intimate and the indefinite in his attempts to overcome the long-standing inchoateness of the ruined medieval shrine.[13]

Back to the present

If he were to come back to Walsingham as one of the ghostly figures whom he occasionally imagined he saw in his lifetime, Patten would note the removal of the old train line to the village, the increase in cars and coaches, and the conversion of village shops from selling everyday necessities into becoming purveyors of cake and kitsch. But he would still recognize much about the material feel of the place. What might surprise him, however, is the shift in the religious and cultural landscape around the shrine, both literally and sociologically. Much remains controversial about Anglican Walsingham, not least its continued opposition to women priests. Yet in 2006 it was voted Britain's favourite religious site in a survey carried out by the BBC;[14] it has been the subject of poetry by a former Archbishop of Canterbury, Rowan Williams; and huge numbers of people visit annually. Many of the more devout come in parish groups or individually to say prayers in front of images of Mary and her child, to process through the streets and to follow stations of the cross, to light candles and take water from the wells at the shrines. The website of the Anglican shrine notes that 'today the Shrine complex welcomes over 10,000 residential pilgrims each year', though this figure should be seen in the context of the further claim that, '[i]n addition, a further 300,000 visitors come to Walsingham each year'.[15] The salient juxtaposition here is not only one of numbers, but also of identities, as we note the shift from 'pilgrims' to 'visitors', indicating how members of Anglo-Catholic parishes throughout the country now mingle with Roman Catholics as well as numerous tourists who come in from the nearby beaches. Roman and Anglo-Catholics celebrate together with a joint pilgrimage in August for the Assumption as well as an Ecumenical Youth Pilgrimage.

We might expect Patten's shade to be delighted by what he would see in the present. His transgressive exemplification seems to have gone mainstream, pointing to a wider whole than he might ever have bargained for. And yet such appearances would be deeply deceptive. Initially, we need to note the irony that Patten lived long enough into the 1950s to see Walsingham grow considerably in popularity, even as Anglo-Catholicism itself began to lose its national impetus as a movement. So the popularity of the site was counterbalanced – and probably aided – by an attenuation and not merely a widening of the ideological, liturgical, and organizational impetus that had prompted its re-emergence in the first place. I think we can go further, however, in thinking about how the present site has come to represent something very different from Patten's vision, but also in exploring how connections between parts and wholes are being made, viewed, and negotiated in very different ways by many of those who visit, as well as those who administer, the shrine.

When I asked one of Patten's successors, an administrator of the shrine, about the priest's contemporary legacy at Walsingham, he noted: 'It's important that his vision is something that we own, if you like ... But it seems to me that Father Patten was never about setting up something that was going to be, you know, cast in stone'. I found this juxtaposition of vision and stone striking as it both evoked and revoked Patten's older tropes. The assertion of succession was expressed through a metaphor of vision, even as the particular image of the fixity of stone was rejected. Of course the idea of casting in stone is a cliché as well as a metaphor that is somewhat apt for Walsingham, but such comments are combined with a questioning of the importance of one of the central features of Patten's restoration of the past: the authenticity of detail, including the very geographical locality of the site. As the administrator put it: 'I don't think I'm very bothered about that … theologically and historically … the whole business of … continuity … that's significant, but it doesn't seem to me that the detail matters very much'.

To judge from my interviews and conversations with Anglican pilgrims,[16] these remarks point to an important thread of discourse that is evident among a significant number of informants, though certainly not all (Coleman & Elsner 1998). What we see here is a Walsingham that exemplifies the *idea* of history and a material connection with heritage, gaining resonance through providing a meta-exemplification of the past *as* past, but without the specific content of that continuity actually mattering very much. Seeking a connection to a sense of the past is consonant with Walsingham as a place; but to focus on the need to both assimilate and verify historical detail runs the risk of destroying the directness of experiencing the site. Thus Richeldis and Mary are sometimes mixed up in people's accounts to me of the origin myth of the shrine. Although archaeology seems finally to have uncovered the location of the original shrine quite a distance from Patten's construction, it is often assumed that the centre of the village is still actually concealing its mystery, that the quest for the shrine continues and that I, as an anthropologist, might be able to shed light on the mystery. Among some visitors I have encountered, there is enough knowledge to know that 'a' shrine exists at Walsingham, but the Roman Catholic site may easily be mixed up with the Anglican one, and vice versa. A remark from a young deaconess in the Church of England sums up some of these positions well:

> I have a sneaking suspicion that Walsingham is probably like Scottish culture and Celtic Christianity. They're both inventions of the nineteenth century … I don't think it matters. I think it expresses something we want to express and can express through that place … It would be false to say this is something we've inherited unchanged from the medieval period. Actually, we've invented it for ourselves.[17]

Apart from its striking echoes of Hobsbawm and Ranger (1983), this view is notable not only because it comes from a member of the Anglican ministry, but also because of its unabashed debunking of, or at least insouciance towards, the specific materiality and the genealogy of the shrine. Both are classed as inventions, but useful inventions – rich but sufficiently inchoate, mouldable vehicles of expression for the concerns of the present. They link with what we might see as a plethora of pilgrimage performances evident in the village, involving both believers and non-believers, sometimes following official liturgy closely, sometimes adopting more creative, ironic, and playful attitudes to the ritual props on offer. At times, even self-identified secular tourists I have followed have attempted to engage with the site – a favourite prop, for instance, is the holy water available in the shrine, which may be used for pouring, sprinkling, or taking home as a souvenir, and which fulfils the generic ritual grammar required of many ancient and holy places. Such engagement corresponds broadly to what Richard Schechner (1985) calls 'restored behavior', performance that draws from some social or individual behaviour and memory from the past rather than mimicking a script *per se*. Contemporary tourists cannot follow any scripted liturgical role because they simply do not know what it is, unless they choose to join a service where they blend liturgically if inexpertly with the devout (see also Coleman 2013).

Although the point cannot be proved, given the lack of comparative ethnographic evidence, I think it is reasonable to assume that the contemporary efflorescence of activities at Anglican Walsingham (and the village as a whole) contrasts broadly with the more liturgically strategic and much more modest pilgrimages among self-identified Anglo-Catholics that Patten encouraged in the 1930s. Not only is the village much more accessible now than it was in the pre-war years, it has taken an important place in the heritage landscape of the country as a whole. The relatively disciplined and often repetitive journeys of the 10,000 or so parish pilgrims who stay in shrine accommodation each year contrast with those of the 300,000 who visit the shrine annually.

What, then, can Anglican Walsingham 'exemplify' in the present? And is this even a relevant question to ask of the site? I want to respond to these questions by juxtaposing Patten with one of his contemporaries, to explore how we can analyse and compare their approaches as orchestrators of pilgrimage but also of exemplification through the site. Such an approach runs the danger of focusing on the exceptional by looking at a liturgical elite rather than the broad swath of pilgrims and other visitors, but the point is to see how their different approaches resonate with as well as help to orientate the very different approaches to Walsingham taken by those engaging with its landscape and relics in the 1930s and in the contemporary period.

Patten produced a number of pamphlets and short articles relating to Walsingham, but he was not an especially skilled writer: his message emerged more powerfully in stone and brick than in words. He was seemingly unable to pass written exams – a characteristic that initially jeopardized his vocation to become a priest when he was a young novice. Martin Warner is a very different figure, in possession of a Ph.D. from Durham University as well as being the current Bishop of Chichester. He was Administrator of the Anglican shrine at Walsingham from 1993 to 2002, and is still Master of the Guardians of the Shrine. As Administrator he was relatively constrained in terms of what he could do to the materiality of the Holy House itself, even if, as noted, Patten's legacy could not be seen as entirely unchanging.[18] What I focus on here is a striking example of Warner's framing of the significance of the shrine, and indeed one of his most explicit attempts to consider how it might form wider spiritual connections for the broad constituency of visitors to the village.

The example is a book.[19] It is called *Walsingham: an ever-circling year*, and was published by Oxford University Press in 1996. It is modest in size, just eighty-eight pages long, and is written in simple language, similar to the kind of address that I watched Warner deliver to pilgrims to Walsingham. It is also aimed at a large audience: the jacket notes claim that it is 'an invaluable companion for pilgrim and tourist', and the text expresses something of a hybrid character, which includes but goes beyond its double address to both pilgrims and tourists. In fact, it is a guide to the site but also a devotional volume – 'an ideal resource for daily meditation', as the blurb puts it. In this sense, of course, it is not remarkable as such: many pilgrim texts in the Christian tradition and beyond have attempted both to anticipate the pilgrim's journey to a holy site and to combine site-seeing and ritual, with the tourist gaze and the sacred gaze converging or at least oscillating (Coleman & Elsner 2003). But what is notable is

Journal of the Royal Anthropological Institute (N.S.), 144-161
© Royal Anthropological Institute 2015

that the text does not try to differentiate between pilgrim and tourist: in the foreword both are called the 'pilgrim-visitor'. The book is also hybrid because it is a single-authored volume in one sense, but also significantly multi-voiced: the foreword is in fact written by the Reverend Alan Williams, Director of the Roman Catholic Shrine at Walsingham – occupying a role that sixty years ago would have explicitly rivalled that of the Anglican Administrator but is now more often devoted to presenting a common religious landscape to all-comers.

What interests me more, however, is the way the book problematizes what it means to make clear connections between materiality and the very history that Patten worked so hard to restore. Warner's first line in his introduction is apparently unequivocal: 'Walsingham', he says, 'is about vision' (1996: xvii). Nothing could be simpler, perhaps? Yet it turns out that vision comes to mean access to some perspectives and not to others. When I first read Warner's words I expected him to be referring to the original hierophanic vision granted to Richeldis in the eleventh century, but there is no mention of that. I then thought it might refer to the visions of Alfred Hope Patten, both his hopes for the shrine and the glimpses of the past that he claimed to have. But again Warner says nothing about those either. In fact, he explains (1996: xvii) that he is focusing our attention explicitly on Mary's vision of her vocation as mother of Christ – a more biblical perspective that resonates with the Annunciation, but also with a 'vision of Jesus' that he describes as being made available to everyone, and not just to a single figure. So in this description vision is not merely shifted from the apparently historical to the biblical, or from Mary to Jesus, but as a faculty it is shifted to us, as well. The 'we' of the text is not Patten's exclusive cadre of Anglo-Catholics but rather a readership that cannot be specified.

This focus on vision takes on extra significance if we realize that it is accompanied by a remarkable set of lacunae in the book as whole, and not just the introduction. Richeldis receives no mention at all in *any* of the text; nor does Patten; in fact the specific history of the site and its contemporary division into two shrines are entirely absent. The Norfolk landscape and the site are revealed to the reader in gorgeous colour, but *only* through the photographs commissioned to complement the text. Such landscape is presented as in a state of constant and chronic deferral to a much wider and more generic landscape: that of the Bible. It turns out that the 'ever-circling year' of the title is a liturgical as well as a seasonal one, guiding us simultaneously through a pilgrimage in the rural Norfolk landscape but also through the biblical story of the nativity, the crucifixion, the resurrection, and so on. Each season of the year forms a chapter of its own but also a 'mystery' of the life of Christ. As readers and viewers we are presented with a juxtaposition that is also a disjunction in terms of both content and medium: pictures lead us into the local landscape of Norfolk, while words lead us to the biblical landscape of prayer and the Bible. Warner's opening chapter does indicate the resonances his approach has with that of the circle of meditations associated with the rosary, but interestingly he does so in a way that leaves open the associations of this Catholic prayer:

> You may have bought this book simply as a pictorial record of Walsingham: if so, I hope that its stories will remind you of the vision which animates the life of this pilgrimage centre ... But you may wish to use these stories, the words of scripture, and pictures of England's Nazareth to pray the rosary, perhaps something you have never done before. Whatever your choice, may the movement of the Holy Spirit upon your imagination enable you to experience through an ever-circling year the

vision of Walsingham in which, with Mary, you gaze upon the glory of God revealed in the face of Jesus Christ (1996: xx).

The liturgical chains of association of the rosary itself are potentially loosened here, as the book may be seen as merely a record of the site, and a link to seasons of the year familiar to atheist and believer alike. At the same time, a certain kind of absence is conjoined with a particular form of presence – looking *at* Walsingham with thinking *beyond* it. If English and biblical landscape intersect, the hierarchy of value is clear: Norfolk points us towards Nazareth and the rest of the Holy Land, even as the Marian imagery of the pilgrimage site is said to point to Jesus himself.

So Warner's book is not a conventional guide, yet in another sense it seems superbly well calibrated to a shifting constituency of pilgrim-visitors. His desire to move our gaze and experience towards the Bible probably remains something of an aspiration in most cases. But his theology resonates with my ethnography in his recognition that current pilgrimage performances at Walsingham often work through spaces that seem overdetermined by relics of history and yet underdetermined by interpretative input from figures of religious authority. The symbolic resources he is drawing on would not have been entirely foreign to Patten, who worked to orientate visitors to Nazareth as well as to England and Englishness. But the connections he draws, as well as the ways of drawing them, are very different, and bypass the specificities of historical detail as suitable mediators to what is seen as the central vision of the site.

We might read such a strategy in various ways. Reference to Patten perhaps risks tactlessness in a text seeking to include Roman as well as Anglo-Catholics. Taking into account Schechner's point about 'restored behavior', we might see Warner as reaching out to the broadest common denominators of his likely readers, assuming the latter's glancing interactions with the landscape in and around the shrine and sketchy knowledge of the Bible. We should also note his likely awareness of the theological politics of vision itself, of the ambiguous status of the holy image in Anglicanism. This point is demonstrated most starkly by the evangelical Christians who regularly visit the site on big procession days and cast their scorn on the Anglican as well as Roman Catholic 'idolators' who persist in worshipping the Virgin Mary through statuary and icon. Such claims are denied by shrine administrators, but Warner's construction of a hierarchy of picturesque image deferring to biblical word still suggests a worry over materiality as the medium of sincere religious commitment (Keane 2002).

For Patten, the inchoateness of the Quaker-owned and blank centre of the original site of the shrine comprised a constant challenge to his attempt to assert direct and detailed sacramental links to the past. Warner, however, complicates much of the polarity between the specified and the inchoate in his sophisticated deployment of mute props of landscape, shrines, and visitor-pilgrims. For it seems that, in the challenge of reaching out to the 300,000 visitors of the mid-1990s rather than the 30,000 of the mid-1930s, relative exegetical and historical blankness now takes on positive qualities (cf. Eade & Sallnow 1991). Under such circumstances, the materiality of Patten's shrine may work best precisely through being rendered inchoate and therefore open to the kind of cultural and imaginative labour highlighted in different ways by Carrithers (2008) and Humphrey (1997). Or again, we are back to another version of a material and social landscape rendered intimate but not cluttered with determining specificity.

The result is that, once more, Patten's work becomes subject to the ironies of history. In the present efflorescence of visitors to Walsingham we see no material dissolution, no physical razing to the ground of its walls and statues; but we are still witnessing a semiotic stripping of the altars that is as effective as that achieved in the Reformation, if not even more so. And this semiotic stripping is not merely coming from without, from the apathies and ignorance of casual tourists or from the accusations of evangelicals; it is also coming from within, from the very 'guardian' of the history and significance of the site within the contemporary Anglo-Catholic landscape.

Concluding remarks: 1922 and all that

Going back to 1922 for a final time, we can add Patten's and Warner's style of making examples, of relating parts – and in their cases also pasts – to wholes, to the list already populated by those other synecdochalists, Eliot and Malinowski. Patten's exemplifying practice, medievalizing as its post-figurative connections appeared to be, was just as modernist in tone and impulse as those of the poet and the anthropologist, even if it was articulated through very different cultural idioms. In accepting this point, we are also noting that Malinowskian anthropology was itself more part of wider cultural modes of practice of the time than is normally acknowledged in a discipline that wrestles with him as both distant ancestor and contemporary paradigm. Meanwhile, the signifiers that Warner's approach evokes float more freely than those of his predecessor, but it would be a mistake to dismiss him as an advocate of an unalloyed post-modern approach to the shrine. His book strips away local history but does so in an attempt to reground the salience of the Anglican shrine within two landscapes, which it also tries to link: that of the social and cultural spaces already inhabited by visitors, whether overtly religious or not, and that of the Bible. He is also engaged in a form of ecclesiastical encompassment whose political and semiotic associations differ significantly from those evoked by Patten. The earlier priest used the materiality of his shrine to house stones from other sites and yet was careful to distinguish himself from 'the Romans'; his later counterpart uses text precisely to incorporate the voice of a Roman Catholic Director of Walsingham within his representation of the total landscape of the pilgrimage centre.

Expressed very specifically in these terms alone, the Patten of the 1920s and 1930s – despite his magpie-like gathering of religious curiosities – becomes somewhat Malinowskian in his faith in a whole (or neatly nested set of wholes) towards which to orientate the self, whereas Warner, the man of the 1990s and beyond, seems almost more Frazerian in his rhetorical gesturing towards multiple and more loosely articulated ideological landscapes in his reflections on the significance of the shrine.[20] In any case, both illustrate how the making of examples can itself be a deeply constitutive practice of self-making. But my own juxtaposition, my own use of such cases as examples, has also provided me with a serendipitous problem in my anthropological understanding of Walsingham as a 'site' of pilgrimage. As Warner's approach in *The ever-circling year* 'exemplifies', contemporary visitors to the shrine and its environs do not engage in the regular circulations of the *kula* but are clearly engaged in lives where Walsingham can be both centre and periphery, both a regular part of the calendar and yet at times semiotically, historically, and theologically indistinct. Given such circumstances, I am forced to ask not only what the shrine itself signifies, but also what to make of a pilgrimage 'centre' becoming re-fractured as its significance is re-inscribed in numerous contexts away from the shrine. So the question now becomes: what are we to make of the fragments of the pilgrimage field that we have now created, as they disperse from Walsingham to engage with the specificities and intimacies of Anglo-Catholic or indeed secular lives that can only be guessed at by the anthropologist?

Journal of the Royal Anthropological Institute (N.S.), 144-161
© Royal Anthropological Institute 2015

NOTES

Many thanks to Andreas Bandak and Lars Højer, to other participants in the workshop 'The Power of Example' (University of Copenhagen, 8–9 September 2011), to Justin Dyer for expert copy-editing, and to anonymous reviewers for their comments on an earlier draft of this paper. Thanks also to Michael Carrithers for his generous and constructive reading, though no doubt much remains in the text that is decidedly non-exemplary in its argumentation.

[1] The ethnographic trope of an ancient Roman shrine that bookends Frazer's vast work.

[2] We might also note the resonances here with Geertz's (1973) distinction between models 'of' and 'for' reality.

[3] Michael Carrithers (pers. comm., 27 May 2013) has also suggested parallels here with the workings of the 'moral imagination' found in discussions around Kaguru story-telling (see Beidelman 1986).

[4] As Lyons notes (1989: 34) any element of historical reality adduced to support a generalization will have characteristics that exceed what can be covered by the generalization. Thus to make an example of an object is to account for only one limited aspect of that object, but also to open the object to other interpretations in the future. (Patten seems to have been a master at this approach.) Brian Massumi (2002: 18) also notes how the example always runs the risk of falling apart, subject to powers of deviation and digression.

[5] Space does not permit a discussion here of how the example evokes connections with and distinctions from notions of assemblage. I point, however, to Marcus and Saka's (2006) useful discussion of how the concept of assemblage has been used by social scientists to negotiate between, on the one hand, drawing attention to the ephemeral, the emergent, the decentred, and the heterogeneous and, on the other, a commitment to the structured and systematic in social life. As in my paper, they juxtapose characteristics of modernist perceptions developed in such humanist genres as literature with what they see as more staid traditions of social theory, looking at how broader modernist sensibilities may permeate empirical research traditions.

[6] An example is that of how the events of 9/11 created a 'situation' – an episode of historicity – followed by a pause before resources of explanation, narration, and clarification were marshalled. We thus see evoked the sense of a gap between happening and response, between historicity and rhetoric (Carrithers 2008: 162).

[7] Drawing on Aristotle, Lyons (1989: 27) notes how the giving of several examples in a row may also lead the audience into a form of engagement by seeking the thread linking the different instances.

[8] The Marian connotations of Anglo-Catholicism certainly contrasted uneasily with the muscular Christianity of a Victorian and post-Victorian evangelicalism. In his novel *Brideshead revisited* Evelyn Waugh noted the assumed connection between Anglo-Catholicism and homosexuality when he had the character Charles Ryder go up to Oxford (once more in 1922) and receive a warning from his cousin Jasper to 'beware the Anglo-Catholics – they're all sodomites with unpleasant accents' (Waugh 1946: 26, quoted in Yates 2010: 145).

[9] The shrine may have been deeply English but for Patten it also represented an English embodiment of the Belgian church, which he saw as exemplary for the way it had never experienced the anti-clericalism of France.

[10] Yelton (2006: 90-1) notes that the altar of the Holy House was formed largely of stones from the ruined priory nearby, but others came from other religious houses. The walls of the Holy House incorporated stones from Augustinian houses in the south wall, and Benedictine in the north.

[11] The ambivalence attached to Walsingham was also almost certainly a function of the somewhat eccentric persona of Patten himself. The following is an extract from an interview I conducted with an older resident of Walsingham, who had worked with Patten as a child: 'Well, he used to go into these so-called trances, you've read about the trances? . . . It amused me, he'd sort of go into a trance and relive history . . . I think he must have read historical novels and act the parts out and you couldn't sort of do anything with him for ages. We were never quite sure about this'.

[12] Massumi notes that: 'The success of the example depends on the details. Every little one matters. Each detail is like another example embedded in it' (2002: 18). It would be difficult to argue that every relic mattered equally to Patten's construction, but we certainly might see each relic as forming a mini-example of a wider whole: not just, say, the body of a saint but the body of the wider church that Patten wished to (re-)create.

[13] Michael Carrithers (pers. comm., 27 May 2013) points out that some of the references Patten was invoking included very broad entities on the edge of the inchoate, such as perhaps 'the Church' or 'Christianity', thus encompassing such multitudes (of people, events, sensations, stories) as to make his project seem all the more important. See also Fernandez (1986) on the polyvalency of the inchoate.

[14] See Janes & Waller (2010: 2); also *http://www.bbc.co.uk/religion/programmes/sunday/features/spiritual* (accessed by the authors 1 February 2009).

[15] *http://www.walsinghamanglican.org.uk/welcome/index.htm* (accessed 20 January 2015).

[16] To date, I have formally interviewed around forty pilgrims to Walsingham, as well as had more informal conversations with many others since the 1990s.

[17] Interviewed summer 1994.

[18] He oversaw some development of the surroundings of the Walsingham shrine while he served as Administrator and also worked to publicize the shrine's activities in schools and other public contexts.

[19] I have not yet interviewed pilgrims or others who have read the book. While many guides to Walsingham have been produced over the past century and more, none has the various hybrid qualities noted in Warner's text.

[20] Space does not permit an overt engagement with Strathern's (1987) juxtaposition of Frazer's and Malinowski's contrasting deployments of detail and 'context' in their respective forms of textual persuasions, though arguably her examination of the relationships between text, author, and readership have analogies here with the relationships between site, administrator, and visitor. However, if Warner is at all equivalent to the shrine priest at Nemi (or indeed to Malinowski) in challenging the work of his predecessor, his act of destruction is surely both partial and ambivalent.

REFERENCES

BEIDELMAN, T. 1986. *Moral imagination in Kaguru modes of thought*. Washington, D.C.: Smithsonian Institute Press.

CARRITHERS, M. 2008. From inchoate pronouns to proper nouns: a theory fragment with 9/11, Gertrude Stein, and an East German ethnography. *History and Anthropology* **19**, 161-86.

COLEMAN, S. 2012. Memory as absence and presence: pilgrimage, 'archeo-theology', and the creativity of destruction. *Journeys* **13**: **1**, 1-20.

——— 2013. Ritual remains: studying contemporary pilgrimage. In *Companion to the anthropology of religion* (eds) J. Boddy & M. Lambek, 294-308. Oxford: Wiley-Blackwell.

——— & J. ELSNER 1998. Performing pilgrimage: Walsingham and the ritual construction of irony. In *Ritual, performance, media* (ed.) F. Hughes-Freeland, 46-65. London: Routledge.

——— & ——— (eds) 2003. *Pilgrim voices: narrative and authorship in Christian pilgrimage*. Oxford: Berghahn.

DILLEY, R. 1999. *The problem of context*. Oxford: Berghahn.

EADE, J. & M.J. SALLNOW (eds) 1991. *Contesting the sacred: the anthropology of Christian pilgrimage*. London: Routledge.

FERNANDEZ, J. 1986. *Persuasions and performances: the play of tropes in culture*. Bloomington: Indiana University Press.

FRAZER, J. 1890. *The Golden Bough: a study in magic and religion*. London: Macmillan.

GEERTZ, C. 1973. *The interpretation of cultures: selected essays*. New York: Basic Books.

GELLEY, A. 1995. *Unruly examples: on the rhetoric of exemplarity*. Stanford: University Press.

HOBSBAWM, E. & T. RANGER (eds) 1983. *The invention of tradition*. Cambridge: University Press.

HUMPHREY, C. 1997. Exemplars and rules: aspects of the discourse of moralities in Mongolia. In *The ethnography of moralities* (ed.) S. Howell, 25-47. London: Routledge.

JANES, D. 2010. Queer Walsingham. In *Walsingham in literature and culture from the Middle Ages to modernity* (eds) D. Janes & G. Waller, 147-64. Aldershot: Ashgate.

——— & G. WALLER 2010. Introduction: Walsingham, landscape, sexuality, and cultural memory. In *Walsingham in literature and culture from the Middle Ages to modernity* (eds) D. Janes & G. Waller, 1-20. Aldershot: Ashgate.

JARVIE, I. 1964. *The revolution in anthropology*. London: Routledge.

KEANE, W. 2002. Sincerity, 'modernity,' and the Protestants. *Cultural Anthropology* **17**, 65-92.

LYONS, J. 1989. *Exemplum: the rhetoric of example in early modern France and Italy*. Princeton: University Press.

MALINOWSKI, B. 1922. *Argonauts of the Western Pacific: an account of native enterprise and adventure in the archipelagoes of Melanesian New Guinea*. London: Routledge & Kegan Paul.

MANGANARO, M. 2002. *Culture, 1922: the emergence of a concept*. Princeton: University Press.

MARCUS, G. & E. SAKA 2006. Assemblage. *Theory, Culture & Society* **23**, 101-9.

MASSUMI, B. 2002. *Parables for the virtual : movement, affect, sensation*. Durham, N.C.: Duke University Press.

ORTNER, S. 1989. *High religion: a cultural and political history of Sherpa Buddhism*. Princeton: University Press.

PATTEN, H. 1934. The site of the shrine of Our Lady of Walsingham (available on-line: *http://www.walsinghamanglicanarchives.org.uk/1934shrinesite.htm*, accessed 20 January 2015).

SCHECHNER, R. 1985. *Between theater and anthropology*. Philadelphia: University of Pennsylvania Press.

Journal of the Royal Anthropological Institute (N.S.), 144-161
© Royal Anthropological Institute 2015

STEIN, G. 1945. *Wars I have seen.* London: B.T. Batsford.

STRATHERN, M. 1987. Out of context: the persuasive fictions of anthropology. *Current Anthropology* **28**, 251-81.

WALLER, G. 2011. *Walsingham and the English imagination.* Aldershot: Ashgate.

WARNER, M. 1996. *Walsingham, an ever-circling year.* Oxford: University Press.

WAUGH, E. 1946. *Brideshead revisited.* Boston: Little, Brown.

WILLERSLEV, R. 2011. Frazer strikes back from the armchair: a new search for the animist soul. *Journal of the Royal Anthropological Institute* (N.S.) **17**, 504-26.

YATES, N. 2010. Walsingham and interwar Anglo-Catholicism. In *Walsingham in literature and culture from the Middle Ages to modernity* (eds) D. Janes & G. Waller, 131-46. Aldershot: Ashgate.

YELTON, M. 2006. *Alfred Hope Patten and the shrine of Our Lady of Walsingham.* Norwich: Canterbury Press.

Tropes anthropologiques et farceurs historiques : du pélerinage comme « exemple » de persuasion

Résumé

L'auteur explore les implications de la création d'exemples pour les informateurs et les ethnographes, en analysant l'histoire de la refondation du sanctuaire anglican de Walsingham au XXème siècle. Il plaide pour une prise en compte des distinctions entre les exemples comme « modèles » et comme « instances », mais aussi pour que l'accent soit mis sur les relations entre l'imparfait et le spécifique dans les processus de création d'exemples. L'article montre comment l'examen de la création d'exemples par les acteurs sur le terrain peut interpeller la création d'exemples dans l'écriture et l'analyse et peut produire des « heureux hasards » plus couramment associés aux rencontres sur le terrain.

10

Of figures and types: brokering knowledge and migration in Indonesia and beyond

JOHAN LINDQUIST *Stockholm University*

This paper takes the broker as an entry-point for considering the problem of exemplification in anthropology. In particular, it approaches this problem by way of the relationship between figure and type, or between example and theoretical exemplar. While the figure is contingent on a specific socio-historical context, the type consciously accentuates particular characteristics in order to form the basis for comparison. More specifically, the paper approaches this relationship by considering the broker as type in relation to two specific figures in the current regime of transnational Indonesian migration, namely the NGO outreach worker and the informal labour recruiter, both identified as 'field agents', or *petugas lapangan*, in Indonesia. By way of juxtaposition the paper discusses the oscillation between figure and type in order to consider biases in the anthropological literature on brokers – most notably that the the broker is inherently amoral if not immoral – while suggesting that the broker is an exemplary methodological starting-point for contemporary anthropology.

Arguably, the broker is an exemplary methodological entry-point for an anthropology concerned with borders, mediation, translation, and transnationalism in 'an already globalized world' (Boellstorff 2003).[1] This claim, however, should be qualified by considering the history of the broker in anthropology, ongoing transformations in the discipline and the contemporary world, and the kinds of problems that the broker appears as a response to. More specifically, arguing that the broker is an exemplary methodological entry-point leads towards a discussion concerning the relationship between the broker as an ethnographically situated example and as a cross-cultural theoretical exemplar. What is the relationship between these two perspectives, and how are we to make productive use of this relationship?

The broker is a classic topic in the anthropological literature, particularly with regard to the study of low-level political and economic relationships (see Bierschenk, Chauveau & Olivier de Sardan 2002: 10), but more generally as an approach to understanding relationships between cultural, economic, and political systems. Clifford Geertz's (1960) 'cultural broker' is arguably most well known in this context. Yet, as in the case of the Balinese cockfight that famously came to function as a synecdoche for Balinese culture (Geertz 1973; see also Clifford 1988), a more specific example underlies his discussion

Journal of the Royal Anthropological Institute (N.S.), 162-177
© Royal Anthropological Institute 2015

of the cultural broker, namely that of the *kijaji*, the Javanese Muslim leader whose local legitimacy was based on experiences in, and relationships with, the centre of the Islamic world, Mecca. With the rise of the Indonesian nation-state, the *kijaji* was drawn into new forms of translocal relations. As Geertz phrased it, while before he was a 'scholar, curer, and mystic teacher, he is now a politician', albeit 'an amateur' one (1960: 247).

The persuasiveness of Geertz's conceptual analysis is based on a well-chosen and ethnographically rich example.[2] More specifically, there is a subtle transition, or perhaps oscillation, between two modes of exemplification, namely the *kijaji* as a specific case and the cultural broker as a more general theoretical exemplar. This can also be phrased as a move from a historically situated figure to a sociological type (Barker, Harms & Lindquist 2013*a*; 2013*b*), a distinction that can be clarified by comparing Walter Benjamin's '*flâneur*', considered specifically against the backdrop of the transformations of nineteenth-century Paris (Benjamin 1986), and Georg Simmel's 'stranger', which consciously accentuates particular characteristics at the expense of historical specificity (Simmel 1971), a form of abstraction comparable to Weber's ideal type (1978). While the social type primarily aims to classify or identify the role that an individual plays in society, thus allowing for comparisons across space and time, the figure is a real person who also is a symbol that embodies the structures of feeling of a particular time and place. While the broker is a sociological type that is recognizable across a wide range of different socio-historical contexts, an understanding of the figure must begin in a particular ethnographic milieu (Barker *et al.* 2013*a*: 162-4).

In this paper I consider the relationship between figure and type through a discussion of the Indonesian *petugas lapangan* (PL for short), or 'field agent', in relation to the broker as type.[3] I do this by juxtaposing two different *petugas lapangan* in ethnographic terms, namely the informal labour recruiter and the NGO outreach worker, who are both important actors in the contemporary regime of transnational migration from Indonesia, but who have nothing to do with one another in practice, and, indeed, are often found in different kinds of locations.[4] More specifically, the *petugas lapangan* is the individual who mediates between the office environment and the field, the *lapangan*, where target populations are found. For recruitment agencies, PL are the actual recruiters who convince villagers to become migrants, while for NGOs PL function as outreach workers in attempts to gain access to the migrants who can be identified as victims. In contrast to the somewhat derogatory Indonesian term *calo*, *petugas lapangan* suggests a formality connected to a bureaucratic office environment. As such the PL ideally mediates between the formal and informal.

These two figures are generally not considered on equal terms, largely because they tend to be seen as inhabiting opposite ends of an ethical spectrum, the former demonized as exploiters and the latter often celebrated as protectors of migrants. In fact, NGOs are frequently used as a source of authoritative knowledge by interested policy-makers and mass media actors with regard to the practices of labour recruiters, thus further reinforcing this normative hierarchy. By way of juxtaposition, this paper begins by disturbing one of the key premises of the anthropological literature, namely that the broker is inherently amoral if not immoral (James 2011: 319), an actor whose primary commitment appears as maximizing individual gain and is therefore deemed untrustworthy. This is phrased clearly in Eric Wolf's understanding of the broker as 'Janus-like' (1956: 1076), as well as in Jeremy Boissevain's definition of the broker as 'a professional manipulator of people and information who brings about communication for profit' (1974: 148). More specifically, in this paper a mode of comparison is created between two different examples that in turn destabilizes and fragments the broker as a type and the narratives that are brought to bear on this type.[5]

As the editors note in their introduction, a good example is 'in-between' and has 'the capacity to make new connections' (p. 14). This could very well be taken as a general description of the broker. From a certain point of view, however – namely that of the broker as a sociological type – we already appear to have an understanding of the manipulative quality of these connections, thus effectively foreclosing the possibility of creating a good example. In order for the broker to become a good example, but retain a comparative potential, I suggest that we move between an understanding of the broker as a disembodied 'type' and a situated 'figure'. It is thus arguably the oscillation between figure and type that offers anthropology an opportunity to engage in a broader comparative discussion.

Geertz's attempt to isolate an emergent dimension of the *kijaji* allowed him to develop the cultural broker as a type that resonated with scholars in other times, places, and disciplines. This is not to suggest, however, that a strict transition from figure to type is possible or even desirable. In the case of the contemporary broker, for instance, my ethnographic eye has been conditioned by a particular anthropological training that comes to suggest a conversation between figure, *petugas lapangan*, and type, the broker; between my specific ethnographic engagements and the anthropology of brokers and brokerage. With this contingent relationship in mind, it is thus worth considering how the anthropologist brokers knowledge between figures and types and to what effect. From that point it becomes possible to return to the question of methodology.

Historicizing the broker

Interest in the broker, as both empirical figure and conceptual type, has waxed and waned in anthropology. While critical in the context of decolonialization and modernization theory in the 1950s and 1960s, in the work of the Manchester School, and later with the rise of transactionalism, the broker largely vanished from view in the late 1970s, before re-emerging in the wake of current engagements with neoliberalism. Early articles by Wolf (1956) and Geertz (1960) were concerned with shifting forms of political authority and the transforming relationship between village and capital following decolonialization. This was a response to the predominance of community-based studies in anthropology and, for Geertz, in particular, the rise of modernization theory, which positioned the new nations within a developmental framework in which the broker was a necessary but temporary actor that would disappear with the rise of rational organizational forms. As the broker came to 'stand guard over the crucial junctures or synapses of relationships which connect the local system to the larger whole' (Wolf 1956: 1075), a new form of ethnographic attention emerged.

Deborah James (2011: 319-20) understands the disappearance of the broker in the 1970s in relation to what Jonathan Spencer (2007: chap. 1) calls the 'strange death of political anthropology', in which the analysis of local-level politics ran into a 'dead end' with the rise of structuralist (particularly Marxist) models of political analysis and a broad-based understanding of the postcolonial state as the primary site of power and domination in the Third World.[6] Even with the rise of post-structuralism during the 1980s, the focus was broadly placed on how social mechanisms disciplined individuals and shaped their subjectivities. In this world, the local-level broker appeared increasingly insignificant in both empirical and analytical terms.

Journal of the Royal Anthropological Institute (N.S.), 162-177
© Royal Anthropological Institute 2015

In contrast to those who have imagined a world of disintermediation characterized by free markets without borders (see, e.g., Ohmae 1990), brokers are arguably proliferating rather than becoming obsolete in the context of neoliberal reform. For instance, James shows the growing importance of brokers in the context of land reform in post-apartheid South Africa, a transitional setting where 'state, market, and patrimonial/patriarchal-style political authority intersect' (2011: 318). David Mosse and David Lewis (2006), in turn, highlight the importance of brokers in the context of a development industry characterized by NGOs, Lawrence Cohen (2003) speculates about the rise of 'bioethical brokers' in the context of the transnational market for organ transplants, Zeynep Devrim Gürsel (2012) notes the proliferation of 'image brokers' in news journalism with the rise of digital media, while Bill Maurer, Taylor Nelms, and Stephen Rea (2013) discuss the rise of the 'mobile money agent'.

These examples suggest not only a renewed interest in brokers, but also a broadened ethnographic scope that includes elites acting on a transnational scale and novel forms of mediation with the rise of digital technologies. This is in contrast to earlier studies that focused on cultural brokers, political players, or 'fixers' firmly situated in a local frame, and on the relationships between rural and urban or centre and periphery. The scale of brokerage has become more complex, not only with regard to new technologies, but also with an increasing unpredictability concerning the spatial mobility of brokers themselves. Furthermore, transformations in the global economy since the collapse of Bretton Woods and ensuing neoliberal reform have increasingly problematized state-centred models of power and sovereignty and pushed for a reconceptualization of the relationship between state and market. It is in this context that we can note the return of the broker in ethnographic terms as an actor positioned along these fault-lines (James 2011).

But there are also historical continuities, as the broker has generally emerged as a theoretical exemplar in the context of state crisis, thus highlighting a move away from structural analysis. Furthermore, and as has already been noted, the presumed moral ambiguity of the broker as an individual who crosses social boundaries and whose motives and loyalties are questioned has remained constant. Both of these points, the latter largely explicit and the former more implicit in the anthropological literature, are of great interest in relation to the coming ethnographic discussion of figure and type, as they reveal basic premises in the study of and interest in brokers and brokerage and suggest problems in constituting the broker as a good example.

The migration broker, an ethnographic starting-point in this paper, has been demonized since the advent of liberalism and the ensuing distinction between 'free' and 'unfree' labor (McKeown 2008). This has become most evident with the contemporary global concern with human trafficking, as the dichotomy between the migrant 'victim' and the broker 'perpetrator' takes shape a priori (Doezema 2010). In contrast, within the field of development and humanitarian aid, NGOs that mediate between donors and targeted populations are widely (though certainly not universally) celebrated as 'grassroots' organizations – most clearly in contrast to the state – that work on behalf of local populations, 'moral fieldworkers' who are 'doing good' (Fisher 1997).[7] In this context, NGOs have emerged as brokers between international donors and local populations. Following the lead of Mosse and Lewis (2006) and others who have highlighted the importance of brokers in development work, it thus becomes possible to think of labour recruitment agencies and NGOs together.

Journal of the Royal Anthropological Institute (N.S.), 162-177
© Royal Anthropological Institute 2015

In Indonesia, private recruitment agencies and NGOs have become critical actors in the contemporary infrastructure of transnational migration across Asia and the Middle East (Rudnyckyj 2004). While recruitment agencies work at the intersection between migrants, state agencies, and employers with the rise of documented circular migration in Asia and the Middle East (Lindquist, Xiang & Yeoh 2012), NGOs focusing on counter-trafficking issues are located at the intersection between international organizations, mass media, state agencies, and migrants (Lindquist 2010a). Although NGOs and private recruitment agencies rarely intersect in practice, except through the former's ongoing demonization of the latter, I want to note that both share a commitment to the migrant and the migration process, albeit in different terms. In this context, it is of more than passing interest that so-called *petugas lapangan* (PL) are key actors in the everyday practices of both recruitment agencies and NGOs.

Brokering migrants

The sun is just rising as we pull over to the side of the road. I have seen Muslim's[8] lone figure at some distance, and as Anton and I step out of the van into the cool morning air, he comes forward to greet us. Muslim is an informal labour broker in his mid-thirties, a PL who recruits prospective migrants – primarily men to the Malaysian palm oil industry – and delivers them to licensed labour recruitment agencies such as the one Anton runs, PT Sinar. We are on our way to the neighbouring island of Sumbawa in order to procure passports, since the process is backed up at the immigration authorities on Lombok, located just east of Bali in Indonesia. Four men are already waiting, while three more have yet to arrive. Muslim has just been in touch with two of the men, who claim that they are on their way, but there is no word from the seventh and final man. He has his cell phone to his ear as we speak.

Muslim is from Central Lombok. His house – located in his extended family's compound – is about 10 kilometres north of the east-west highway that cuts across the island. In contrast to the main highway, the small roads that run north and south are in disrepair and it takes nearly an hour to drive to the village. Muslim's family is well-off in the context of the village and owns gardens and land that yield three harvests of rice per year. Not far away, however, the Wallace line becomes evident and divides the greener western half of the island from the drier eastern part, where only one harvest of rice per year is the norm. This efficiently creates a poverty line that makes East Lombok the main source of migrant labour on the island. It is also in this direction that Muslim focuses his recruitment.

Like most other PL, Muslim is constantly on the move, attempting to extend his geography of recruitment beyond already existing social relations and create links to potential collaborators who might become sub-brokers (or sub-PL), visiting prospective migrants, while shuttling back and forth between recruitment agencies in the main commercial city of Mataram. To be a PL thus demands a steady cash flow, a cell phone, and a vehicle of some kind, at least a motorcycle but preferably a mini-van to move larger groups of migrants, and some connection to the place of recruitment.

Muslim first went to Peninsular Malaysia in the mid-1990s as an undocumented migrant and spent several years working on rural palm oil plantations and urban construction sites in the booming Malaysian economy. Whenever he returned to Lombok during Ramadan, his employers would ask him to bring new workers, thereby allowing them to bypass middlemen and to assert some control over the recruitment process. In his home village, he would generally find at least a few friends willing to join him as he promised stable wages not available on Lombok. Within a couple of years, Muslim turned to recruitment full time as it proved to be more lucrative than any form of migrant labour. In this process, he came to collaborate with a string of intermediaries between Lombok and Malaysia who had the knowledge and resources to move migrants further along, for instance through access to speedboats and payments to officials or thugs in key harbours.

This was the era of the *tai kong* (literally 'ship's captain' in Chinese), or migrant smuggler, as Indonesian border islands such as Batam, Bintan, and Karimun in the Riau Archipelago became hubs, both through the undocumented transport across the Straits of Malacca by night and through the production of passports that allowed for documented crossing but undocumented employment (Ford & Lyons 2011; Lindquist 2009). The 1997 Asian economic crisis and the fall of Indonesia's President Suharto the following year was a watershed for Indonesian migration to Malaysia, however, with the intensification of deportation campaigns (Chin 2008). In the wake of these processes, a faciliated work visa process and Memorandums of Understanding (MOUs) between the Indonesian and Malaysian governments aimed to protect the migrants and regulate their mobility between the two countries, most notably by means of extensive demands for documentation. In Indonesia, the formalization of temporary labour migration was matched by the deregulation of the labour recruitment market and a growing number of private labour recruitment agencies (Pelaksana Penempatan Tenaga Kerja Indonesia Swasta [PPTKIS] – Private Placement Managers of Indonesian Workers), which followed the dismantling of monopolies after the fall of Suharto – in neoliberal terms a parallel 'rolling back' and 'rolling out' of the state (Peck & Tickell 2002). In this process of state regulation and market fragmentation, the bureaucratized *petugas lapangan* came to replace the *tai kong* as the key broker in the new migration regime.

Following the crisis, Muslim moved back to Lombok, as the intensifying regulation of cross-border mobility made it increasingly difficult to engage in migrant smuggling. In contrast to the 1990s, when he escorted migrants across great distances to the Indonesian border or to Malaysia, his space of action became increasingly constricted to Lombok, as he began to deliver migrants to a few licensed agencies on the island. In other words, while his role as a local recruiter and cultural broker who could convince villagers to become migrants remained in place, a new form of engagement with the micropolitics and logistics of documentation took shape as the PL also came to handle much of the paperwork that became necessary in the new regime of documented migration.

By 2009, however, the labour recruitment industry had become increasingly competitive with more than 500 registered agencies in Indonesia; most having multiple branch offices across the country. Today there are several thousand labour recruitment offices in Indonesia.[9] On Lombok alone there are over 150. Each of these in turn uses even greater numbers of PL, who generally come from the region in which they recruit, or collaborate with sub-brokers who do, and thus control access to migrants. Competition is stiff. In fact, the success of any licensed recruitment agency is entirely dependent on the success of these informal brokers. Notably, the number of people engaged in labour recruitment has steadily increased as a certain form of legitimacy has emerged that was not prevalent during the era of undocumented migration. Furthermore, the delivery of migrants to licensed agencies allows for a deferral of responsibility in a migration industry rife with subcontracting in both the recruitment and employment processes.

As we stand on the side of road, waiting for the three remaining men to arrive, Muslim shows Anton that the paperwork is in order. Beyond accessing documents, a significant problem in becoming a migrant is accessing capital. To work in the palm oil plantations, the fee is around four million rupiah (US$400), which migrants often have to borrow at up to 100 per cent interest, while they make over $200 per month in Malaysia, compared to $1 to $2 per day on Lombok. Like other PL, Muslim works without a contract and his income depends on how much he can extract from the migrant, usually up to 300,000 rupiah, or $30, as market prices have stabilized. In order to get the process going, sometimes PL such as Muslim will act as moneylenders. This entails a risk since it is difficult to guarantee that they will not drop out along the way after significant investments have been made.

After around half an hour the rest of the men arrive and Muslim shows obvious signs of relief. He has spent a lot of time with them, smoking cigarettes, drinking tea, and discussing what it is like to work in Malaysia, gradually convincing them that he is the right person to recruit them. Now it is time for Anton and his agency to escort the men to the immigration office and have the passports made that are necessary for getting work visas from the Malaysian consulate. The men will return to their villages and wait for the agency's job order of fifty workers to be filled before airline tickets are booked for them and they can take part in a mandatory government-run three-day pre-departure training programme. We all get into the van for the four-hour drive and ferry ride to Sumbawa.

Soon thereafter I leave Lombok, returning the following year in 2010. When I visit Muslim, he is weary and confused. The group of migrants he had recruited the previous year have ended up on a plantation where their contracts have not been respected and several have absconded from their employers. Muslim, who is carrying a large part of their debt, says that he has lost around 15 million rupiah, or about $1,500. He tells me that it is increasingly difficult to recruit because of the growing number of PL, many of them returning migrants. Many women are now travelling to Saudi Arabia to work as domestic servants and broker fees are much higher in that sector, but as he puts it, 'I have never been to Saudi. What am I going to tell them?'

Muslim has two children and needs to make one million rupiah per month to survive – equivalent to the fees from about four palm oil plantation migrants – but since he has limited cash flow, he is considering other options. He has occasionally brokered car and motorcycle sales, but more recently he has turned his attention to land, especially in the southern areas of the island, hoping to make money more quickly, with up to 30 per cent commissions. He tells me he has contacts with people who have contacts with foreigners and he is on the hunt for possible land acquisitions. He believes that once the new airport in southern Lombok is finished, land prices will skyrocket as the island will be able to compete with Bali as a tourist destination. But at the same time he has recently been pushed out of a couple of deals once a buyer and seller have agreed. In the next breath he tells me that he is considering going back to Malaysia as a migrant.

Brokering trafficking

I am sitting with Adi on the floor in his house on the Indonesian island of Batam, just across the border from Singapore. He is shaking his head and becoming increasingly agitated as we watch a film on my laptop, a 2005 award-winning documentary film, *Inside the child sex trade*, originally made for the Australian current affairs programme *Dateline* by television journalist Olivia Rousset. In the film we are introduced to Batam through the work of the local NGO PRAI (Perhimpunan Rekan Anak Indonesia, Association of

Journal of the Royal Anthropological Institute (N.S.), 162-177
© Royal Anthropological Institute 2015

the Friends of Indonesia's Children). Ramses, the man who runs PRAI, leads Rousset to Diana and Lina, two teenage girls from the island of Madura (located just off the east coast of Java) who have become prostitutes in Batam's largest quasi-legal brothel area. The central plot of the film is their ensuing rescue and return from the brothel to their families in their home villages (e.g. Lindquist 2013).

'Those were our *kelompok dampingan* [literally 'support group']!' Adi and YMKK (Yayasan Mitra Kesehatan dan Kemanusiaan, the Partnership in Health and Humanity Foundation), the local NGO he works for, had been carefully beginning to negotiate to get Diana and Lina out of the brothel when PRAI, together with the film team and one of the girl's uncles, raided it without telling the girls beforehand. For Adi, as a PL[10] in charge of approaching support groups in the ongoing counter-trafficking programme, long-term contacts with brothel owners were critical in order to gain access to potential victims and under-aged prostitutes. After the raid, relations with brothel owners had become antagonistic, and seeing the images for the first time served to intensify his anger towards PRAI.

Adi comes from the South Sumatran city of Palembang and travelled with his uncle to Batam in the years after the economic crisis as the island retained its reputation as a site of rapid economic development. After working at a restaurant for a couple of years, Adi came into contact with YMKK, which needed a group of PL to work on a large World Bank-funded HIV programme, as Indonesia, and Batam in particular, had been widely identified as the next epicentre of the Asian epidemic. What is generally valued in a PL is not any formal education but rather a particular form of 'street knowledge' that is critical for the legitimacy of NGOs that work with marginalized groups.

YMKK had already been running reproductive health projects in Batam for over a decade, targeting mainly two key groups, young female factory and sex workers who dominate the island's formal and informal economies, respectively. These economies developed in tandem as Singapore was transformed into a financial hub and factories were relocated to offshore locations such as Batam throughout the 1990s (Lindquist 2009). Like many Indonesian NGOs that are dependent on the ebb and flow of international funding, the number of staff at YMKK and the actual projects have varied at any given time depending on their economic circumstances.

Intermittently over the course of a number of years, I spent many days shadowing Adi and other PL as they knocked on the doors of factory dormitories, entered brothels and karaoke bars, and visited freelance sex workers in their residences in the context of a wide variety of projects. The outreach work was concerned with gaining the trust of indviduals – often in collaboration with 'peer educators' recruited from the support groups – distributing information about reproductive health issues and HIV/AIDS, informing about the location of health clinics, as well as collecting information about these perceived risk groups.

When the expected HIV epidemic failed to emerge in Indonesia, funding for prevention programmes dried up. After 2002, however, YMKK began to be approached by donors and collaborators interested in developing projects on *trafficking*, a term that was directly inserted into the Indonesian language. Human trafficking quickly emerged as a global problem at the beginning of the millennium. In this process, funding for counter-trafficking programmes was increasingly made available to Indonesian NGOs through donor agencies, while there was ongoing pressure on the Indonesian government to address trafficking on a national scale.[11] Batam, a border zone and high-risk area for the spread of HIV in Southeast Asia's humanitarian geography, was identified as a hotspot for trafficking and thus plugged into a new form of global circuit (cf. Ford & Lyons 2012).

This shift in focus was relatively uncomplicated for YMKK since its support groups, female prostitutes in particular, overlapped in reproductive health, HIV prevention, and counter-trafficking projects (Lindquist & Piper 2007). During outreach trips to brothels and karaoke bars, Adi and other PL merely added a few more survey questions to ascertain how women entered prostitution and if they wished to exit. The bulk of the outreach work was thus spent collecting data, which were later transferred to computers in the office through data-entry. Creating lists with signatures was critical in this process since target goals for projects were achieved by informing a certain number of individuals each week. The signatures and information collected, in turn, became evidence included in funder reports, which showed that the project had been fulfilled. Field surveys were translated into datasets as a geography of trafficking was mapped on to the island and across the region, thereby adding to a regime of evidence used by donors and policy-makers to demonstrate that trafficking was a problem that demanded attention. At the same time, such documentation validating YMKK's work was a donor requirement, and, like many other NGOs increasingly caught up in an auditing apparatus, YMKK dedicated significant amounts of time generating this type of computerized paperwork (Power 1999).

PL such as Adi became key points of access to women identified as victims of human trafficking. In this context, in particular, there was ongoing competition among NGOs on Batam for trafficking victims in relation to two different types of actors. First, there were international donors such as the IOM (International Organization for Migration), whose Victims of Trafficking programme has offered support to over 6,500 Indonesian migrants since 2004, and, as an effect, the NGOs that collaborated with them in this process.[12] In fact, the IOM increasingly came to prioritize collaborations with NGOs that were most successful in delivering victims in real numbers. Second, there were increasing numbers of journalists and filmmakers who turned to YMKK in order to gather filmed interviews with trafficking victims, as moving images had become a critical technology in circulating testimonials of trafficked women (Lindquist 2010a). Diana and Lina, featured in *Inside the child sex trade*, were iconic in these terms, but far from a common story in Batam's sex industry. Many of the journalists and filmmakers were referred by international NGOs and donors working on trafficking issues in Jakarta or across the border in Singapore. The opening vignette in this section offers a poignant example of how competition works across both these fields (cf. Yea 2013).

In interactions with journalists and filmmakers from Indonesia and abroad, women from YMKK's support groups came to stand in as examples of trafficking. These visits took a standard form, which included particular elements. Visitors were asked to be escorted to 'red-light districts', most often a brothel village (*lokalisasi*) or a karaoke bar. At the centre of these reports were interviews with female prostitutes, preferably the youngest available; meetings that Adi would usually organize. In fact, he saw himself as doing the women a favour since they would often be paid as much as for sexual services. In other words, Adi and the women I talked with understood an interview and sexual service as roughly equivalent. One of the women had been interviewed four separate times and compared them not in terms of the quality of the final visual product, but rather according to how well she had been treated and been paid. Other critical elements were interviews and shots of PL such as Adi and the head of the NGO in her office or when she was speaking in public. Most asked the same questions: How many cases of trafficking are there on Batam? Are the numbers going up or going down? In general, interviewing members of the NGO therefore became a standard strategy in the creation of a legitimate narrative.

More recently, funding for counter-trafficking projects has been scaled down. It is currently not clear if this situation is temporary. YMKK has since experienced a crisis of management and currently there are only a couple of people working there, including Adi. He is still a PL, and spends time among different support groups, but without funding there is a constant demand to look for new kinds of projects and possibilities within or outside the sphere of humanitarian work, for he too has children to feed. Most notably, he has come to broker in government documents, such as identity cards, but also become a scribe for neighbours, writing formal letters directed to the state.

Mediators of migration

Preconceived notions concerning brokers as manipulative and morally ambiguous mediators in a neoliberal landscape arguably constitute a 'bad exemplar' for generating new ethnographic perspectives. Instead I suggest that we take the renewed interest in the broker as a cue for considering the relationship and dynamics between figure and type, between example and theoretical exemplar. More specifically, I have begun to do this by approaching two ethnographically situated figures that inhabit different ends of an ethical spectrum but work on a comparable scale and along a similar temporal horizon, while indeed sharing the same name, *petugas lapangan*, or 'field agent'. Rather than using the one to comment on the other – thus creating a hierarchy of interpretation – I have brought the two into the same frame in order to allow them to speak to one another as figures and by extension understand the broker as a sociological type that comes to encompass them both. Juxtaposing the practices of brokers who are vilified with those who are celebrated allows for the problematization of a priori ethical distinctions, thereby allowing us to consider them as part of the same economy and thus drawing attention to the importance of considering the moral and material together (Peebles 2010).

The two ethnographic accounts were developed and written in relation to one another. In this process, certain similarities have become evident on an individual level. First, Muslim and Adi share a particular social position. We might even imagine them as replacing one another. Both have graduated from high school and are part of a broad cross-section of Indonesians who have gravitated away from village life and become unskilled migrants within the field of service or affective rather than manual labour. The experience of migration has offered them forms of knowledge and expertise that have facilitated their entry into their respective fields of brokerage. Because they both lack capital, connections, and tertiary education, their value lies precisely in their ability to navigate the relationship between the *lapangan*, the field, and the NGO and recruitment agency they work for. Second, and following directly from the previous point, it is not only their ability to engage with paperwork that is of central importance to their labour, but also their capacity (real or perceived) to establish rapport with migrants. There is a critical performative element in this process as both come to enact not only particular forms of expertise (Carr 2011) but also forms of friendship that in an important sense are instrumental, but not as 'lopsided' as patron-client relations (Pitt-Rivers cited in Wolf 2001: 179). Third, Muslim's and Adi's existences are precarious in the sense that their labour depends on the inherently unpredictable circulation of capital that in different ways set migrants in motion. Both cases describe processes of boom and bust, in Muslim's case following from the risks associated with moneylending, and in Adi's because of the nature of funding cycles from international organizations. Finally, Muslim's move to land brokerage and Adi's to brokering documents suggest a broader field of brokerage characterized by similar forms of expertise and uncertainty. The alternative would appear to be a return to unskilled migration rather than village-based labour.

These points, in turn, illuminate broader similarities. The social position and particular competences of the *petugas lapangan* suggest a general problem that NGOs or recruitment agencies have in engaging direcly with targeted populations, either as prospective labour migrants or as migrant victims. This can in part be understood in relation to recent transformations of the development and labour recruitment industries. In the wake of the Asian economic crisis and the fall of President Suharto, political spaces were opened for the expansion of NGOs, which had previously been highly regulated by the state, and licensed recruitment agencies, which emerged in full force following the liberalization of the market economy after a history of crony capitalism. Both fields are thus characterized by processes of neoliberalization in the context of ongoing political decentralization.

Yet the history of the PL precedes that of neoliberalism. The PL was introduced by the Indonesian state to deal with the cultural intimacies of birth control in the context of large-scale family planning programmes beginning in the late 1960s, brokers who were paid for each villager they were able to transform into an acceptor.[13] In the contemporary era, the PL emerges as a figure that embodies particular local cultural competences in the context of a complex relationship between state and market and offers access to groups that can be transformed into migrants or victims, respectively, thereby allowing them to enter into a frame of exchange with both recruitment agencies and NGOs. These transformations should therefore arguably be considered primarily in neo-patrimonial rather than neoliberal terms (see Barker & Van Klinken 2009: 27).[14] In other words, the problem of accessing migrants and victims depends on the establishment of new forms of patronage rather than technologies of market reform. This highlights a more enduring historical problem of mediation between a wide range of state, market, and civil society actors in relation to local populations across Indonesia. But while PL such as Adi and Muslim are therefore deemed necessary by recruitment agencies and NGOs, they are also considered untrustworthy, as they are capable of diverting migrants, and the capital they embody, to competing agencies and NGOs. Processes of formalizing the informal (as in the term PL itself) and thereby capturing the PL are thus considered critical in controlling the economies at hand.

For recruitment agencies, the transformation of the villager into migrant via the PL sets labour and capital in motion, while the debt/credit relationship and the risks associated with it remain largely concentrated on the village level.[15] For NGOs, the transformation of the migrant into a victim allows for the circulation of capital in similar terms, at least in relation to the IOM programme discussed above. Furthermore, in contrast to the work of recruitment agencies, NGOs are governed by a general regime of audit, which is largely concerned with the 'management of appearances' (Power 1999). This is particularly evident in the context of data-entry and in relationships with journalists and filmmakers, as statistics and images come to function as evidence that trafficking is a problem that demands continued response (Lindquist 2010a). In contrast, it is, for instance, striking to note the economic equivalence of interviews and sex work posited by Adi and the prostitutes who were part of his support group. In other words, beyond the ethical economy of counter-trafficking – in which prostitution is exploitation – is an alternative form of moral economy that runs against the grain of the dominant discourse of the victimization. More generally, it is clear that relationships between PL, and migrants and victims, respectively, are based on forms of trust that cannot easily be reduced to exploitation.

The ethnography at hand thus allows us to return to the question of ethics that has defined the a priori distinction between the celebrated NGO activist and the demonized labour recruiter. As Cohen has phrased it, '[C]ertain ethics travel well precisely because of the flexibility of their reductive transactional frame' (2003: 672). Activists and recruiters are both critical to a form of ethics that reproduces an understanding of the migrant as a rational actor constrained by poor information flows, illegal actors, and various forms of coercion. The power of this transactional frame is precisely the ease with which it is reproduced across cultural, economic, and political divides. Centring our attention on the practices of PL such as Adi and Muslim, however, allows us to move beyond this form of 'ethical publicity' (Cohen 2003) and consider how both the recruitment of labour migrants and responses to abuses against migrants should be considered, not in opposition, but in an important sense as constituitive of one another. While it is clear that NGOs come to define themselves as ethical in relation to the apparently unethical practices of recruiters and traffickers, the strikingly similar practices of PL highlight the importance of building rapport and mobilizing subjects across a common divide.

Both figures perpetuate the forms they are engaged in within a common temporal horizon. Successfully transforming a villager into a migrant or a migrant into a victim in the face of competition strengthens their individual positions while expanding the economies in which they are engaged. Taken together, these figures reveal a broader economy that depends heavily on similar forms of brokerage located at the strikingly modern intersection between trust and paperwork. More specifically, they highlight a shift of ethnographic attention in which it becomes possible to conceptualize transnational migration as a field characterized by multiple forms of brokerage and mediation, as recruiters and NGOs enact various forms of expertise in relation to migration (Carr 2011).

In line with the work of scholars such as James (2011), the paper argues that the broker can be considered as an exemplary methodological starting-point for a contemporary anthropology. In this process, however, it is important to begin to unpack biases that I have outlined. A new anthropology of the broker or brokerage should remain initially agnostic with regard to the relationship between brokerage and ethics. Furthermore, it should be attentive to how the broker appears – both empirically and analytically – in the context of state crisis, previously in the era of decolonialization and currently in the era of neoliberalism. From this perspective, there is a risk that the broker is considered as an effect of state crisis rather than in relation to a specific socio-historical context. Finally, it is important to note that while historically it was generally clear what the broker was mediating between, the village and the national capital, or, more generally, encapsulated political structures (Bailey 1969: 167), in the contemporary context of unbounded fieldsites this is not immediately obvious.

These points allow for a more complex understanding of the relationship between figure and type, not least in methodological terms. Arguably, it is not the broker *per se* that is of primary concern for contemporary anthropology but rather what the broker might reveal in ethnographic terms. From this perspective, it is possible to avoid the pitfalls of methodological individualism and consider the broker as an ethnographic entry-point and methodological fetish that comes to illuminate broader contexts and processes from particular positions of mediation (cf. Appadurai 1986: 5). Figure and type can thus come to temporarily converge. As such, this renewed focus on the broker considers scale and temporality as emergent in relation to the ethnography at hand. The problem of how to describe and conceptualize what the broker mediates between is therefore primarily ethnographic, as is the more specific question whether the broker is better understood as an intermediary or mediator – an actor or entity that makes a difference or no difference in the transaction, respectively (Latour 2005; Maurer *et al.* 2013).

This suggests a position from which we might reconsider the relationship between figure and type, or between example and theoretical exemplar, as one not of opposition or antagonism but rather of conversation. Taken together, figure and type, in this case *petugas lapangan* and broker, leads us towards a point of convergence that offers an ethnographic starting-point for considering historically situated systems of brokerage. It is through this conversation that a form of comparative ethnography might emerge.

NOTES

Thanks to Rebecca Empson and Maple Razsa for reading and commenting on earlier versions of this essay. I am particularly grateful to Andreas Bandak and Lars Højer for doing so several times and for the effort they have put into this edited volume. Ongoing work and discussions with Joshua Barker and Erik Harms have formed the basis for the argument.

[1] I consider the broker as a specific type of middleman, mediator, or intermediary. Most generally, the broker is a human actor who gains something from the mediation of valued resources that he or she does not directly control, which can be distinguished from a patron, who controls valued resources, and a go-between or a messenger, who does not affect the transaction. For a more general review of the anthropology of brokers and brokerage, see Lindquist (2015).

[2] It is worth noting the contrast between Geertz's use of a vernacular example, the *kijaji*, and other earlier discussions of brokers that utilize more general examples such as the 'African chief' (Fallers 1955).

[3] *Petugas* literally means 'a subordinate who is given an order or task', while *lapangan* means 'field'. Although 'field agent' is not an ideal translation, arguably it is preferable to 'field operative' or 'field worker', since the word 'agent' highlights to a greater degree the form of brokering that the *petugas lapangan* engages in.

[4] This paper is based on intermittent and ongoing fieldwork in Indonesia. While I have been conducting fieldwork on counter-trafficking NGOs since 2005, work on labour recruitment agencies was initiated in 2007.

[5] Although this is not quite the same as Lazar's (2012) notion of 'disjunctive comparison', I am engaged in a similar attempt to compare that which is not generally considered comparable, and through this process to reframe ethnographic research that has been gathered in different contexts over an extended period of time.

[6] Talal Asad's (1972) critique of Fredrik Barth's transactionalism would be an example of this shift of concern.

[7] I would argue that within the field of counter-trafficking the positive moral discourse surrounding NGOs remains largely intact, in contrast to other forms of development organizations, for instance.

[8] Pseudonyms are used for informants throughout the paper.

[9] Interview with office manager at the head office of APJATI, the Indonesian Manpower Services Association (Asosiasi Jasa Tenaga Kerja Indonesia), in Jakarta, 4 June 2014. Of the 546 licensed companies, 461 were members of APJATI, and these had a total of 3,227 licensed branch offices.

[10] In this context, *petugas lapangan* is sometimes translated as 'outreach worker', a term widely used in the social services and NGO sectors. For a brief historical description of the outreach worker in the United States, see Rowe (1999). Occasionally the term PO, or *petugas outreach*, is used.

[11] In its annual Trafficking in Persons (TIP) report, the United States Department of State (various years) ranks countries into three tiers according to how they deal with trafficking. In 2001, the first TIP report identified Indonesia as a (worst-offender) Tier 3 country – which carried the threat of withdrawal of all non-humanitarian aid from the United States (*http://www.state.gov/g/tip/rls/tiprpt/2001/3930.htm*, accessed 22 January 2015). A national counter-trafficking commission was quickly established and plans were made to

draft new counter-trafficking legislation enabling Indonesia to reach Tier 2 (countries whose governments do not fully comply with minimum standards but are making significant efforts to do so) by the following year.

[12] The programme has generally been considered a success and even a 'model for the world' by the director of the US State Department's counter-trafficking programme (*http://www.iom.or.id/ news.jsp?lang=eng&code=102&dcode=4*, accessed 20 February 2009, no longer available on-line).

[13] For instance, in 1971 a PL was paid 5,000 rupiah per month as a flat salary and a further 200 rupiah for each IUD acceptor and 100 rupiah for each birth control acceptor recruit (*Kompas* 1971). See also Pemberton (1994: 229-30) for a description of the reach of the state in the context of birth control.

[14] Edward Aspinall (2013) argues in the context of contemporary Indonesian political life that patronage and neoliberalism should be understood as intertwined. Generally speaking, I would not disagree with this argument, but in the context of this paper I am more specifically concerned with highlighting how the practices of the PL are critical to a particular form of brokerage that, as I have noted above, precedes neoliberalism.

[15] This is most generally the case for men. For a more extensive discussion of how debt/credit relations differ in terms of gender, see Lindquist (2010*b*).

REFERENCES

APPADURAI, A. 1986. Introduction: commodities and the politics of value. In *The social life of things* (ed.) A. Appadurai, 3-63. Cambridge: University Press.

ASAD, T. 1972. Market model, class structure and consent: a reconsideration of Swat political organization. *Man* (N.S.) **7**, 74-94.

ASPINALL, E. 2013. A nation in fragments: patronage and neoliberalism in contemporary Indonesia. *Critical Asian Studies* **45**, 27-54.

BAILEY, F.G. 1969. *Stratagems and spoils: a social anthropology of politics*. Oxford: Blackwell.

BARKER, J., E. HARMS & J. LINDQUIST 2013*a*. Introduction to special issue: figuring the transforming city. *City & Society* **25**, 159-72.

———, ——— & ——— (eds) 2013*b*. *Figures of Southeast Asian modernity*. Honolulu: University of Hawai'i Press.

——— & G. VAN KLINKEN 2009. Reflections on the state in Indonesia. In *State of authority: the state in society in Indonesia* (eds) G. Van Klinken & J. Barker, 17-46. Ithaca, N.Y.: Southeast Asia Program Publications, Cornell University.

BENJAMIN, W. 1986. Paris, capital of the nineteenth century. In *Reflections: essays, aphorisms, autobiographical writings* (ed. P. Demetz), 146-62. New York: Schocken Books.

BIERSCHENK, T., J.-P. CHAUVEAU & J. OLIVIER DE SARDAN 2002. Local development brokers in Africa: the rise of a new social category. Working Paper # 13, Department of Anthropology and African Studies, Johannes Gutenberg-Universität.

BOELLSTORFF, T. 2003. Dubbing culture: Indonesian gay and lesbi subjectivities and ethnography in an already globalized world. *American Ethnologist* **30**, 225-42.

BOISSEVAIN, J. 1974. *Friends of friends: networks, manipulators and coalitions*. Oxford: Basil Blackwell.

CARR, E.S. 2011. Enactments of expertise. *Annual Review of Anthropology* **39**, 17-32.

CHIN, C. 2008. 'Diversification' and 'privatisation': securing insecurities in the receiving country of Malaysia. *Asia Pacific Journal of Anthropology* **9**, 285-303.

CLIFFORD, J. 1988. On ethnographic authority. In *The predicament of culture: twentieth-century ethnography, literature, and art*. Cambridge, Mass.: Harvard University Press.

COHEN, L. 2003. Where it hurts: Indian material for an ethics of organ transplantation. *Zygon* **38**, 663-88.

DOEZEMA, J. 2010. *Sex slaves and discourse masters: the construction of trafficking*. London: Zed.

FALLERS, I. 1955. The predicament of the modern African chief: an instance from Uganda. *American Anthropologist* **57**, 290-305.

FISHER, W. 1997. Doing good? The politics and antipolitics of NGO practices. *Annual Review of Anthropology* **26**, 439-64.

FORD, M. & L. LYONS 2011. Travelling the *aspal* route: grey labour migration through an Indonesian border town. In *The state and illegality in Indonesia* (eds) E. Aspinall & G. van Klinken. Leiden: KITLV Press.

——— & ——— 2012. Counter-trafficking and migrant labour activism in Indonesia's periphery. In *Labour migration and human trafficking in Southeast Asia: critical perspectives* (eds) M. Ford, L. Lyons & W. van Schendel, 75-94. London: Routledge.

GEERTZ, C. 1960. The Javanese kijaji: the changing role of a cultural broker. *Comparative Studies in Society and History* **2**, 228-49.

———— 1973. Deep play: notes on the Balinese cockfight. In *The interpretation of cultures*, 412-53. New York: Basic Books.

GÜRSEL, Z.D. 2012. The politics of wire service photography: infrastructures of representation in a digital newsroom. *American Ethnologist* **39**, 71-89.

JAMES, D. 2011. The return of the broker: consensus, hierarchy, and choice in South African land reform. *Journal of the Royal Anthropological Institute* (N.S.) **17**, 318-38.

Kompas 1971. Tiap seratus kundjungan kerumah-rumah hanja hasilkan rata-rata 4 akseptor [Every 100 home visits generally results in only 4 *akseptor*]. 29 December.

LATOUR, B. 2005. *Reassembling the social: an introduction to actor-network-theory.* Oxford: University Press.

LAZAR, S. 2012. Disjunctive comparison: citizenship and trade unionism in Bolivia and Argentina. *Journal of the Royal Anthropological Institute* (N.S.) **18**, 349-68.

LINDQUIST, J. 2009. *The anxieties of mobility: migration and tourism in the Indonesian borderlands.* Honolulu: University of Hawai'i Press.

———— 2010a. Image and evidence: human trafficking, auditing, and the production of illicit markets in Southeast Asia and beyond. *Public Culture* **22**, 223-36.

———— 2010b. Labour recruitment, circuits of capital and gendered mobility: reconceptualizing the Indonesian migration industry. *Pacific Affairs* **83**, 115-32.

———— 2013. Rescue, return, in place: deportees, victims, and the regulation of Indonesian migration. In *Return: rethinking mobile subjects and nation-states in globalizing Asia* (eds) B. Xiang, B. Yeoh & M. Toyota, 122-40. Durham, N.C.: Duke University Press.

———— 2015. Brokers and brokerage, anthropology of. In *International encyclopedia of social and behavioral science* (Second edition). Amsterdam: Elsevier.

———— & N. PIPER 2007. From HIV prevention to counter-trafficking: discursive shifts and institutional continuities in Southeast Asia. In *Human trafficking* (ed.) M. Lee, 138-58. Cullompton, Devon: Willan.

————, B. XIANG & B. YEOH 2012. Opening the black box of migration: brokers, the organization of transnational mobility and the changing political economy in Asia. *Pacific Affairs* **85**, 7-19.

McKEOWN, A. 2008. *Melancholy order: Asian migration and the globalization of borders.* New York: Columbia University Press.

MAURER, B., T. NELMS & S. REA 2013. 'Bridges to cash': channelling agency in mobile money. *Journal of the Royal Anthropological Institute* (N.S.) **19**, 52-74.

MOSSE, D. & D. LEWIS 2006. Theoretical approaches to brokerage and translation in development. In *Development brokers and translators* (eds) D. Lewis & D. Mosse, 1-26. Bloomfield, Conn.: Kumarian.

OHMAE, K. 1990. *The borderless world: power and strategy in the interlinked economy.* New York: Harper Business.

PECK, J. & A. TICKELL 2002. Neoliberalizing space. *Antipode* **34**, 380-404.

PEEBLES, G. 2010. The anthropology of credit and debt. *Annual Review of Anthropology* **39**, 225-40.

PEMBERTON, J. 1994. *On the subject of 'Java.* Ithaca, N.Y.: Cornell University Press.

POWER, M. 1999. *The audit society: rituals of verification.* Oxford: University Press.

ROWE, M. 1999. *Crossing the border: encounters between homeless people and outreach workers.* Berkeley: University of California Press.

RUDNYCKYJ, D. 2004. Technologies of servitude: governmentality and Indonesian transnational labor migration. *Anthropological Quarterly* **77**, 407-34.

SIMMEL, G. 1971. The stranger. In *On individuality and social forms* (ed.) D.N. Levine, 143-9. Chicago: University Press.

SPENCER, J. 2007. *Anthropology, politics, and the state: democracy and violence in South Asia.* Cambridge: University Press.

WEBER, M. 1978. Basic sociological terms. In *Economy and society*, Vol. **1** (eds G. Roth & C. Wittich), 3-62. Berkeley: University of California Press.

WOLF, E. 1956. Aspects of group relations in a complex society: Mexico. *American Anthropologist* **58**, 1065-78.

———— 2001. *Pathways of power: building an anthropology of the modern world.* Berkeley: University of California Press.

YEA, S. 2013. Mobilising the child victim: the localisation of human trafficking in Singapore through global activism. *Environment and Planning D: Society and Space* **31**, 988-1003.

Figures et types : négocier savoir et migrations en Indonésie et au-delà

Résumé

L'article fait du courtier un point d'entrée pour examiner le problème de la création d'exemples en anthropologie. Plus précisément, il aborde ce problème par le biais de la relation entre figure et type ou entre exemple et exemplaire théorique. Alors que la figure est inscrite dans un contexte sociohistorique donné, le type accentue consciemment des caractéristiques particulières afin de constituer la base de la comparaison. Plus précisément, l'article aborde cette relation en examinant le courtier comme un type en relation avec deux figures spécifiques du régime actuel de migrations transnationales des Indonésiens : l'envoyé en mission sur le terrain des ONG et le recruteur de main-d'œuvre informel, appelés tous deux « agents de terrain » ou *petugas lapangan* en Indonésie. Par juxtaposition, l'auteur examine, par une discussion de l'oscillation entre figure et type, les biais de la littérature anthropologique sur le courtier (en particulier le fait qu'il serait, par essence, amoral sinon immoral), tout en suggérant que celui-ci constitue un point de départ méthodologique exemplaire pour l'anthropologie contemporaine.

Index

Journal of the Royal Anthropological Institute (N.S.), 178-182
© Royal Anthropological Institute 2015